PRAISE FOR *DESIRE*

"*Desire* is the most important sexuality book of the last decade."

—BARRY MCCARTHY, PhD, author of
Couple Sexuality After 60

"This book is useful for lovers and those who work with lovers therapeutically. . . . I recommend this for anyone who is seeking to strengthen their relationship and for any professional who is working to help lovers find more success in intimacy."

—LEXX BROWN-JAMES, PhD, LMFT, CSE, CSES,
author of *The Black Girls' Guide to Couple's Intimacy*

"Drs. Fogel Mersy and Vencill have written the most comprehensive book on sex and desire that I've read as a couples therapist. . . . This book should live on the shelves of every therapist and person curious about sex and desire."

—ELIZABETH EARNSHAW, LMFT, CGT,
author of *I Want This to Work*

"*Desire* does a wonderful job distinguishing desire from arousal, addressing sex science and theory in an approachable way, and offering prompts for sexual self-reflection. I can't wait to use this as a reference for years to come."

—CANDICE NICOLE HARGONS, PhD, associate professor
of counseling psychology, University of Kentucky

"Essential . . . Fabulous . . . Superbly written and refreshingly inclusive, it is a must-read for clinicians and the general public."

—MORAG YULE, PhD, CPsych, founder and
director, Ontario Sex Therapy

desire

desire

AN INCLUSIVE GUIDE
TO NAVIGATING
LIBIDO DIFFERENCES
IN RELATIONSHIPS

LAUREN FOGEL MERSY, PSYD, AND
JENNIFER A. VENCILL, PHD, ABPP

BEACON PRESS, BOSTON

Beacon Press
Boston, Massachusetts
www.beacon.org

Beacon Press books
are published under the auspices of
the Unitarian Universalist Association of Congregations.

Materials and/or excerpts from the work of Dr. Betty Martin;
the Gottman Institute; Rosemary Basson/Royal College of Obstetricians
and Gynaecologists, "Rethinking Low Sexual Desire in Women,"
BJOG (UK), Jan. 1, 2000; Sexual Health Solutions, LLC; and
Vaginismus.com are printed here with permission.

Printed in the United States of America

27 26 25 24   8 7 6 5 4 3 2 1

This book is printed on acid-free paper that meets the uncoated paper
ANSI/NISO specifications for permanence as revised in 1992.

Text design and composition by Kim Arney

Library of Congress Cataloging-in-Publication Data is available for this title.
ISBN: 978-0-8070-2029-6 (paperback); e-book: 978-0-8070-0680-1;
audiobook: 978-0-8070-1288-8

Lauren Fogel Mersy:
To a future that's free from sexual shame,
one where everyone has access to good sex education.

Jennifer A. Vencill:
Desire has often been compared to a dance,
an intertwined and intimate weave of push and pull,
back and forth, step and counterstep. To the partners
with whom I've danced—thank you for the lessons.

And to my patients and students,
who inspire me every day.

CONTENTS

Part III

AUTHORS' NOTE

All case examples are either composites or fictional in order to protect privacy. Any similarity to actual persons is coincidental.

The information in this book is for informational and educational purposes. It is not a substitute for individual psychological or medical care and does not constitute therapeutic services or medical advice. It is recommended that you consult your medical or mental health provider with any questions or concerns about your healthcare.

The authors have made every effort to make sure that the information in this book is accurate and well researched. It is current as of the date of publication.

The views expressed are the authors' personal views and do not necessarily reflect the policy or position of Mayo Clinic.

IT'S COMPLICATED

Prisha and Donovan sit down for their first sex therapy session. A young couple in their early thirties, they are seeking help to address their growing libido differences. They have been together for three years and married for one. At the beginning of their relationship, they seemed to have the same level of interest in sex. They were sexual together a few times per week and felt satisfied and comfortable with that frequency. Over the past year or so, since getting married, Prisha has not been feeling as interested in sex as she once did. She still finds Donovan attractive and loves him dearly, but she just doesn't think about sex very often anymore. When Donovan tries to initiate sex, she often turns him down, stating that she isn't in the mood. There are times when she wants to cuddle or kiss Donovan, but she worries it will turn into more. She has started to avoid even general physical touch and affection, especially since she doesn't want Donovan to feel turned on and then rejected.

Prisha wonders what's wrong with her. She feels as if there's a part of her that is broken. Donovan has started to worry that Prisha doesn't find him attractive anymore or perhaps that she even has feelings for someone else. The more Donovan tries to initiate sex, the more Prisha feels pressure and stress around sex. The more Prisha turns Donovan away, the more hurt and frustrated he becomes. It feels like a never-ending cycle without a solution. If this is the pattern after only one year of marriage, how will they be able to sustain a long-term intimate connection?

What's more, Donovan has noticed that now, when he is sexual with Prisha, his mind often wanders to anxious thoughts about her interest or his performance. Since sex is not as frequent as he would like, when an opportunity does arise he tends to focus on quickly getting to intercourse. Unfortunately, this has gotten Donovan increasingly stuck in his head, leading to performance anxiety and occasional problems with erections. Rushing into intercourse has also meant less pleasure and fewer orgasms for Prisha, further lowering her libido.

Prisha and Donovan's sexual dynamic is, unfortunately, one we see every single day in our therapy offices. In fact, difficulties with desire are the number one reason people seek sex therapy. Sexual desire discrepancies affect people of all ages, genders, sexual orientations, cultures, and religions. Because most of us didn't receive comprehensive sexual health education growing up, nor were we taught how to talk about sex in an open and healthy way, figuring out how to manage such a discrepancy can be extraordinarily difficult. And when sexual desire discrepancies aren't well managed, other sexual and relationship problems (such as sexual pain, erection difficulties, resentment, and hostility) often follow.

Sex therapy is an excellent way to address these problems. However, many people can't access or afford such services due to a limited number of providers (at the time of this writing, there are fewer than 1,100 certified sex therapists in the entire United States!). This is why we've written this book.

When people find out that we're sex and relationship therapists, we usually get one of two reactions: folks either get a little nervous and quiet or, on the flip side, they become excited and start asking a lot of questions. As therapists and educators, we love questions! We've talked to many people about their relationship worries. We have answered questions about the sex lives of fellow plane passengers, more than a few taxi and Lyft drivers, and even once on a boat while on vacation in Vietnam. These conversations don't just happen on various forms of transportation. We've also spent a lot of time answering questions and talking about sex and relationships in classroom settings, at professional conferences, and with our therapy clients. Across all of these experiences, one concern tends to emerge more than all others: "I've lost interest in sex." Over the years, we've heard many variations of this worry, including:

- "I want to be sexual with my partner/spouse/lover, but sex doesn't really cross my mind. I want to want it."
- "I used to want sex all the time, but lately I don't. Why isn't sex the way it used to be?"
- "My partner/spouse/lover is super attractive and I love being sexual with them, but they mostly reject my advances. I'm not sure what to do anymore."
- "If I never have sex again, I'd be fine. But that's definitely not okay with my partner/spouse/lover."
- "I know my partner/spouse/lover is really attracted to me. They want to be sexual all the time, but I don't. What's wrong with me?"
- "My body has changed and I don't feel attractive anymore."
- "I've never really been a sexual person and I'm not sure what the big deal is."
- "I enjoy sex when it's happening, but outside of that, I don't really think about it."
- "My partner is not very interested in sex and I worry they might want to be with someone else."

If any of these worries or situations sound familiar, this book is for you.

WHO'S HAVING DESIRE CONCERNS?

Concerns about sexual desire cut across gender, sexual orientation, and age.[1] In fact, desire differences in relationships are actually the norm rather than the exception. Let's repeat that: differences in desire are a normal part of a relationship. Some of us have low libido during select times or phases of life, whereas others experience this on a more regular basis. On the other hand, many people describe consistently high libido across the course of their lives, or in certain phases of their lives. Encountering libido changes over time with oneself, or within a relationship, is a common experience. And, as it turns out, libido is quite complicated!

A sexual desire discrepancy does not necessarily mean that anything is wrong in a relationship. In fact, it's quite natural that people—with individual needs and interests—will have differences around sexuality. As partners move out of the honeymoon phase of a relationship—which typically lasts between six months to two years—and as the stresses and demands of life persist, it can certainly be difficult to maintain an active sex life. Sex can often fall lower and lower on the priority list and may start to feel like a chore or obligation for some people. Often, sex doesn't feel spontaneous anymore. Or it's not as fun or exciting as it felt early in our relationships. When this is the case, sexual activity typically becomes less frequent, and sometimes, physical touch with partners decreases or stops altogether. This book is for anyone facing this common situation.

Before diving in further, we want to discuss why this book felt so important for us to write. Plainly put: we've written the book we want to give our clients as a starting point for navigating libido concerns. Sexual desire is complicated, yet so few of us learned the ins and outs of libido (or any sexual topic, for that matter) while growing up. We also aren't usually taught how to talk about sex and sexual desire in open, healthy ways with our partners, spouses, or even our healthcare providers. Libido concerns most often tend to emerge in a relational context, typically with our sexual and romantic partners. Despite popular narratives to the contrary, this is not just an individual problem but often is a relational difference. Desire discrepancies require navigating the preferences of each partner.

We offer this book as a resource that both explains the many factors that affect sexual desire and also provides you with a path forward. This book also aims to be comprehensive and inclusive of everybody and every body. Most books on sexual desire cater to a readership of cisgender heterosexual women. (If some of these terms are new for you, don't worry! We review them in the next section.) While these women are, of course, important, people of all genders and orientations experience difficulties with sexual desire, and many have trouble finding resources that speak to them. This book is meant to provide a wider lens, inclusive of many different experiences and people, and we hope you'll see yourself reflected in these pages.

Last, but certainly not least, we've written this book with some important sexual health foundations in mind:

1. You are responsible for your own pleasure.
2. You are the expert of your own body.
3. Intercourse is not the goal for everyone.

4. There is no one-size-fits-all approach. Use what works
   and leave the rest.
5. Consent is key.

These are concepts that we'll return to throughout the book.

WHO ARE WE?

We met at the University of Minnesota Medical School's Institute for Sexual and Gender Health, where we both completed our postdoctoral training. Over dinner one night, we discussed the need for a more inclusive book to help people navigate desire discrepancies— almost like an encyclopedia about libido. Given our balance of clinical and academic experience, we realized, "Hey! We might actually be the team to write this book!" While Lauren focuses exclusively on clinical work in sex and relationship therapy, Jennifer is a scientist practitioner with therapy, research, and teaching roles.

In the world of research, the term *reflexivity* is used to describe the process of locating oneself within the research process: to identify strengths, particular viewpoints, and potential biases that we bring to scientific endeavors. In clinical practice, this is similarly referred to as the *location of self*: an examination of our sociocultural, interpersonal, and individual roles and positions and how they may impact the therapeutic process. Writing a book is neither research nor the practice of therapy; however, as authors, we feel it's important to offer at least some acknowledgment of the many ways that our own social and professional positions have impacted what you're about to read.

Lauren: I am an Ashkenazi Jewish, Canadian American white woman who was born and raised in Toronto, Canada. I am cisgender, sexually questioning, married, graduate school–educated, upper-middle-class, nondisabled, and an elder millennial. In my teen years, as I noticed the lack of open conversation about sex and sexuality in our culture, I developed a growing interest in breaking the stigma, shame, and taboo around sex. My curiosity about human sexuality and partnerships grew throughout college and graduate school, which led me to pursue a two-year postdoctoral training program at the University of Minnesota's Institute for Sexual and Gender

Health. Though I am part of a religious minority, I have experienced privilege in most other aspects of my identities.

Jennifer: I am a white, nondisabled, cisgender woman, born and raised in a middle-class family in Virginia, United States. I also identify as a bisexual femme: I am attracted to many different types of people, regardless of gender. *Femme* is a word with a multitude of meanings, grounded in the history of queer activism and femininities. For me, my femme identity reflects this crucial history, upon which my own life and career have developed, as well as a nod to gender expression that both celebrates and subverts traditional femininity. Growing up, my interest in human sexuality developed through understanding and embracing my own identity and, in large part, from witnessing the deep shame, anxiety, and stigma that many of my peers experienced when it came to sex, sexuality, and gender. This stood in stark contrast to my (mostly) sex-positive experiences and upbringing, and it didn't take me long to figure out that my experiences were perhaps not the norm. I pursued a career in psychology with a focus on sexual and gender health so that I could provide support and care to those struggling with these topics—and to also help work toward a more sex-positive world.

We want to acknowledge that we are both currently located in the United States and that our viewpoints have been shaped by living and working here. Though we suspect that much of the information in this book will be useful for folks in other countries and societies, we understand that there are always cultural and geographic limitations to our perspectives. Additionally, in this book we discuss types of oppression that we have not personally experienced—for example, racism, transphobia, allosexism, and ableism. Individuals and communities with identities and experiences different from our own are referenced throughout this book so that it can be as inclusive and wide-reaching a resource as possible.

WORDS ARE IMPORTANT

Remember that old rhyme: "Sticks and stones may break my bones, but words will never hurt me"? Though it's true that words alone don't have the ability to physically harm us, language does have the power to express ideas, respect, and inclusion—or alternatively, disrespect, hostility, and exclusion. At the end of the day, words are actually critically important.

This book is written for anyone concerned about libido, regardless of gender, sexual orientation, relationship orientation, race, religion, age, or ability, and you may come across some words (and hopefully some ideas) that are new to you. To make sure we're all on the same page, here are some of the terms we'll be using and elaborating upon throughout this book.

Allosexual: Someone who experiences sexual attraction to others; someone who is not asexual. *Allosexism* is a type of discrimination or cultural exclusion that occurs based on the assumption that everyone is allosexual.

Arousal non-concordance: When there is a difference between the level of physical arousal in your body and your awareness of this arousal; or, when there's a difference between your mind and your body with respect to arousal.

Asexual: Someone who experiences little to no sexual attraction to others, though they may feel attraction in different ways (e.g., romantic attraction; see below). Asexual folks often use the abbreviated term *ace.*

Cisgender: Someone whose gender identity matches the gender they were assigned at birth. You may also hear or see this term abbreviated to *cis.*

Desire discrepancy: A common occurrence in which there are different levels of libido between sexual or romantic partners.

Gender identity: An internal sense of one's gender, which may or may not align with one's gender assigned at birth. Some gender identities include woman, man, agender, bigender, nonbinary, genderqueer, gender fluid, gender nonconforming, Two-Spirit, and many others. It's important to note that *woman* is an umbrella term for both cisgender and transgender women. Likewise, *man* is an umbrella term for both cisgender and transgender men.

Libido: The original term for sexual desire and one that, depending on culture and context, may now be used interchangeably with *sexual desire* or *sexual interest/motivation.* We use the terms *libido* and *sexual desire* interchangeably throughout this book.

LGBTQ+: An acronym used to describe the lesbian, gay, bisexual, transgender, queer, and questioning community. The + is used to acknowledge the multitude of other marginalized sexual and gender identities included within the community—for example, asexual and intersex individuals.

Monogamous: Someone who is romantic and/or sexual with one person at a time.

Nonbinary: Someone whose gender identity does not fall within the traditional gender binary of *man* or *woman*. Some people who are nonbinary may also identify as transgender, while others may not.

Non-monogamous: Someone who is in romantic and/or sexual relationships with more than one person at a time. The term *non-monogamous* implies ethical or consensual non-monogamy in which all partners are informed and have given consent.

Penetrative sex: This can include penile-vaginal, penile-anal, or other types of genital penetration. Penile-vaginal penetration is often what folks are referring to when they say "sex" or "intercourse" but, as noted below, in this book we define *sex* and *sexual activity* much more broadly.

Person with a penis: Simply put, someone who has a penis. It's important to recognize that not all people with penises identify as men, and not all men have penises.

Person with a vulva/vagina: Someone who has a vulva and/or vagina. Not all people with vulvas/vaginas identify as women, and not all women have vulvas/vaginas.

Queer: An umbrella term often used for someone who identifies as LGBTQ+. Not everyone in the LGBTQ+ community uses this term.

Romantic attraction: Interest in or motivation toward a romantic connection with others. This may or may not coincide with sexual attraction.

Sex (verb): Sexual activity that brings a sense of pleasure, connection, and often (but not always) a feeling of sexual release. Sex is not synonymous with penetration—it can include a wide variety of sexually pleasurable experiences. Sex may be solo or partnered.

Sexual attraction: One's interest in, or motivation toward, sexual activity with others. This may or may not align with romantic attraction.

Transgender: Someone whose gender identity does not match the gender they were assigned at birth. You may also hear or see this term abbreviated to *trans*.

Vagina: Internal genitals, also known as the vaginal canal.

Vulva: External genitals that can include the labia majora, labia minora, clitoris, urethra, and opening to the vagina/vaginal canal.

Words can be challenging! These are the definitions we'll be using, though we also recognize that they won't always capture everyone's personal definitions or experiences. Language around sex and gender is fluid and can rapidly change. We value inclusivity *and* we also know it's not possible to speak to every person's individual experience. You know yourself and your situation best, and while we strongly encourage you to challenge yourself with new ideas and concepts, some suggestions or concepts may not work for your particular circumstances. Our goal is to provide you with knowledge and tools to better navigate your concerns related to libido. In service of that goal, we encourage you to take what fits from this book and leave what doesn't.

Throughout this book we will refer to sexual health research and how it can inform your navigation of libido concerns. That said, it's important to acknowledge that sex research has several major limitations. For example, most sexual health research has focused on cisgender heterosexual people and is heavily dominated by white participants. Additionally, the bulk of research in our field pulls from WEIRD populations, an acronym for Western, educated, industrialized, rich, and democratic societies, which only represent an estimated 12 percent of the global population.[2] What all this means is that research results are commonly based on a narrow selection of the population and, as such, may not be universally applicable. We make it a priority in this book to specifically talk about populations that have been historically left out of sexual health research, including People of Color, disabled people, LGBTQ+ people, and other marginalized groups, and to include relevant research as possible.

WHAT TO EXPECT

As we've noted, this is a book for people with sexual desire concerns. We're here to provide information about the numerous factors that can impact libido, many exercises and ideas that can help you navigate sexual desire concerns, and also a chapter to help you decide where to go for additional support, should you want it. Some readers will find that this book is helpful in and of itself, whereas others may need to reach out to a healthcare provider (or team of providers) for further assistance with their concerns. For example, this book alone is not able to fully address medical issues impacting libido, though some of the exercises will likely be helpful alongside medical treatment. We include the most current research and evidence-based information available, but it's also important to recognize that science and medicine are constantly evolving. While we discuss healing from trauma, an important disclaimer is that this book does not address relationships where there is current, ongoing abuse or interpersonal violence between partners. This includes physical, emotional, verbal, and/or sexual abuse. If you are in an abusive relationship, please seek support from a local organization, healthcare provider, or hotline focused on interpersonal violence. In the United States, the National Domestic Violence Hotline number is 1-800-799-7233 or you can text START to 88788 from a mobile phone. All of the exercises and recommendations in this book are based on a foundation of consent and safety between partners.

To be most user-friendly, we've divided this book into three main sections. Part I will cover the history and basics of libido (though that's not to say that *basic* means easy—remember, sexual desire can be quite complicated!). We review both medical and nonmedical factors that can impact libido and lead to desire discrepancies between partners. This is important foundational information, because sexual desire is multifactorial in nature, meaning there are typically many things that contribute to it changing. In part II, we take a deep dive into specific strategies and important tools for addressing libido concerns and/or a desire discrepancy between partners. The book concludes with part III, which contains two chapters: the first specifically addresses partners who have higher libido, and the second offers guidance to readers who are considering seeking additional support around sexual desire differences. For example, if you suspect that changes in libido occurred as a side effect of a certain medication, as part of aging, or as a result of stressors in your relationship, we'll help direct you to the most relevant type of provider to continue addressing these factors.

Throughout this book, you'll encounter exercises and reflection questions. We recommend that you create a **sexual health journal** and keep it handy as you read. That way, you can use the journal to write about your reactions and to participate fully in the exercises that we've included. The sexual health journal is a tool we often ask our clients to use to better reflect on their own sexual thoughts and feelings. It also serves as a written record of your sexuality concerns, which can be used to further explore these topics with partners, a therapist, and/or a relevant medical provider.

Most chapters in this book include short case examples or vignettes to help illustrate how sexual health concerns and concepts might be applied in the real world. All case examples are composites; they don't reflect one person or relationship, but rather are an amalgam of client concerns we have encountered over our time in the field of sexual health. Details have been changed to ensure confidentiality and anonymity are fully protected.

Lastly, as clinicians and researchers, we have some biases to acknowledge upfront. We approach the subject of libido from a sex-positive framework. That means we support all individuals in choosing what is best for them sexually, and we don't assume that there is one solution that fits for everyone. Some folks are monogamous, some are non-monogamous. Some folks are allosexual, some are asexual. Some folks are queer, some are heterosexual. Some folks are kinky, some are not. We believe in treating all of these experiences equally and with respect. Whatever your identity, sexual practices, or reason for picking up this book, we hope that it helps you reach your personal sexual health goals.

desire

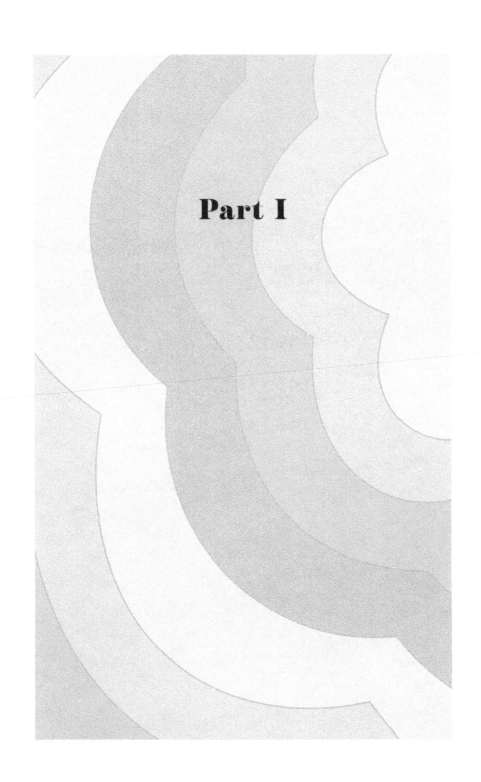

Part I

chapter 1

THE LOWDOWN
ON LIBIDO

Let's start with some important information and concepts about sexual desire. There is so much that our culture does not teach about sex and libido and, unfortunately, many of us have also picked up misinformation along the way. We've seen that access to this critical and foundational knowledge in and of itself can be transformative for many people.

LIBIDO BASICS

The term *libido* is derived from Latin for *desire* or *lust*. It was popularized by Dr. Sigmund Freud in his *Three Essays on the Theory of Sexuality*, first published in 1905.[1] He used the term *libido* to conceptualize sex as an internal physiological drive, like hunger, thirst, and fatigue. In fact, thanks to Freud, it's still very common to hear people refer to a "sex drive." Sounds like a good theory, right? Unfortunately, biomedical and psychological research suggest that Freud missed the mark here.[2] What we understand today is that sex is *not* a drive. Surprised? Let's break down this common misconception about libido.

Biologically speaking, *drives* exist to keep us alive. A drive is a human need that will result in death if not addressed within a certain time frame. For example, if we go without food, water, or sleep for a certain number of days, we literally cannot survive—thus we experience very strong drives like feeling hunger, thirst, and fatigue. When it comes to sex, however, the reality is that none of us will die from a lack of genital stimulation or orgasms. We know that's certainly not how it feels to some people . . . stay with us here! Of course, at a population level, humans need to be sexual and procreate to survive as a species. But as individuals, sex is not required for us to live, and no one is dying from a lack of orgasms. It may feel that way for some folks, but libido just doesn't work like a drive.

If libido is not a drive, then what is it, and how does it work? Sexual desire is what's known as an *incentive-motivation system*, meaning we all require an incentive or motivator to provide or reinforce desire for sexual activity.[3] (To be clear, *incentive* doesn't mean to be coerced into sex—that is never okay. Here, *incentive* is another way of saying *motivator* or *reason*.) For many folks, major motivators for sex are physical pleasure or a sense of intimate connection, but others may experience different motivators. The bottom line is that if sexual activity—especially with a partner—is not motivating to us in some way, or if we are not consistently getting something positive out of the experience, sexual desire can be difficult to experience. This is especially true in long-term relationships, where the novelty and initial excitement of being sexual with somebody new has likely decreased or faded altogether over time. It's also important to note that some motivators are more sustainable than others. For example, some people are solely motivated to be sexual in order to please a partner, which can make libido challenging to maintain over time. Recognizing or finding your own unique motivations for sex, then, becomes critically important for sexual desire.

It may surprise you to learn that people engage in sexual activity for lots of different reasons. Because sex is based on an incentive-motivation system, it's important to realize that there are many distinct and personal sexual motivations in the world. In fact, one study on this very topic found that participants identified over two hundred different reasons for having sex with a partner![4] A common motivator is that sex (and/or orgasm) feels physically good. But sometimes the motivation is to feel more connected to our partner(s), to reduce stress, or even to have a spiritual experience. However, these reasons alone may not sustain your motivation for sexual contact with another person over the long term.

Time for your first exercise! In table 1 are just some of the many reasons or motivators for being sexual with another person. Place a check mark next to the ones that have been motivating for you (both currently and in the past).

TABLE 1. I AM MOTIVATED TO BE SEXUAL . . .	
❑ Because I feel attracted to someone	❑ To feel close to someone
❑ To relieve stress	❑ To help fall asleep
❑ To feel attractive or desired	❑ To feel alive
❑ To help combat symptoms of depression	❑ To improve or maintain physical health
❑ To be physically active	❑ To express love
❑ To experience pleasure	❑ To get pregnant
❑ To feel a sense of spiritual connection	❑ To maintain a sense of physical intimacy
❑ To reconnect after conflict	❑ Because I'm feeling horny
❑ To celebrate something	❑ To help grieve/mourn
❑ To boost self-esteem	❑ To reduce pain
❑ To help reduce menstrual cramps	❑ To feel good
❑ For physical touch	❑ To alter my mood
❑ To be playful or have fun	❑ To experiment or try something new
❑ To feel a sense of comfort	❑ To feel loved
❑ To act out a fantasy	❑ To relax
❑ Write in your own:	❑ ❑

Here are few questions to reflect on in your **sexual health journal:** Are any of your sexual motivators missing from this list? Did any of your answers surprise you? Why or why not? Consider writing more about your responses in your sexual health journal.

Some people feel like their sexual desire exists without stimulus, much like Freud's concept of a sexual drive. Others may feel like their desire doesn't exist at all, despite lots of stimuli. Exploring and identifying your individual motivators is an important goal in the path to better understanding your own libido. Perhaps more important, however, is understanding that everybody's sexual desire is a bit different. If you have been feeling like you're missing

SEXUAL DESIRE VERSUS AROUSAL

Desire and arousal are often conflated—people use these terms interchangeably without realizing they are speaking about two different sexual health concepts. *Sexual desire* is a mental and psychological process. It's defined by our interest in seeking out and engaging in sexual activity. This is altogether different from *sexual arousal*, which refers to our bodies getting turned on. Arousal is a physiological process that might involve genital swelling, tingling, erections, and/or lubrication, as well as hardening of the nipples and perhaps looking and feeling flushed. Many people experience sexual desire and arousal simultaneously, and this common overlap is likely why the terms get confused. It's very important to know, however, that these processes aren't always in alignment. For example, we can be quite mentally interested in sex (desire), but struggle with physical arousal (e.g., difficulty with lubrication or erection). Alternatively, we might also experience physical arousal but little to no mental interest in sex. This is referred to as *arousal non-concordance* (a term also mentioned earlier, in the introduction) and demonstrates that what our bodies are doing doesn't always tell the whole story.[5] We have seen arousal non-concordance be the source of many conflicts between partners in therapy. To learn more, we recommend Dr. Emily Nagoski's TED Talk called "The Truth About Unwanted Arousal." She also writes about it in her groundbreaking 2015 book *Come as You Are: The Surprising New Science That Will Transform Your Sex Life*.

some internal drive that fuels your sexual desire, we want to reassure you that there is nothing wrong with you and that you are normal.

THE TWO TYPES OF SEXUAL DESIRE

How medical and psychological communities conceptualize sexual desire has shifted enormously over time, especially as sexual science has evolved past Freud's idea of a sexual drive. Let's look at how the concept of desire has changed over the years—and how these concepts can help you learn more about your own libido.

The first modern conceptualization of the sexual response cycle was proposed by Dr. William Masters and Virginia Johnson, an American research team who became well-known during the 1950s and '60s. Their model includes the phases of excitement (that is, physical arousal), plateau, orgasm, and resolution. As you can see in figure 1, sexual desire was not actually mentioned in this original model!

Masters and Johnson were mostly interested in studying the biology of sex—that is, what happens to our physical bodies during sexual experiences. It's perhaps not surprising, then, that they charted our sexual response as starting with physical "excitement" and arousal—things like lubrication, genital swelling, and erection—rather than psychological factors like desire. While this model was truly groundbreaking at the time, it has since been heavily critiqued, both for ignoring the psychological and emotional aspects of sex and for assuming that everyone experiences the same sexual response cycle (spoiler alert—we don't!).

It was Dr. Helen Singer Kaplan—a physician, psychologist, and early sex therapist—who first included desire in a model of human sexual response. In her 1979 book *Disorders of Sexual Desire and Other New Concepts and Techniques in Sex Therapy*, Dr. Singer Kaplan recognized the importance that psychological influences exert on our sexual response.[6] She argued that, for many people, mental interest or desire for sex occurs *before* bodily arousal. To this day, it is Dr. Singer Kaplan's model that shapes most people's

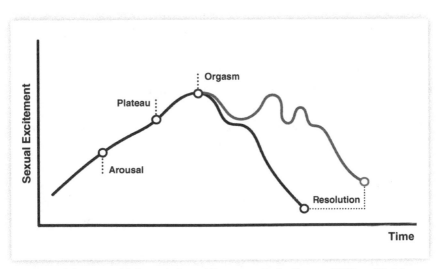

FIGURE 1. Masters and Johnson's Sexual Response Cycle. Source: William H. Masters and Virginia E. Johnson, *Human Sexual Response* (Boston: Little Brown, 1966).

ideas about sexual response. We suspect this is because the Singer Kaplan model—combined together with the Masters and Johnson model—is still commonly taught in courses on human sexuality and sexual medicine. Culturally, this has privileged a conceptualization of sex that starts with psychological desire.

In 2000, twenty-one years after the Singer Kaplan model was introduced, physician and sexual medicine specialist Dr. Rosemary Basson provided the next critical shift in our understanding of sexual response. Her research suggests that for many folks, sexual desire is an *outcome* of physiological arousal: interest in sex does not necessarily just occur out of nowhere and then lead to physical arousal.[7] This means that often, libido may not be like an on-off light switch but more like a dimmer switch, with some physical arousal and warming up required for sexual interest to activate. If we return to the original Masters and Johnson sexual response cycle, this would mean that for many people, desire is located *after* the initial excitement/arousal phase of the cycle (rather than *before* the arousal phase, as in Singer Kaplan's model).

Importantly, Dr. Basson did more than just update past sexual response models. She recognized the strengths of these past models and addressed their limitations to better account for individual variety and diversity. Basson's model (figure 2) is able to explain the enormous complexity involved in our sexual responses, acknowledging that while there may be some core commonalities to our sexual response, at the end of the day, we are all a bit different.

Perhaps the most important concept that Dr. Basson illuminated is the existence of two different types of libido: spontaneous sexual desire and responsive sexual desire. Because her model covers a complicated topic—libido—it can be confusing at first. Let's dig a bit more into this important model and the two types of sexual desire that it depicts.

Spontaneous Sexual Desire

As you can see, at the center of Basson's model is *spontaneous desire*. This is in line with Dr. Singer Kaplan's original notion of psychological desire preceding sexual arousal and activity. Spontaneous desire sounds like what it is: an interest in sex that comes on suddenly. Many people experience spontaneous sexual desire simultaneously with physiological arousal (perhaps lubrication, erection, or a tingling in the genitals; a sense of being horny).

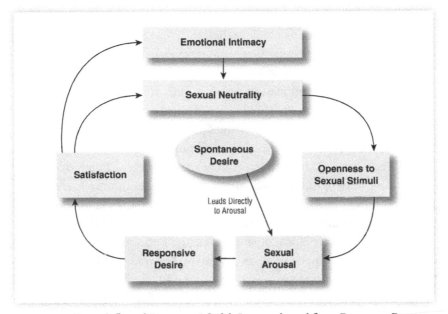

FIGURE 2. Basson's Sexual Response Model. Image adapted from Rosemary Basson, "Rethinking Low Sexual Desire in Women," *BJOG: An International Journal of Obstetrics and Gynaecology* 109, no. 4 (April 2002).

The combination of desire and physical arousal is often a powerful experience. Notably, spontaneous desire is the main—if not the only—type of sexual desire that we see depicted in our culture. In the movies and shows we watch, and in the books and magazines we read, partners become "turned on" and then have sex. In these portrayals, sex happens quickly, passionately, and without much lead-up time. Spontaneous sexual desire is treated culturally and psychologically as our main cue for sex to begin: we experience a sense of horniness and react by pursuing sex with a partner or self-stimulating (or doing nothing and feeling sexually frustrated for a while!). What's left out of this narrative, however, is that some people experience little to no spontaneous sexual desire and often find themselves waiting long periods of time for this sexual cue. Spontaneous sexual desire is usually what folks are referring to in our therapy offices when they say they have "lost" their desire, or that their libido is "low."

Though there is still much that is not understood about spontaneous sexual desire, we do know some important things about it. First, spontaneous sexual desire appears to be influenced—at least partly—by sex hormones such as estrogens and androgens (aka testosterone). Though everyone has both estrogen and testosterone in their bodies, there can be notable variability in levels from person to person. There is some evidence to suggest that higher levels of testosterone are associated with higher levels of spontaneous sexual desire but, because hormones are complex, this is not always true.[8] Additionally, changes in hormone levels—which may be triggered, for example, by menstrual cycles, pregnancy, menopause, or certain medications—may intensify or diminish one's experience of spontaneous sexual desire (more on this in chapter 4). It's important to acknowledge that much of our understanding of the role hormones play in libido comes from animal models. The mechanisms underlying the influence of sex hormones in human sexual behavior remain quite unclear, and all reputable sexual medicine clinicians, researchers, and professional organizations understand that libido is multifactorial in nature—not solely based on these hormone levels.[9]

In addition to hormone levels, we also know that spontaneous sexual desire can be influenced by neurotransmitters, the chemicals that send signals in our brain.[10] Research here is also still quite limited, but perhaps the best illustration of this phenomenon is the honeymoon period of a new relationship. Also referred to as *new relationship energy* (NRE) or *limerence*, this is the period early on in our partnerships in which spontaneous sexual desire is typically high and sexual activity is more frequent.[11] This is also the point in relationships in which we tend to have a flood of neurotransmitters, such as dopamine and norepinephrine, when we are around our new partners. You may recall this period in your own relationships. It's often associated with feelings of infatuation. We tend to view our partners with rose-colored glasses, placing them on a pedestal and feeling as if they can do no wrong. This stage naturally comes to an end, as does the rush of neurotransmitters, in a process known as *habituation*. When we habituate to our partners, there is often a corresponding decrease in spontaneous sexual desire. That's not to say that sexual desire completely tanks with habituation, but it will likely level off to some degree as you get to know your partner better over time (including those endearing but maybe also annoying habits they have). Depending on the partnership, this honeymoon period and heightened spontaneous sexual desire may last anywhere from a few months to a few years.

Not only is it normal for spontaneous sexual desire to decline somewhat as relationships progress, it's also quite predictable due to the biological and psychological process of habituation. Spontaneous sexual desire can feel powerful and positive, often leading to distress when it fades or levels off. Because humans like to find and make meaning of our everyday experiences, we tend to read into such changes in ways that may be quite unhelpful. For example, if a partner's spontaneous libido has declined over time, we might start to believe that they no longer find us attractive, that we have fallen out of love, or that they may have found someone else. These are common interpretations that we hear from clients as they try to make meaning of changes in their or their partner's spontaneous sexual desire. And while it's certainly possible that some of those fears are true, we find that shifts in spontaneous desire are more likely related to identifiable physiological changes or psychological and relational factors.

BOOSTING SPONTANEOUS DESIRE

The search for a medical method to increase spontaneous desire has long been the holy grail of the sexual health world. Hormones—especially testosterone—and neurotransmitters have been the main focus of this search, since we know that both play a role in spontaneous sexual desire. Two medications—flibanserin and bremelanotide—were approved by the FDA to increase cisgender women's spontaneous sexual desire. They have unfortunately not yet been studied in other populations. Flibanserin was put on the market in 2015 and bremelanotide in 2019. Flibanserin, a daily oral medication, began as a failed antidepressant before being marketed for decreased sexual desire. Its mechanism of action is the disinhibition of neurotransmitters (dopamine, norepinephrine) that are known to be excitatory factors of sexual desire. Bremelanotide, which is injected prior to sexual activity, is theorized to stimulate dopamine, though its exact mechanism of action remains unknown. There is still a lot to learn about these medications and existing research has been mixed. A major challenge is that these medications cannot address common barriers to libido, such as relationship concerns, sexual pain, anxiety, and many other factors that we will discuss in this book.

Returning to Dr. Basson's model, remember that spontaneous sexual desire is only one type of libido. It's also a type of libido that may naturally be low for some people and that also tends to fluctuate over time depending on one's physiology and other life factors, such as stress. For many people, simply waiting around for spontaneous sexual desire to kick in on its own might mean that they'll be waiting forever! This leads us to the very important, yet often overlooked, second type of libido: responsive sexual desire.

Responsive Sexual Desire

Responsive sexual desire also sounds like what it is—libido that occurs in *response* to some type of physical sensation. Importantly, this means that this type of desire happens *after* receiving stimulation, not before, as with spontaneous desire. Because we rarely educate people about responsive sexual desire and infrequently see it reflected in the culture around us (remember all those movies featuring only spontaneous desire!), it's easy to be unaware of this key piece of information about libido. In responsive desire, the order of desire and arousal are the reverse of Dr. Singer Kaplan's model. This means that for many folks, significant physical arousal may need to happen before sexual desire occurs (or rather, responds).

Basson's model was the first to really recognize the critical role of responsive sexual desire—and the fact that this type of desire is incredibly common. For many people, responsive sexual desire is their predominant experience of libido. Unfortunately, responsive sexual desire doesn't seem to be discussed much outside the offices of sex therapists. This is somewhat shocking given that Basson's model of sexual response is not all that new—it is now twenty-plus years old! It wasn't until the publication of Dr. Emily Nagoski's book *Come as You Are* that knowledge of responsive sexual desire became more mainstream.

As we've noted, the culture around us tends to insist that spontaneous desire is the norm for everyone when it's not. This means that the libidos of a large percentage of the population are misrepresented and misunderstood. Those with a more responsive type of sexual desire can be made to feel "broken," or like something is wrong with them. This leads many folks to present to sex therapy with the goal of transforming their responsive desire type to a more spontaneous one, due to the mistaken belief that this is how they are "supposed to" experience libido. This is often not a goal that we can accomplish, since an individual's sexual response type is typically just a result of how their body works.

That said, many barriers to libido can be addressed and, often, removed. The goal, then, becomes helping partners satisfactorily navigate sexual desire and pathways to arousal, especially if folks are in a relationship where one partner is more spontaneous and another is more responsive. As Jennifer is fond of saying to such folks: "This is a *difference* in desire but not necessarily a deal-breaker!" Navigating different types of sexual desire first and foremost requires education and understanding, so let's dig into responsive desire a bit more.

If responsive sexual desire is a response to a stimulus, how does that work exactly? We have found that there are at least four foundational requirements for responsive desire:

1. Consent
2. Pleasure
3. Focus
4. Time

Starting with the first requirement, it's clear that something explicitly nonconsensual—like sexual assault—will not trigger responsive sexual desire. Of course! However, the concept of consent is far more wide-reaching. For responsive sexual desire to occur, we must truly be open to receiving stimulation (that is, something that sparks arousal from any of our physical senses). We don't need to feel turned on or horny, but an openness to engaging in physical stimulation is key to developing responsive libido. This is what Basson's model references as a sexually neutral starting point. Pressure from a partner, or self-pressure to engage in physical or sexual touch, is not a neutral starting point, is not fully consensual, and is unlikely to trigger responsive desire.

The second key requirement for building responsive desire is that the physical stimulation must be pleasurable. Stimulation that is (unintentionally) painful, or that causes physical and emotional discomfort, is unlikely to result in responsive desire. In fact, we address pain as a major barrier to libido in chapter 4. Moreover, touch that feels simply neutral to us is also unlikely to build responsive sexual desire. In order to reliably develop our sexual response, physical stimulation has to feel good!

Moving into the third foundational requirement, we must be able to focus on the stimulation that we are experiencing (read: responding to). We might be fully open to physical touch (consent) and it might feel great (pleasure), but if our minds are elsewhere and we're experiencing "busy brain," we're distracted from our ability to perceive physical pleasure. Learning how to better focus during positive, pleasurable sexual experiences can be a game changer for folks with more responsive libidos (more on that in part 2 of the book!).

Lastly, time (and timing) is a major requirement in building responsive desire. For some people, the stimulation that triggers their response could be a quick thought, image, or fantasy. It could be someone attractive walking by, a brief image while scrolling on social media, or a scene from a TV show or movie. That could be it! Brief stimulus → sexual desire response. For others, responsive desire might require longer exposure to a stimulus, or multiple stimuli. Longer stimulus → sexual desire response. Still others might need a different set of stimuli: lots of touching and kissing with a partner, for example, or enjoying a lot of quality time and emotional connection with them. Regarding timing, context plays an important role in both our openness and our responsiveness to stimulation. The amount of time and the context required to build responsive desire varies considerably from person to person, making this an important area of self-discovery in your libido journey.

Basson's model has been groundbreaking for our understanding of the diversity and complexity of sexual desire and response. She showed that many individuals' libido springs not from spontaneous desire but from a place of sexual neutrality—they are open to either seeking out or receiving sexual stimuli. As their body experiences pleasurable stimulation and becomes physiologically aroused, desire emerges in response to that arousal, which leads to a sense of satisfaction and emotional intimacy. Understanding this responsive type of libido is critical for managing desire differences in partnerships. There's a metaphor we've heard that suggests that some people's sexual desire operates like a microwave: it's quick to get turned on. For others, though, desire might be more like an oven: it takes more time to warm up or preheat, if you will. If your sexual response operates more like a microwave, that's likely just how your body works. This may change over time with circumstance or aging, but for now, it's the way it is. Similarly, if your sexual response operates more like an oven, that's likely an intrinsic part of who you are—a quality that may not suddenly change. The goal here is not to turn microwaves into ovens or vice versa. The goal is to better understand what works for you and how to use that knowledge in your relationships.

Before we continue, take a moment with your **sexual health journal** to reflect on what you've just read about spontaneous and responsive sexual desire. Do you see yourself in either of these desire types? Have you experienced one type more than another? Neither? If you have a partner or partners, do you and your partner(s) have different types of libido? Have you noticed your desire type changing over time, or throughout the course of a relationship?

THE WILLINGNESS MODEL

Our culture's emphasis on spontaneous desire often leads folks to think, "If I don't have the desire, I can't be sexual." But what if that spontaneous desire never surfaces? What if that lightning bolt of horny erotic feelings never seems to strike? We turn here to the *willingness model*, which is a major component of responsive sexual desire. This concept is included in Basson's model of sexual response, and it stems from the important (and often overlooked) work of sex therapist and author JoAnn Loulan, who wisely stated: "Willingness may be the most important part of your sexual response, not desire or orgasm."[12]

In neutral situations where you aren't yet feeling sexual, you may find that you're open to sexual contact, even if you aren't necessarily feeling turned on. Returning to our microwave and oven metaphor: The willingness model involves asking yourself, "Am I willing to go turn on the oven?" rather than, "Is the oven already on?" Those are two very different questions. The willingness model is helpful for folks who predominantly experience responsive desire (which is why Basson incorporated the concept into her model of the sexual response cycle). It's a framework that can help us move from a neutral context to a sexual context. Willingness can lead to desire, arousal, pleasure, none of those, or all of those.

Perhaps the best way to think about the willingness model is using a very simple 0 to 10 scale to answer the question: Are you willing to see if your sexual desire will arise (respond)? When you're at a 0, you aren't feeling willing to try to create responsive desire. And that's okay! We all have days that are a 0 on the willingness scale, when perhaps you don't feel well, or are stressed and overwhelmed. At the other end of the willingness scale is a 10, meaning that you feel open to physical engagement of some kind to create responsive sexual desire. Importantly, a willingness rating of 10 does *not* mean that you are already turned on or experiencing spontaneous desire; rather, that you are open to cultivating responsive desire.

Of course, there are lots of potential ratings between 0 and 10. What happens, for example, if you rate your willingness at a 4 or 6 on the scale? It may be helpful for you to think about what your own personal willingness scale looks like. What, for example, is your own personal midpoint? For one person, a 5 on the willingness scale might mean a willingness to get into bed and cuddle and then evaluate additional physical contact from there. For someone else, a 5 might mean that they are a definite "no" for genital sexual contact, but a "yes" for something else that is intimate—for example, spooning naked together.

One of the benefits of using the 0 to 10 willingness scale is that we can use it to self-assess *as well as* to communicate with our partners about our level of willingness to sexually engage. Willingness ratings won't always be as easy as a 0 or 10, however, so it's important to consider which factors move us back and forth along the scale. Take some time in your **sexual health journal** to reflect on this: what experiences or activities help move you closer toward 0? Alternatively, what experiences move you closer to a 10? These factors are referred to as *brakes* and *accelerators*, respectively, and we'll talk more about them in the next section.

Willingness goes both ways. It's important that we don't just fixate on whether one partner is willing to have the type of sex the other partner wants. For example, people are often labeled as having "low libido" if they don't desire frequent intercourse. But what if they are frequently interested in other types of sex? And what if, rather than asking the "low libido" partner to be willing to have intercourse on a more frequent basis, we ask the "higher libido" partner to work on broadening their definition and experiences of sex? Or to perhaps give more value to physical and sexual touch that doesn't lead to penetration or orgasms? This involves dismantling a strong, culturally held, hierarchical view of sexual activity, something we'll discuss further in the next chapter.

We want to make clear that the willingness model is rooted in consent. Willingness is something that comes from within. It cannot and should not be pushed for by a partner. Consent cannot be coerced: by definition, it needs to be freely given and is revocable at any time. Consent is the underpinning for responsive desire and a concept that we'll return to throughout this book.

THE DUAL CONTROL MODEL: ACCELERATORS AND BRAKES

You've probably heard the terms sexual *turn ons* and *turn offs*. The dual control model, proposed by Dr. Erick Janssen and Dr. John Bancroft in 2007, essentially explains the same ideas in more scientific terms.[13] They suggest that we have an internal sexual excitation system (SES) and sexual inhibition system (SIS): a certain set of variables that move us toward sex, and another set of variables that move us away from sex. This concept works extremely well in conjunction with the willingness model. Accelerators and brakes—the factors that move us back and forth along the willingness scale—can be conceptualized as the turn ons and turn offs of Janssen and Bancroft's SES and SIS.[14]

Some accelerators and brakes are more predictable and common than others. For example, feeling relaxed and well-rested is a fairly typical accelerator for our libidos (both spontaneous and responsive), whereas experiencing pain or fatigue tends to put the brakes on desire. Beyond that, however, most accelerators and brakes are highly individualized—they are specific to you and your relationships. This means that it's important to consider your personal accelerators and brakes in order to learn more about your libido and how to use the willingness scale. This then opens the door to better communicating your needs to sexual partners.

Accelerators and brakes can behave differently from person to person (just like cars!). Some folks have very sensitive accelerators, which means that it doesn't take much to arouse them or spark a willingness to be sexual. Some folks have very sensitive brake pedals, which means that it doesn't take much to turn them off or to shut down willingness to be sexual. Folks with concerns about low libido often try to rev on the accelerator. They go on vacations, play sexy or romantic music, buy flowers, and light candles, all with the hopes that this will ignite the spark of desire. For many, though, revving the accelerator is simply not enough. It doesn't take a car expert to know that we can rev the gas all we want, but if there's still a heavy foot on the brake, you aren't going anywhere! For this reason, it is also critically important to address the factors that may be pressing down our sexual brakes.

We invite you to consider some of the factors that impact your sexual desire. As we've seen, sexual accelerators and brakes form the building blocks of your libido and influence willingness in the absence (or decrease) of spontaneous desire. It's also critical for us to discuss sexual accelerators and brakes with our sexual partners. To help you get started, we've provided examples based on what some of our clients have shared with us. Again, while some accelerators and brakes tend to be fairly common (e.g., most people's sexual desire is negatively impacted by feeling sick), these factors are also individual and involve both your personal preferences and, if partnered, the unique aspects of your relationship. Some people's accelerators are other people's brakes, and vice versa! No two lists are the same.

Take out your **sexual health journal** and list the factors that impact your sexual brakes and accelerators in table 2.

TABLE 2. BRAKES AND ACCELERATORS	
Brakes	**Accelerators**
Kids being noisy in the next room	Being well-rested
Feeling ill	Feeling close to my partner(s)
Pain with sex	Pleasurable stimulation

PLEASURE, SATISFACTION, AND SEXUAL DESIRE

As we discuss the basics of libido in this first chapter, we would be remiss not to include sexual pleasure and satisfaction. While we'll return to this particular topic again and again (it's that important!), let's start here with some foundational facts.

Sexual pleasure and satisfaction play a critical role in libido differences between partners. Studies have repeatedly shown that high sexual satisfaction is a strong predictor (in some studies, the number one predictor) for desiring partnered sex in long-term relationships, regardless of gender.[15] This consistent finding has fueled criticism of the pharmaceutical industry's quest to develop biomedical cures or treatments for "low" desire: often we find that desire is "low" not because of a physiological issue, but because the sex that folks are having simply isn't all that good! From a sex therapy perspective, the "low" desire in these cases is more accurately a sign of good judgment—after all, who gets excited to have sex that's painful, boring, or generally unsatisfying? Research—inclusive of heterosexual people, lesbian women, and gay men—has shown that high sexual satisfaction is associated with either no sexual desire discrepancy or unproblematic sexual desire discrepancy between partners.[16] While we can't necessarily establish cause and effect from these studies, it is certainly safe to say that high sexual satisfaction has strong positive value when it comes to libido. Indeed, we often find that positive and satisfying sexual experiences can effectively "build" on one another to create stronger libido.

There are, of course, many reasons why sexual satisfaction might be low in a relationship—lack of knowledge, sexual pain, poor technique, performance anxiety, and relationship tension to name a few. The most important thing is that these are behavioral and psychological factors that can be addressed and improved. Pleasurable and satisfying sex is a skill that can be learned and practiced, and sometimes, decreased libido is a sign that we need to do just that!

SEXUAL MESSAGES AND CULTURAL SCRIPTS

As we've seen, there are many cultural messages that mislead us into believing that something is wrong with our libido. Many of these messages are delivered to us based on gender and assumed sexuality. Let's explore a few.

Cisgender heterosexual women are typically socialized to believe that their sexual interest will decrease with age, that sex is mostly for men, and that men should be the pursuers and initiators of sexual activity. Furthermore, heterosexual women are often taught that men who aren't pursuing sex may have lost interest (or may even be seeking sex outside of the relationship). They have been taught that penile-vaginal penetrative intercourse is what sex is all about and that it is important to keep men sexually satisfied in order to keep the relationship secure. Many women internalize cultural messages that their own pleasure or orgasm is not as important as men's and that sex ends with his orgasm. Importantly, these messages hurt people of all genders.

Cisgender heterosexual men are typically socialized to believe that they should *always* be interested in sex and that they should have a constantly high libido. They have often learned that men are the pursuers of sex, and that part of a man's overall worth is determined by how often he has partnered sex or how many sexual partners he's had (consider, for example, how a "stud" or "player" receives social clout in our culture). Erections and orgasms are depicted as the main goals of sex. Much like women, men are also typically taught that if a partner is not interested in sex, it's because of a loss of attraction. Again, these messages are harmful for people of all genders. We will continue to explore the roots of such messages throughout this book.

If you are transgender, nonbinary, and/or queer, many of these cultural messages about cisgender heterosexual men and women—and sex in general—may not fit for you and can perhaps lead to feelings of erasure. That said, you were probably still exposed to—and may have internalized—many of these messages throughout your life. You might have already figured out that these messages just don't reflect your own feelings and experience. Our culture's messages about sex and queer, trans, and nonbinary folks tend to be more openly hostile: that sex outside of a cisgender heterosexual relationship is unacceptable or immoral. There are also some harmful sexual stereotypes specific to the LGBTQ+ community, such as pervasive messages that gay men and bisexual people are always promiscuous, or that relationships between lesbian women will ultimately become nonsexual, leading to "bed death."[17] Bisexual and other plurisexual people are often culturally erased while also facing a unique host of negative sexual stereotypes: they are often portrayed as unable to be monogamous, as sexually confused and indecisive, or as vectors of sexually transmitted infections. Trans and nonbinary people in our culture tend to be either sexually erased or fetishized. All of these stereotypes and negative cultural messages diminish the complexity of the human sexual experience and, as we hope you'll see throughout this book, are incredibly harmful to people of all genders and sexual orientations.

For centuries, cultures and religions across the globe have dictated such messages around sex. Women in particular have been heavily shamed around sex: the purity movement, for example, popularized by evangelical Christianity in the United States, celebrates and prizes women's "virginity" (a term we do not like and no longer use, which we expand on in chapter 2). The general social message has been overly binary, praising men for their sexuality (as long as it falls into the standard heterosexual model) while shaming women for theirs. Women and girls have been taught to hide and police their bodies and sexualities for fear of arousing the men and boys around them. Many women and girls have been taught that men and boys cannot control their sexual desires (something, by the way, for which there is absolutely no scientific evidence). And men and boys who don't have a particularly high desire for sex have been made to feel inadequate or abnormal.

For folks who have been taught by their culture or faith to wait until marriage to be sexual, it can be difficult, once they are married, to simply flip a switch and begin to relax and enjoy an activity that, for years, they were told to fear and distrust. We have seen many clients wait until marriage to have sex, only to find it difficult to transition into enjoyable sexual activity after a lifetime of messages that sex was off-limits, bad, or "dirty." For the record, it's absolutely okay to wait until marriage to be sexual with a partner. The problem is that we are often not adequately prepared for that transition—physically, mentally, and emotionally. We'll discuss this further in chapter 2, where we dive much deeper into sex and faith traditions.

THE SEXUAL SPECTRUM: FROM ASEXUALITY TO HIGH SEXUALITY

Like many aspects of human sexuality, libido is a spectrum (or, for you science-minded readers, a statistical normal curve). On this spectrum, most people fall somewhere in the middle, but there are individuals whose level of libido places them at one of the far ends. Depending on life stage, personal circumstances, and aspects of biology, many of us shift slightly back and forth along the spectrum throughout our lives. Our sexual partners also shift along the spectrum of libido. This libido spectrum is one place where sexual desire discrepancies between partners can occur. (As we've seen, different libido types—spontaneous and responsive—are another.) Sometimes the discrepancy on the libido spectrum is temporary, while other times it's a perpetual difference that requires thoughtful attention.

One end of the spectrum is not just low, but absent desire for some or all sexual activity—sometimes referred to as *asexuality*. A person who is asexual does not experience, or very rarely experiences, sexual attraction to others. Many asexual people report that they rarely, if ever, experience spontaneous or responsive desire. To be clear, this doesn't mean that their bodies are incapable of sexual arousal, or that they are unable to enjoy genital stimulation. As author Julie Sondra Decker discusses in her book *The Invisible Orientation*, some asexual people may, in fact, engage in sexual activity—solo or with partners—and their reasons for doing so are numerous (remember the importance of sexual motivators!).[18] For some asexual people, masturbation feels unrelated to sex and may, for example, represent a method of relaxation. Partnered sex might still occur, not necessarily due to libido, but rather as a way to connect with a partner.

Some asexual people may be willing to have partnered sex, and some may not. Remember, every person's reasons or motivations for being sexual are unique to them. It depends on the individual. If you discover while reading this book that you or your partner(s) are asexual, it may be a discrepancy that requires ongoing discussion and negotiation. We'll cover strategies for approaching these discussions in depth throughout the book. Some examples include:

- The asexual partner is sometimes willing to be sexual (with consent, of course).
- The allosexual partner addresses their sexual desire via self-stimulation (with or without the asexual partner present).
- The partners, if monogamous, open up the relationship so that the allosexual partner can explore their sexual desire with others.
- The partners practice mutual masturbation as part of their sexual activity.

WHAT IS COMPULSORY SEXUALITY?

The phrase *compulsory sexuality* is inspired by Adrienne Rich's famous essay "Compulsory Heterosexuality and Lesbian Existence."[19] In it, she discusses the cultural assumption of heterosexuality: our wider culture erases other sexualities, treating them as if they don't exist and, therefore, cannot be explored. This concept, initially applied to gay and bisexual exploration and identities, has been expanded to address the concerns of the asexual community. As author Angela Chen writes, "Compulsory sexuality is a set of assumptions and behaviors that support the idea that every normal person is sexual, that not wanting (socially approved) sex is unnatural and wrong, and that people who don't care about sexuality are missing out on an utterly necessary experience."[20] In essence, compulsory sexuality contributes to stigma against those whose desire for sexual activity is low or perhaps even absent—regardless of whether they identify as asexual. We certainly find that among sexual health professionals, the assumption of allosexuality is deep-seated and can erase—or even potentially cause harm to—asexual individuals.

On the other far end of the libido spectrum, some individuals experience very high spontaneous sexual desire. For folks who are highly sexual, it is often frustrating to have a partner with lower or a more responsive type of libido. Some people have been labeled "sex addicts" or have been harshly judged for having high sexual desire. It's important to note that, just as having low sexual desire is not inherently a problem, having a high desire for sexual activity is not in and of itself an issue. (We dedicate an entire chapter to this topic in part III of the book.) Masturbating or wanting to be sexual every day can be a normal and healthy form of sexual expression for some, but not for others. If the type or frequency of an individual's sexual activity leads to unwanted or harmful consequences (e.g., missing work, violating the boundaries of one's values or relationship, depression, anxiety, not getting enough sleep), there may be good reason to seek out therapy or support. Otherwise, there is no one appropriate level of desire for everyone.

Recall that an important foundation of this book is that everyone is responsible for their own pleasure. For the individual who wishes to be sexual much more frequently than their partner, taking responsibility for this may involve more self-stimulation to bridge the libido gap. Or it may involve finding nonsexual ways to connect with a partner to experience more physical touch. Some partners choose to become consensually non-monogamous so that the higher-libido partner can have more partnered sexual experiences. We recommend approaching this strategy with a lot of thought and support and review the complex topic of opening up a relationship in chapter 3.

REFLECTION EXERCISE Let's think more about the spectrum of libido. In your **sexual health journal**, take a moment to describe your own libido. Notice what emotions, thoughts, and body sensations come up as you think about this and how it impacts your life. Let's look at a few more questions for your journal:

- If you have "low" libido, what exactly do you have low libido *for*? That is, what specific sexual behaviors (e.g., kissing, oral sex, intercourse) feel less or least interesting to you? Is there a specific feeling or experience that you are hoping to avoid?
- What does low libido mean to you?
- If you have "high" libido, what specific sexual activities do you have high libido for (e.g., kissing, oral sex, intercourse) or feel most

interested in pursuing? Is there a specific feeling or experience that
you are seeking?

- What does high libido mean to you?
- When you think about or say the word *sex*, do you really mean
  penile-vaginal penetration, or do you mean something else? What
  does sex mean or look like for you?
- Do you enjoy the sex that you're having, or have had in the past? Is
  it physically and emotionally pleasurable to you? Why or why not?

The point of this book is not to exactly match you to someone else's libido
or sexual response style. Biologically and psychologically, this is difficult—if
not impossible—to do. Rather, the goal is to understand what works best
for you, to learn how your own unique body works, and to find ways to
honor that both for yourself and within your relationship. We find that this
process requires cultivating self-awareness and reflection about the many
factors that can impact sexual desire, as well as the development of healthy
communication skills so as to be able to discuss this topic with partners.

SEXUAL HISTORY EXERCISE Part of beginning to understand what works best for
you and how your sexual patterns have developed is to look backward.
Understanding our own unique trajectories of sexual development—the
education we received (or didn't), the cultural messages we adopted, when
changes in our sexual health occurred—is an important task. To this end,
we strongly encourage you to create a time line of your sexual history,
from your earliest experiences related to sex and sexuality up to the present
moment. In this exercise, we invite you to write about significant events
regarding your sexuality, including your level of sexual interest at different
points in time. This time line will also be helpful for reference and to refine
as you continue reading this book. Get out your **sexual health journal** and let's
get started!

In creating your sexual history time line, we challenge you to go above
and beyond simply listing chronological dates and events. We encourage you
to also write about important aspects of your social, emotional, and mental
development, including events or memories that significantly impacted your
sexuality. This is an important part of beginning to understand the development of your sexual patterns, values, and beliefs. Here are a few suggestions
and questions to consider in creating your sexual history time line:

1. To get started, it may help to break up your time line into segments (e.g., decades starting with 0–10 years old, 10–20 years old, and so on, up through your current age). As you write, you will probably remember events that happened in other time periods. Allow this to happen and fill in the gaps. It doesn't have to be in exact order.
2. Include both positive and negative events or memories.
3. Include any religious or faith-based influences on sexual health.
4. Include family messages or attitudes about sex and sexuality, such as those specific to your own sexual development. These messages or attitudes may have been overt (spoken) or covert (unspoken but still understood).
5. Include cultural, racial, and/or ethnic influences on your sexual health.
6. When did you discover or first become aware of your sexuality?
7. When did you begin to self-stimulate? How did you learn about it? What messages did you receive about masturbation and where did these messages come from?
8. When was your first crush? How old were you when you first started dating? If you didn't date, what was that like for you?
9. How old were you when you first became sexual with a partner? How did you feel about the experience?
10. How did you feel about your body as you were growing up? Did those feelings change over time or at different points in your life?
11. What messages did you get from your family, culture, and community about gender and what it means to be masculine or feminine? Did you receive messages regarding sexual experiences with your own gender? Were they positive, negative, or neutral?
12. Did your family members ever talk about sex or sexuality? What kind of sexual health education did you receive growing up?

DESIRE DISCREPANCY AND THE AVOIDANCE CYCLE

Most partners have a sexual desire discrepancy at some point in their relationship. For some partnerships, desire discrepancies arise from time to time and are temporary. For others, a desire discrepancy is a more perpetual dynamic in the relationship. For example, one partner may ideally enjoy sexual activity three times per week, whereas the other partner may enjoy sex once a month. One partner may prefer intercourse every time they are sexual, whereas the other partner may prefer intercourse infrequently, or not at all. While it's very common for people to have different preferences around sexual frequency and activities, this is not typically how we are taught to consider sexual relationships—and it's certainly not what's represented in movies, television shows, books, and other media that we consume. Nevertheless, desire discrepancies are quite common and, for better or worse, it's unrealistic to think that we can exactly match up our own sexual ideals with our partner's.

One pattern that's very common among partners with a desire discrepancy is that the partner labeled as lower libido will try to meet their partner's sexual ideal. Let's use an example to illustrate this:

Rivka likes to have sex about once a week and ideally prefers intercourse. Chaim generally feels like being sexual about once a month. Chaim's preference is to skip penetrative intercourse to focus more on oral sex, which is his favorite sexual activity. If Chaim chooses to be sexual once per week to satisfy Rivka, and if they engage only in the type of sex that Rivka prefers each time, it won't be long before Chaim experiences a further lowering of his desire, as sex becomes all about and for Rivka. Remember that sex is not a drive—it's an incentive-motivation system. If Chaim does not have an incentive for sexual activity other than pleasing Rivka, it is likely that over time, he will lose interest altogether. Sex that satisfies only one partner is extremely difficult to sustain long-term.

Let's consider a metaphor here and, instead of sex, use watching movies as our example. Imagine that every time Em and Rory watch a movie, Em chooses the movie and Rory just goes along with it. Em loves action and adventure movies, whereas Rory enjoys drama and documentaries. If Em chooses an action film every time, how long will it be before Rory comes to the conclusion that they'd rather not watch a movie at all? What develops over time for Rory is a negative association to movies. *Movies = I don't get to experience what I enjoy.*

One of the greatest challenges of a desire discrepancy is that the cycle can perpetuate itself very quickly. The higher-libido partner wants sex more, perhaps, in part, because for them it does not feel readily available. The lower-libido partner wants sex less, perhaps, in part, because for them sex feels too available or pressured. Another way of saying this is that the supply and demand may be very different for each partner, which can reinforce the pattern and become even more frustrating over time.

Another variable may be that the higher-libido partner, in an attempt to cope, is trying to think *less* about sex. Meanwhile, the lower-libido partner, in their own attempt to cope, may be trying to think *more* about sex to meet the higher-desire partner. This creates an interesting effect. According to ironic process theory, developed by social psychologist Daniel Wegner, trying to suppress a thought actually has the opposite effect and instead tends to strengthen that very thought! In Wegner's famous "white bear study," officially titled "Paradoxical Effects of Thought Suppression," one group of research participants was asked *to* think about a white bear whereas the second group was asked *not* to think about a white bear.[21] Both groups then verbalized their thoughts—stream-of-consciousness style—for five minutes. Each time they thought about a white bear, they were instructed to ring a bell. Despite the instructions they'd received, the second group thought about white bears more than once per minute on average.

In the next part of the study, this second group was then instructed *to* think about a white bear and again to verbalize their thoughts for five minutes, ringing a bell every time they thought of the bear. This group thought about the white bear much more often than those in group one, who did not suppress their thoughts in the first place. It seems, then, that when we try to suppress our thoughts, we experience a rebound and think about that thing even more. This is part of what makes desire discrepancies so challenging for many relationships. For the higher-libido partner, trying not to think about sex might leave them thinking about it even more! Of course this can lead to frustration for all partners involved.

Importantly, when folks have come to us seeking help with low libido, we tend to see greater progress if they have one or more internal motivators to change, rather than if their goal is solely to satisfy a partner. If you feel you have lower libido, motivation to meet your partner's level of sexual interest may be what initially brought you to this book, which is perfectly understandable. We hope that, along the way, you might also identify and discover some additional, personal motivators for sexual activity. If not though, that can be okay and we include resources for you too.

THE MENTAL CHECKLIST FOR SEX AND THE STRESS RESPONSE

Many folks have a mental checklist of conditions that they go through before deciding whether to be sexual. You may or may not be aware of doing this. It's like your mind goes through a list before considering sex, and if any items on the checklist are not satisfied, sex can feel like it becomes off-limits. Here's a sample of what we mean:

- I must be feeling confident about my body
- I must not be too hungry
- I must not be too full
- I must have my to-do list completed
- I must feel energized
- I must not feel too stressed
- I must be in a good mood
- I must feel connected to my partner
- I must be "in the mood"
- There must not be any distractions in the home
- I must feel physically healthy
- The kids must be asleep

Do any of these sound familiar? If they do, you're in good company. And how often do all of these circumstances perfectly line up? Very rarely, if ever. If we wait for the perfect time to have sex, we may be waiting . . . and waiting . . . and waiting. The mental checklist is an excellent example of sexual brakes that can disrupt libido. Folks tend to find that these boxes are rarely all checked—perhaps only on vacations. The rest of the time, it's a lot to expect and largely unrealistic for our day-to-day lives. The question is not necessarily how to check all of the boxes—though certainly some may need attention—but rather to figure out how to maintain a healthy sex life amidst the chaos of our daily lives.

Stress affects sex. No shocker there, right? When our bodies are in a constant state of stress, all aspects of sexual functioning can be disrupted, especially spontaneous or responsive desire. The *stress response* involves the nervous system registering a sense of threat or danger. These stressors may be real or perceived. As Drs. Emily Nagoski and Amelia Nagoski explain in their book *Burnout: The Secret to Unlocking the Stress Cycle*, stressors are "anything you can see, hear, smell, touch, taste, or imagine could do you

harm." These can be external factors like work problems or family obliga-
tions, or internal stressors like negative self-talk or feelings of shame. Stress,
then, is "the neurological and physiological shift that happens in your body"
when faced with a stressor.[22] For some folks, stress provides an incentive to
seek out sex, as sexual activity helps them to reduce tension and feel good.
For other folks, stress *inhibits* their sexual interest, as sexual activity feels
out of reach based on their state or capacity.

The stress response is known by many different names, including *fight-
flight-freeze, survival mode, dysregulation, being activated or reactive,* and
others. For the sake of consistency, we'll refer to it as our *stress response.*
When we experience a stress response, our bodies are essentially detecting
a threat, either real or perceived, and our behavior is often an attempt to
seek safety. Some people cope with a stress response by seeking out sex.
For others, however, this process shuts down sexual desire or the ability to
get aroused. This is one reason (though certainly not the only reason) why
some folks have difficulty becoming sexually aroused, staying aroused, and/
or having an orgasm. It's also why some folks may not have spontaneous
desire, or may struggle to cultivate responsive desire.

Though we've come a long way from our prehistoric, cave-dwelling days,
in many ways our bodies don't recognize the difference between the threat
posed by a predatory animal and the threat posed by a partner who is upset
with us. It can all register the same way in our nervous system. What happens
for many of us, then, is that we get stuck in the stress response and have
difficulty returning to a state of calm and safety. Back in the days when we
were being chased by lions, if we survived—by running away, fighting off
the animal, or collapsing and being overlooked—there was an identifiable
point at which the threat would end.

In our modern lives, our bodies don't often get the message that the threat
is resolved. (Sometimes, that's because it isn't—more on this in chapters 2
and 4.) We may constantly find ourselves in a stress response. The link
between libido and the stress response is critical for many people. As such,
we'll return to this concept again and with additional detail in later chapters.

Libido, as it turns out, is much more complicated than most people
realize. This is true regardless of your desire type or where you may fall on
the libido spectrum. In the next few chapters, we'll explore more of the
factors—from individual differences to large-scale sociocultural systems—
that can impact libido.

chapter 2

CULTURAL AND SOCIETAL FACTORS

S ex and sexuality are complex. As we've noted, they involve a great many factors and layers of experience. This is especially true when it comes to libido. Over the next few chapters, we'll be using an important model to discuss and explore how these factors overlap and intersect to create differences in libido. Specifically, we'll focus on what's called the *ecological systems* model, first proposed by psychologist Urie Bronfenbrenner in the 1970s.[1] Bronfenbrenner's theory illustrates how the different, complex systems of our world can influence our development on an individual, personal level. It's considered a biopsychosociocultural model because it combines elements from all of these aspects of our experience (the biological, psychological, social, and cultural).[2] The ecological systems model was not specifically designed with libido in mind but is a useful tool for considering the complexities of human sexual experiences. For the purposes of this book, we've broken things down into three main levels: the sociocultural (society + culture), the interpersonal (relationships with others), and the individual (personal), and we will discuss impacts to libido in that order.

First, let's look at a quick overview of the model, in figure 3. The sociocultural level encompasses our society and culture as a whole, and how our interactions with cultural messages, systems, and institutions impact us. The interpersonal level concerns our relationships with others (partners, family, friends, co-workers, kids, etc.) and how they affect us. Finally, the individual level pertains to what's happening in our own bodies and minds. When it comes to libido, the focus is often exclusively on the individual

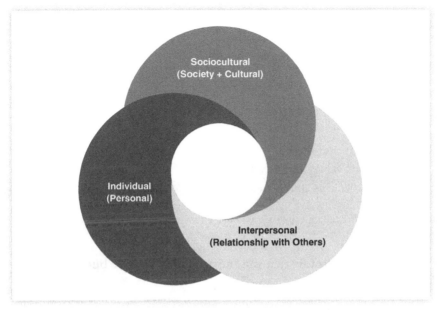

FIGURE 3. Ecological Model, adapted from Urie Bronfenbrenner, *The Ecology of Human Development: Experiments by Nature and Design* (Cambridge, MA: Harvard University Press, 1979).

level and medical or psychological treatment for libido concerns often reinforce this narrative. This mindset ignores the critical influences of interpersonal and sociocultural factors on a person's libido.[3] It's important to recognize that while sociocultural, interpersonal, and individual factors can operate separately to impact libido, more often they interconnect and overlap. The beauty of the ecological systems model is that it reflects the complexity of who we are as human beings. Rather than just one factor or level of experience, it allows us to consider the many nuanced variables that affect our overall sexuality. Below are some examples of sociocultural, interpersonal, and individual factors that can influence libido. Take a moment to review them and use your **sexual health journal** to write down which factors may apply to you.

Sociocultural factors that can impact libido may include, but are not limited to:

- Sexual education
- Heteronormativity

- Compulsory sexuality
- Oppression and discrimination
- Racism and white supremacy
- Transphobia
- Homophobia
- Biphobia/binegativity
- Ableism
- Misogyny and sexism
- Religious values and beliefs
- Food insecurity and poverty
- Media
- Politics

Interpersonal factors that can impact libido include but are not limited to:

- Relationship concerns
- Communication style and effectiveness
- Parenting stressors
- Workplace stress or conflict
- Friendship and/or family difficulties
- Emotional labor and mental load imbalances between partners

Individual factors that can impact libido include but are not limited to:

- Medications
- Medical conditions or illnesses
- Physical limitations
- Chronic pain and/or fatigue
- Sexual/genital pain
- Pregnancy and postpartum
- Physical activity
- Sleep
- Hormones
- Menstrual cycle
- Cancer and cancer treatment

- Aging
- Malnutrition/food insecurity
- Sexually transmitted infections (STIs)
- Alcohol and other substances
- The stress response
- Depression
- Anxiety
- Performance anxiety
- Trauma
- Body image
- Grief and loss
- Sensory sensitivities (e.g., sensitivity to smell, touch)
- Miscarriage
- Sexual shame or guilt
- Gender dysphoria
- Sexual interests and preferences

All of these factors (and more) can impact libido and our overall sexual health. Some are things we can control and change; others are consistently present factors that we have to navigate. Recall that many of these variables overlap and are interconnected. For example, food insecurity relates to both individual and sociocultural levels of the ecological systems model. Drug and alcohol use has a biological effect on the individual and is also shaped by interpersonal and sociocultural dynamics. Gender dysphoria is often both felt individually and reinforced socioculturally. Though one's challenges with libido can feel very individual—and, at times, lonely—these difficulties typically don't exist in isolation. The rest of this chapter will focus specifically on the sociocultural factors that can impact libido. In chapter 3 we'll review interpersonal barriers to libido, and chapter 4 will look at in-dividual challenges. In this way, we'll be taking a top-down approach from the broadest to the most specific levels of the model.

THE "SEXUAL RECESSION"

There have been media reports in recent years about an overall reduction in sexual activity in the United States. News coverage of this so-called "sexual recession" seems to stem from a study published in 2017.[4] In this project, researchers looked at sexual health information from 1989 to 2014 that was provided by over 26,000 American adults. This large, nationally representative data set allowed the researchers to track and describe sexual trends over time, and the results were certainly interesting. First, in comparing the early 1990s to the early 2010s, American adults reported having sex about seven fewer times per year. When comparing the late 1990s to the early 2010s, the number was nine fewer times per year. Perhaps not a drastic decrease, but a decline for sure. The researchers found two main factors involved in this sexual decline: (1) an increase in the number of Americans *without* a steady partner, and (2) a decline in sexual frequency among individuals who *are* steadily partnered (both married and unmarried).[5]

Let's break down these results a bit further. Relationship and sexual health research has long documented that individuals who are partnered have more sex than single folks. This has sometimes been referred to as the *marriage advantage*, though it certainly extends to unmarried partnerships. And this consistent finding makes some sense based on partner availability—you're simply more likely to have partnered sex when you have a steady partner. In recent years, however, we've seen more people choosing to delay long-term partnerships. Marriage, too, has been on the decline. With more single people in the country, there has been an overall decline in reported sexual frequency. Importantly, however, on a case-by-case basis, the sexual frequency rates for single Americans do not appear to have changed much over time.[6]

What is perhaps most interesting about that 2017 study is that the marriage advantage seems to be on the decline. Specifically, partnered people have reported lower sexual frequency in recent years. Meanwhile, for single people, the rate of sexual frequency has remained consistent (though there are now more single people overall driving down the frequency numbers). So, the question is: Why might sexual frequency be decreasing among partnered people?

One potential answer relates to the fact that, in the 2017 study, *sex* was not explicitly defined. That is, we don't really know *which* sexual activities have declined. As sex therapists, we've already noted that we consider *sex* to be an expansive term, one that includes everything from penile-vaginal penetration to oral sex to masturbation to anal stimulation to using a vibrator and more. These different types of sex—especially oral and anal sexual activity, and the use of sexual aids—are quite common and tend to become more common with age.[7] In our culture, however, the many varieties of sex are often overlooked—unless specifically asked about—and the average American is most likely to define sex as penile-vaginal penetration only. For the 2017 study then, if participants were only considering intercourse as sex, it's possible that they may actually have underreported other types of sex that they were having, creating the *appearance* of a sexual recession. Sex between partners may appear to be on the decline because folks are continuing to discover a wider range of sexual activities that the study did not explicitly ask about.

Even if we read the 2017 study with an expansive definition of sex in mind, however, there are some important sociocultural forces that may be reducing the frequency of sex (broadly defined) within partnered relationships. For instance, as cultural norms have shifted, many folks have become more empowered to reject the notion that sex is an obligation or a duty in their relationships; this is perhaps most true for cisgender women partnered with cisgender men. Also, as a society, we are now more explicitly addressing sexual consent: marital/spousal rape was finally criminalized in the United States in 1993 and is increasingly recognized by our culture as the violation that it is.[8]* Thus, many people—again, cisgender women in particular—have more power to decline sexual activity with their partners. Though there are still many relationships where this is sadly not true (we'll discuss this in greater detail in chapter 6), and though there is still much work to be done to achieve gender equity, we suspect that this increased freedom from sexual coercion may account for at least some of the observed decline in partnered sexual activity. If so, the "sexual recession" may in fact be a positive cultural shift.

While we're on the subject of the sexual recession, we would be remiss not to address the critical difference between *quantity* and *quality* of sex. Although frequency has perhaps declined, it's certainly plausible that sexual quality may have remained constant among the study population—or even increased as varied sexual activities have become more normalized. This is a fundamental concept that we often discuss in working with our clients: *quality over quantity*. Sex research strongly supports this approach. Sexual frequency does *not* necessarily equate to sexual or relationship satisfaction and, indeed, some research finds there may be a point of diminishing

---

* It is important to note that, in many countries, sexual assault between partners—especially married partners—is still neither socially recognized nor outlawed.

returns.[9] Returning to the importance of an expanded definition of sex, researchers have found that sexual satisfaction is related to receiving more oral sex, having more consistent orgasms, incorporating a greater variety of sexual acts into one's partnered experiences, and strong sexual communication.[10] As noted in chapter 1, research also shows that sexual satisfaction is the number one predictor of desire for both solo and partnered sexual activity.[11] Despite all the press, at the end of the day, it may be that the "sexual recession" doesn't matter all that much. We much prefer quality over quantity and suspect that you probably do too!

THE CULTURAL ROOTS OF SEXUAL SHAME

One factor that can severely disrupt the quality of our sexual experiences is *shame*. Shame is the worry that some part of us is unacceptable, wrong, or bad in the eyes of others. It's a feeling that we'll be rejected because of some aspect of who we are. This is related to, but different from, guilt. Guilt refers to feeling remorseful about something we've done. In this sense, guilt is about an action that we have or have not taken (behavior), whereas shame is focused on who we are (character). When it comes to sex, many people worry that their sexuality is not "normal" or is unacceptable in some way. That's shame.

Sexual shame is often triggered by two main factors that are sociocultural in nature: (1) a lack of accurate education about sex, sexuality, and gender; and (2) an inability to speak openly and honestly about sexual health topics. After all, what better way to discover whether you are sexually "normal" (spoiler alert: you are!) than by learning more about sexuality and by talking with others to gain perspective. This is part of what psychologists call *social referencing*: using knowledge about what others are doing to understand our own behavior and give it context.[12] Sadly, we live in a culture that deprioritizes sexual education and also actively discourages open and healthy discussions about sex and gender. Taken together, this is a sociocultural recipe for widespread sexual shame that can trickle down into the interpersonal and individual levels of experience to impact libido.

Sex Education and Shame

We routinely ask our clients how they learned about sex, gender, and sexual health over the course of their lives. Who or what played an important role in their sex education, and how do they feel now about that education? Unfortunately, the vast majority express dissatisfaction, frustration, and often regret. Many of our clients describe their sex education as openly shame-based in various ways (more on that ahead) but, even more frequently, clients relate an educational experience that reflects a *null environment*. That is, they grew up in an environment in which sex, gender, and sexual health were never mentioned. Though they may not have heard specifically shaming things about sex, they recognize that their null environment actually sent the same message: "We don't talk about these topics because they're bad, embarrassing, or shameful."

A common saying in the sex therapy world is that we are sexual beings—in some capacity—from birth to death. Our relationship with our sexuality—and, unfortunately, often shame—starts at a young age. In our first few years of life, we begin to explore our bodies and will likely experience some pleasure while doing so. We naturally move toward what feels good, and this commonly involves genital self-exploration. Early on as children, we don't understand the sexualized aspect of this behavior—we just know what feels good.* Though it's actually common for children and adolescents to engage in genital self-touch, many are scolded for these behaviors and taught to avoid them, particularly when adults assign sexual meaning to such exploration. Children and adolescents may be punished for these behaviors or told that they are bad, dirty, or gross. Shame is often a side effect.

Miseducation—or, more often, no education—about sex, sexuality, and gender make this problem much worse because we don't know where to even begin the conversation. In the United States, the lack of accurate sexual health education is a long-standing and systemic sociocultural problem. For example, at the time of this writing, only twenty-nine states plus Washington, DC, require sexual health education for adolescents. Out of these, only eleven states require that, if sex education is provided,

---

* As an example, we've reassured many a worried parent who noticed their toddler rubbing their genitals against a car seat. This is very common! The biggest questions from parents tend to be whether such behaviors are normal or are potentially a sign of concern, including abuse. Obviously, we all want to keep children safe so it's important to know which behaviors represent healthy exploration and which behaviors are concerning. We strongly recommend the excellent "Sexual Behaviors in Childhood Guide," available for free at www .sexpositivefamilies.com.

the information must be medically and scientifically accurate.* Some states legally *prohibit* teachers from answering students' sexual health questions when those questions don't adhere to a narrow, state-approved curriculum.

As sex therapists, we regularly see the negative impact of such state- and local-level (e.g., school board) policies around sexual health education. Clients often tell us that sexual topics were extremely taboo when they were growing up and were never discussed by their parents or caregivers (the null environment). In school, they similarly learned very little about sex, sexuality, or gender. There was perhaps a discussion about remaining abstinent from sexual activity until marriage, and some remember scare tactic education techniques, such as viewing disturbing photos of sexually transmitted infections (STIs). Neither of us can recall, however, a client telling us that they learned accurate and inclusive information about genitals and reproductive systems (e.g., that a clitoris and a penis are homologous—made of similar tissue and nerve endings), information about sexual development, or how to talk about sexual likes, dislikes, consent, and safe sex practices with potential partners. Lack of information about these basic sexual health topics leave us without a frame of reference for our desires and behavior and, in turn, increases the risk of experiencing sexual shame and guilt. Shame and guilt thrive in secrecy. Accurate sexual health education is part of the antidote to sexual shame. Education removes the secrecy and helps us build skills to talk about these important topics.

PUMP UP THE POSITIVITY!

To increase your sexual health knowledge *and* decrease sexual shame, consider inviting more sex-positive messages and education into your life. *Sex positivity* is the practice of respecting our own and others' sexual interests and activities, as long as they are consensual and respect the bodily autonomy of all involved. There are many ways to welcome more sex positivity into your day-to-day experiences. Follow sexual health providers on social media. Read medically accurate

---

*In case you're interested—we were!—Guttmacher Institute, a nonprofit research organization, carefully tracks sexual health education policies in the United States and provides up-to-date information about each state on its website. At writing, the states that both mandate sex education and require it to be medically accurate are California, Hawaii, Iowa, Maine, New Jersey, North Carolina, Oregon, Rhode Island, Tennessee, Utah, and Washington state.

websites and add books about sex education and sexuality to your reading list. Listen to sexual health podcasts. (We've listed a bunch of our favorite resources at the end of the book.) Perhaps most importantly, talk more openly about sexual health topics to a few close friends or your partner(s). This may feel strange (and difficult!) at first but can really help to normalize sexuality. We're betting you'll be surprised by how much you have in common!

Purity Culture and Shame

One common source of sexual shame is the faith-based messages we receive at a young age and, indeed, throughout our lives—often regardless of religious or faith affiliation. Even people who are not raised in a religious household often internalize negative faith-based messages about sex due to their pervasive presence in American culture and media (though this is by no means exclusive to the United States). In 1949, Canadian neuropsychologist Dr. Donald Hebb proposed that our learning and memory are based on the repeated activation of the same neural pathways in our brain. That is, when stimuli are paired together over and over again—such as sexual topics and negative messages—our brains create a shortcut (literally) and we quickly learn to associate whatever has been paired together.[13] Now known as Hebb's law, this neurobiological process was later summarized by Dr. Carla Shatz with the memorable saying "What fires together, wires together."[14] For many, repeated exposure to religious viewpoints that associate sexuality with shame is enough to forge this strong connection between the two: sex = shame. For those who are part of a faith community, it's certainly possible to remain in that community *and* also cultivate a healthy relationship with sex, gender, and sexuality. That said, for many folks, negative faith-based messages about sex can create barriers to sexuality and are thus critical to consider with regard to libido. One of the most predominant faith-based contributors to sexual shame is purity culture.

Purity culture is perhaps most associated with the American Evangelical Christian movement, though similar beliefs can be found across many different faith traditions (elsewhere called *honor culture*, for example), and have actually become deeply ingrained in secular society as well.[15] Purity beliefs place high importance on sexual abstinence until marriage—specifically, marriage between two cisgender heterosexual people, as purity culture leaves no room for sexual or gender diversity. There is an expectation of absolute sexlessness prior to marriage. It is believed that purity—and therefore moral goodness—is achieved by those who not only abstain from sex but who also rid themselves of all sexual thoughts and emotions.[16] The immense difficulty here, of course, is that most people (even asexual folks) have sexual thoughts from time to time. Purity culture teaches that those who can't purge these thoughts and emotions are flawed and unworthy of God's love. This can be a particularly shame-inducing paradox for adolescents trying to navigate their emerging sexual feelings.*

Years of psychological and behavioral research tells us that trying to focus people on what *not* to do rarely has the desired effect. Remember the white bear study from chapter 1 and what happens with repressed thoughts? Purity culture teaches that abstaining from all sexual activity, thoughts, and feelings (again, a losing battle for most) will be rewarded after marriage with an effortlessly pleasurable sexual relationship with one's spouse. Unfortunately, even if someone follows the "rules" and abstains from sex until after marriage, it can be extraordinarily difficult to simply switch on sexual desire after years of active suppression and being taught to associate sex with anxiety and fear. Author Linda Kay Klein writes beautifully about this pattern in her book *Pure*, drawing on dozens of interviews with individuals who were raised in purity culture. She points out the common "brain trap" that, for many folks, often forms between sex and shame: "Even if we eventually come to understand that our sexual nature is natural, normal, and healthy, we may find that our upbringing in purity culture, which has dedifferentiated [made the same] shame and sex over years of messaging, observation, and experience, ensures that our brain fires those shame neurons when the subject of our sexuality arises, with or without our permission, trapping us in a shame spiral."[17]

For individuals raised within purity culture who then go on to marry, libido can be low or absent, and pleasure can be tough to experience. We see many newly married partners in sex therapy who are struggling with their

---

* Importantly, we're not suggesting that waiting to be sexual until after marriage is an incorrect choice. In fact, that's part of being sex positive—supporting and respecting people for doing what works best for them. However, we do want to highlight these common themes and messages about premarital sex that folks often struggle to reconcile. If waiting until marriage is part of your value system, perhaps there are ways to increase your education and understanding of sex and sexuality, or to explore sexuality prior to marriage, in a manner that fits within your value system while also decreasing any potential sexual anxiety and/or shame.

sexual functioning due to a narrow definition of sex, inaccurate information, and years of built-up anxiety and shame related to purity culture messaging. These are broad sociocultural influences on sexual health that trickle down into our relationships and individual lives.

Religious messages about sexuality, particularly within purity culture, are often strictly gendered and reflect what's known as *complementarianism*: the belief that cisgender men and women have been assigned specific, complementary gender roles by God. Men are expected to be strong, tough, self-sufficient, masculine leaders of a household. Women are expected to support men by being submissive, sweet, feminine, and pretty (but not *so* attractive as to veer into appearing overtly sexual—a confusing and constantly moving target). Communities that adhere to purity culture beliefs routinely punish and ostracize those who do not fit into these stereotyped gender binaries, whether through behavior and/or appearance. Sexual expectations are also strictly gendered. Children raised in purity culture are taught that girls and women are responsible for the sexual thoughts, feelings, and behaviors of the boys and men around them.[18] For example, girls are taught to constantly monitor their appearance and to dress "modestly" so as not to cause men to experience sexual desire and thus sinfulness. The message here ends up being that cisgender women's bodies are dangerous, in need of constant control and vigilance so as not to lead men into immorality. Accompanying this is the message that cisgender men are inherently hypersexual—with an inexhaustible amount of sexual desire—and cannot be expected to control themselves if sexually "tempted."

When it comes to sexual health, these gendered purity culture messages are concerning for several reasons. First, the strict gender binary demands an unattainable rigidity that sets people up for failure and also ignores natural sexual and gender diversity. These messages are also inherently shaming in their dehumanization: men are full of animalistic, uncontrollable desire, and women are either a God-given "outlet" for this desire or a threat to men's morality. Such a view of sexuality erases our sexual agency and provides little to no opportunity to address individual or partnered sexual wants, desires, likes, and dislikes.

In considering the sociocultural influences on libido, it's important to recognize that gendered messages and beliefs about sexuality are widespread in our culture even outside of purity culture. We often see purity culture beliefs represented in the secular world via damaging sexual double standards: for example, praising men for their sexual activity ("studs"), but condemning women for the same behavior ("sluts"). Purity culture also props up the widespread myth that men should be good at sex and automatically know how to please a partner (as if there is some kind of universal formula). This sets many people up for feelings of failure and shame, while also neglecting to teach them the important sexual communication skills that actually do build sexual confidence and satisfaction. Similarly, the stereotype that women have low desire compared to men permeates secular society, completely erasing what we know about the complexities of libido. In fact, research shows that in mixed-gender couples, cisgender women and men are equally likely to report being the lower-libido partner![19] But because our society does not acknowledge this reality, when men have low libido, their partners tend to assume that *they* have done something "wrong," or that the man is being unfaithful. Remember, all people experience fluctuations in their libido—this includes cisgender men.

THE MYTH OF VIRGINITY

Virginity can be a touchy subject but one that is important to address within the framework of sociocultural influences on sexual health. A *virgin* is generally understood to be someone who has not had a sexual partner, though in fact nailing down the specifics of this definition is quite difficult and really depends on who you ask. Some might say that virginity means there is no history of any sexual behavior (solo or partnered). Others say that refraining from penile-vaginal intercourse is the marker of virginity (ignoring the validity of other sexual activities, as well as the people who may not be interested in this particular type of sex). Still others might say you're a virgin if you masturbate alone, but not if you've been sexual with a partner (does kissing count?). Despite the widespread belief (and misinformation—for example, about hymens) in the importance of virginity, there is no medical definition for the term.[20] It's an example of a socially constructed idea—something that does not exist in objective reality but has been built by sociocultural interactions and belief systems. This is why pinpointing an exact definition is so tough.

Many raised in purity culture, which emphasizes virginity via the abstinence-until-marriage requirement, report that the ambiguous nature of this concept created confusion, guilt, anxiety, and shame. This makes a lot of sense. With no concrete definition, how do folks (typically, young people) know where the line of virginity gets crossed? This ambiguity tends to result in what might be considered sexual loopholes, such as the practice of "soaking," in which partners engage in some variety of sexual activity but still feel able to say they have maintained virginity (read: purity and goodness) per their unique definition of sex.

The concept of virginity is rooted in both faith traditions and historical attempts to guard paternal lineage and bloodlines, particularly for royal and noble families.[21] The idea is that if a cisgender woman can somehow prove that she has had no sexual partners before marriage, the paternity of any children she has after marriage is assured. This, of course, relies on some pretty big assumptions: (1) the flawed belief in an objective definition of virginity and (2) unquestionable monogamy. What's important to take away here is that cultural messages around virginity are enormously mixed and can negatively impact sexual relationships, functioning, and even safety. Virginity is viewed as something to prize and is equated with goodness, purity, and morality, but, per purity culture, this message is often targeted more toward girls and women than to boys and men. The notion of "losing" one's virginity upholds the myth that sexual activity changes a person's value and is, indeed, something that even exists to be "taken." If there is no agreed upon definition of virginity, what exactly is being lost or taken anyway?

Consider spending a moment reflecting on these points in your **sexual health journal**. What messages about virginity did you receive growing up? Do you hold different values now from those you were raised with? How do you define virginity, and why might that be the case? Does your definition of virginity include LGBTQ+ people, or does it focus only on cisgender heterosexual people? Why or why not?

To override the sex = shame connection that many have learned through purity culture messages, it becomes critically important to create new and positive experiences. This can be difficult, especially at first, as purity culture tends to have an anti-pleasure stance in general. One of Jennifer's former students nicely summarized this often anxiety-provoking conundrum: "To the adults in my childhood environment, pleasure was a red flag that could mean you were engaging in sin or just not focusing on what was 'really' important in life." Within purity culture, any form of pleasure—sexual or otherwise—tends to be discouraged and viewed with suspicion. We'll talk much more about strategies to begin disrupting the sex = shame connection in part II of this book.

Not all faith-based messages around sex are rooted in purity culture, and there are indeed sex-positive religious traditions. That said, the lasting impact of purity culture messages is an extraordinarily common sociocultural contributor to sexual shame and thus a sexual brake for many people. As always, our goal is to help you find what works best for you in terms of navigating libido, and that includes taking into account your own faith tradition. One of the most difficult things to grapple with is trying to be and understand your authentic self while also receiving messages from the culture and institutions around you that your authentic self is wrong, bad, or immoral.

A NOTE ABOUT SOLO SEX

While we're on the topic of shame and purity culture, let's take a moment to touch base about self-stimulation, also known as *masturbation* or *solo sex*. This is an aspect of sexuality that, for many, is associated with feelings of both shame and guilt due to faith-based messaging. Learning about self-stimulation as a potentially pleasurable activity that is best enjoyed in private (solo or with consenting partners) is an important aspect of sexual health education.

Looking back, what were the messages you received about masturbation while growing up? What do you remember learning, either explicitly or implicitly? If you haven't already, feel free to add these experiences to your sexual history time line and to write more about them in your **sexual health journal**. We'll cover this important topic in more detail in chapter 5.

MINORITY STRESS

Perhaps one of the most widespread yet unacknowledged societal-level influences on sexual desire is *minority stress*. Members of marginalized groups experience chronic stress—above and beyond stressors associated with everyday life—related to being stigmatized by the dominant society.[22] Minority stressors tend to be categorized as *distal* (external in origin) or *proximal* (internal in origin). Distal stressors influence proximal stressors, which in turn can negatively impact health in a number of ways. For example, the discrimination faced by many LGBTQ+ individuals (distal stressors) can lead folks to internalize the stigma around their identity (e.g., internalized homophobia, monosexism, cis-sexism), conceal their identity (being in the closet), or expect rejection by others. These proximal stressors are sometimes referred to as *felt stigma*—that is, the way in which individuals who have been marginalized feel and internalize the stigma they receive from the larger culture.[23]

Minority stress is socioculturally based. Of course, any number of marginalized and stigmatized identities can exist—such as those related to race, sexual orientation, gender, disability, religion—depending on time and place. Distal stressors, such as being a target of racism or sexism, are often exacerbated for individuals who hold multiple marginalized identities. Like many sociocultural factors, minority stress often has a trickle-down effect on interpersonal and individual health.[24]

Research on minority stress has exploded over the past twenty-five years and has been especially important in helping us understand why so many people from marginalized groups experience higher rates of physical and mental health concerns. For example, chronic exposure to minority stress has been linked to a higher risk of heart disease and other metabolic disorders, as well as to symptoms of depression and anxiety due to increased stress hormones like cortisol.[25] Particularly troubling is the accumulating body of research that links the chronic stress of racial discrimination to accelerated physical and health decline at the DNA level, specifically via the shortening of protective DNA sequences known as telomeres.[26] Adding to minority stress–related health disparities is the fact that social inequities often create barriers to accessing necessary healthcare, perpetuating a vicious cycle.

You may be wondering why the topic of minority stress has shown up in a book about sexual desire. Well, as you probably know from your own busy life, most of us are quite tired after a long day of work, school, or managing daily responsibilities. For folks who face cultural stigma and marginalization, there are often added stressors to deal with each day. This might involve monitoring things like how we speak, move, interact, or come across to others in order to avoid the pain of distal minority stressors, including outright discriminatory behavior.[27] You can imagine, then, the lack of energy that may be left for sexual intimacy and connection. Proximal stressors such as internalized racism, sexism, ableism, sizeism, and others can further disrupt spontaneous or responsive desire processes via sexual shame. That's because identities that have been marginalized are culturally othered and treated as bad, shameful, or otherwise not "normal." As we've discussed, struggling with shame—general or sexual—related to who you are can be a major libido disrupter.

MINORITY STRESS AND LIBIDO

Unfortunately, minority stress is a chronic experience for folks with identities that have been marginalized. And we know, without a doubt, that chronic stress negatively impacts our sexual health.[28] We typically think of this impact as being *psychological* in nature: chronic stress often results in our thoughts being heavily focused on worries, taking us away from other aspects of our lives (including potential sexual accelerators). This is certainly a common pattern that we see in sex therapy. However, researchers have also proposed a *physiological* link between chronic stress and libido via hormones like cortisol.[29] Often referred to as the stress hormone, cortisol is released by our adrenal glands. Chronic high stress can overstimulate the adrenal glands, leading to consistently high levels of cortisol and, ultimately, disrupted adrenal gland production. Over time, this process is believed to dampen sexual arousal, which, of course, is an important cue for many people's libido. More research is needed on this possible link between low libido and high cortisol production. Suffice to say, however, that experiences of stigma and oppression are not doing anything to help our libidos!

Minority stress is often a new consideration for folks learning more about sexual desire. Let's consider some examples.

Joyce is a Black, queer, cisgender woman who works full time as the director of human resources at a large healthcare company. She has a partner and two children. Within Joyce's relationship, she has lower sexual desire than her partner. Additionally, her partner tends to initiate sex at times when Joyce is less open to it, such as at night—after a long workday—when their kids are asleep. Joyce has learned that she has a predominantly responsive style of libido, which, as you'll recall, is heavily influenced by context, including stress and energy levels. Part of Joyce's job is to help manage the work-related concerns of her company's employees. These can include issues of racism, sexism, bullying, and relational dynamics. She recognizes that she also navigates many of the same concerns as the employees with whom she works. For example, Joyce finds that she needs to consistently monitor her speech and communication strategies while at work. She refrains from using African American Vernacular English (AAVE) because it's viewed by her mostly white colleagues as "unprofessional."* Joyce is also one of very few openly LGBTQ+ employees at her company. Though her co-workers are generally accepting, Joyce tends to avoid topics in conversation that highlight her sexual identity (e.g., attending a Pride celebration, discussing her partner). Monitoring her communication and speech all day at work can feel emotionally exhausting, leaving Joyce with less energy at the end of the workday compared to her white and heterosexual colleagues, who don't have to monitor their words and actions in the same way.

Here's another example:

Gautam is a gay cisgender man whose parents immigrated to the United States when he was very young. Though he is out as gay to immediate family and friends, he is not out at his retail sales job: he has heard his supervisor and some of his co-workers make homophobic jokes, and he worries that they would not be accepting. Based on their jokes and behaviors, Gautam suspects his supervisor and co-workers will view him as more competent if he presents as more traditionally masculine. At work, therefore, he deepens his voice and wears loose-fitting clothes, whereas in his personal life, he enjoys wearing more fitted clothing and will occasionally wear mascara. He finds this identity concealment to be very draining day after day, however, and tends to come home from work feeling tired and invalidated. Likely his heterosexual co-workers have never had to consider such factors.

Whether directly or indirectly, minority stress can seriously disrupt our physical and mental health and, of course, our sexual relationships. Remember the stress response that we talked about in chapter 1? For folks whose identities have been marginalized, distal and proximal minority stressors are often frequent and unresolved, leading to a chronic stress response. Though being stuck in a stress response is an individual-level factor when it comes to libido—which we discuss further in chapter 4—it's critical to recognize that many people live with a chronic stress response that is rooted in sociocultural-level discrimination. Though there are several different types of minority stressors, in the next section we'll cover one that can be especially pervasive. Before we do, take a moment to reflect on the following questions in your **sexual health journal.**

---

*This is referred to in linguistics as *code-switching*—alternating between two (or more) languages depending on the social context or setting.

JOURNAL PROMPTS What emotions came up for you while reading about minority stress? Did any of the information or examples resonate with you? Has one or more of your identities been marginalized? If yes, how do you feel that has affected your general and sexual health?

HETERONORMATIVITY

As the word suggests, *heteronormativity* refers to sociocultural values and structures that position heterosexuality as the default—normal, healthy, and preferred—in comparison to all other sexualities.[30] Heteronormativity relies on a strict gender binary that positions cisgender men and women as heterosexual reproductive partners who are complementary—"naturally" opposite but unequal.[31] In this way, heteronormativity involves both sexual orientation and gender. You may recall that heteronormativity is also a key feature of purity culture values and belief systems. Heteronormative systems legitimize the stigmatization of, discrimination against, and fear of gay and lesbian individuals (homophobia), bi+ communities (binegativity or biphobia), and transgender people (transphobia). And it's not only LGBTQ+ people who are harmed by heteronormativity. Sociocultural messages and scripts based in heteronormativity affect people of all genders and sexual orientations.[32] Here are some common examples of heteronormativity in action:

- Worry that interest in anal play "makes you gay"
- Complementarianism: Men believing they must be sexually dominant; women feeling like they can't or shouldn't initiate sex; men being told they "should," or are expected to, have higher libido; having sex out of a sense of "duty" to a partner or spouse
- Dominant sexual scripts that position penile-vaginal intercourse as the only type of "real sex"
- Beliefs that sex that falls outside of cisgender heterosexual norms is less-than, deviant, or "doesn't count"
- Viewing men's level of desire as the default in cisgender heterosexual relationships, often positioning "low" libido as a woman's problem to be fixed
- Assuming that women in cisgender heterosexual relationships are responsible for running the household and being the primary parent

As you can see, heteronormativity is embedded in many areas of our relationships and sexual assumptions. Let's look at a common scenario we see as sex and relationship therapists:

Alexis and Jasper have been married for six years. They have two small children and both work full-time jobs. Alexis picks up their children from daycare on her way home from work, prepares dinner, gives the kids their baths, reads them a story, and tucks them into bed. By the time she has a moment to herself, it's usually pretty late. Jasper typically wants to spend evening time with Alexis and sometimes have sex after the kids have gone to bed. For Alexis, sex is the last thing on her mind, as she's mentally and physically exhausted by this point in the day. She cares about Jasper and wants him to be happy, so she often says yes to sex in an effort to please him. Because she's usually so tired though, Alexis doesn't often engage in stimulation that would feel pleasurable for her and, in fact, has gotten into a habit of rushing through sex—focusing on Jasper's orgasm and declining his offers to focus on her pleasure. Over time, she begins to feel less and less inclined to say yes to Jasper's advances—not only is Alexis rarely experiencing spontaneous libido, but her responsive desire also has become suppressed.

Recall from the last chapter that there are four foundational elements for building responsive sexual desire: consent, pleasure, focus, and time. In the case of Alexis and Jasper, we see that while Alexis is generally open and willing to be sexual, she ignores opportunities to experience sexual pleasure, struggles to focus during sex due to exhaustion and stress, and agrees to be sexual at a time that is not optimal for her. Three out of our four foundational elements are missing, making it no surprise that her libido has declined over time.

What does this have to do with heteronormativity? A closer look reveals that Alexis has internalized a belief that sex is primarily for men, and that her role as a wife includes giving sexual pleasure to her spouse (also known as "duty sex"). In these moments, she sees herself as the provider of sex, rather than a participant in sex who is equally deserving—and equally in need, at least for responsive desire—of pleasure. This view of sex is a direct result of heteronormative thinking. Additionally, Alexis—like many cisgender heterosexual women—carries an enormous mental load (see chapter 3). This pushes heavily on her sexual brakes, inhibiting both spontaneous and responsive sexual desire.

Often, in therapy, reexamining heteronormative views of sex and relationship expectations is critical for addressing libido discrepancies. In the case of Alexis and Jasper, Alexis started to realize just how much her nighttime routine with the kids was negatively impacting sexual experiences with Jasper. Creating a more equitable split of the evening household responsibilities allowed Alexis to spend time with Jasper. She felt less exhausted and freer to become a more equal partner in terms of both giving and receiving sexual pleasure. As sex became more enjoyable again, her responsive sexual desire became more consistent.

THE DILEMMA OF THE GENDER BINARY

Western culture has historically promoted the concept of two—and only two—genders: men and women. For many years, European and American cultural systems, including the medical community, dictated that a baby's gender be assigned based on external genitalia. If a baby was born with a penis, that child was considered a boy. If a baby was born with a vulva, that child was considered a girl. This long-standing practice still occurs with regularity, and gender often continues to be conflated with genitals. Thankfully, we've come a long way in our understanding of gender, and science now recognizes the complex, overlapping constructs of sex and gender. The terms used to describe these constructs may be confusing at first, so let's take a moment to review them.

Sex can be defined in several ways: First, as a physical act, but also historically as a way to designate gender identity. As noted above, babies with penises were labeled male and babies with vulvas were labeled female. At times, an infant's internal genitals (the presence or absence of a uterus or prostate, for example) and genetics (e.g., chromosomes) may also have come into play. This was especially true if a baby was born with external genitalia that did not fit neatly in the traditional binary boxes of "boy" or "girl" (see the Intersex Identities box for more detail). Sex and gender were conflated. We now know that it's not that simple, and typically it's most accurate to refer to a person's *sex assigned at birth* (which may differ from their gender).

Research shows us that gender is separate from, but related to, sex assigned at birth. Gender is a deeply felt sense of one's identity with biological underpinnings and may or may not align with one's sex assigned at birth. Gender is as diverse as all of humankind! A person may identify their gender as woman, man, gender fluid, nonbinary, bigender, agender (no gender at all), or any number of other potential gender identities. As discussed in the introduction, we use the term *cisgender* to refer to individuals whose gender identity aligns with their sex assigned at birth, and the term *transgender* to refer to the many individuals whose gender identity does not align with their sex assigned at birth. Folks who fall outside of traditional binary gender categories do not necessarily ascribe to a trans identity, particularly those from non-Western cultures that conceptualize gender beyond the binary.

Much like heteronormative messages emphasize heterosexuality over other sexual orientations, *cisnormative* messages often stigmatize or erase those who are not cisgender. It's important to highlight that many groups of people—particularly those of Indigenous, African, and Asian cultures—have long recognized the existence of more than two genders. This includes the *fa'afafine* of Samoan societies, the *Nádleehí* of Native American Navajo culture, the Filipino *baklâ*, the *mashogu* in East African cultures, and many, many more. In many of these cultures, gender diverse individuals are considered spiritual leaders and hold places of high honor in their communities. Though these traditions have endured throughout the world, gender fluidity and diverse gender expression was largely repressed—often violently—during the colonization of many of these cultures by Western nations. Indeed, Western colonization was a major force in spreading the now-dominant cisnormative sociocultural values that we see today.[33]

As you may have guessed, heteronormativity and cisnormativity are deeply and intricately related. In many of the same ways that heteronormativity can limit our sexual health, so too can cisnormative beliefs and values. At a sociocultural level, cisnormative systems contribute to unique minority stressors for transgender and nonbinary folks. Indeed, the minority stress framework that we discussed earlier has been adapted to specifically address the *gender* minority stressors that trans and nonbinary communities face.[34] These commonly include discrimination in interpersonal, workplace, and housing settings; high rates of anti-trans violence; and day-to-day microaggressions, like filling out trans-exclusionary paperwork at the doctor's office. As previously discussed, minority stress is chronic, and it is believed to contribute to numerous physical and mental health concerns over time. Chronic stress does not help anyone's libido! In the case of trans and nonbinary communities—who continue to fight for basic rights in many places—the exhaustion of dealing with cisnormative systems can understandably impede sexual health.

The rigidity of the gender binary and cisnormativity are sociocultural factors that, like many other factors at this level, can trickle down to impact libido in both interpersonal and individual ways. In chapter 4, we'll review how cisnormativity can be internalized (via internalized transphobia), as well as how experiences like gender or anatomical dysphoria can disrupt libido.

INTERSEX IDENTITIES

Did you know that an estimated 1 in 4,500–5,500 babies are born with variations in their sexual and/or reproductive anatomy that fall outside of the strict male/female binary? For example, this could be a child born with a penis who also has ovaries or a baby with XX chromosomes but no uterus. Some healthcare professionals believe the prevalence to be even higher.[35] In the medical world, such conditions are referred to as *disorders of sex development*, though we prefer the more affirming *intersex*. *Intersex* is an umbrella term that includes many different conditions that can affect someone's anatomy and/or reproduction. Intersex conditions may be observable at birth, but for some people, they don't become apparent until later in life (e.g., during puberty, when trying to have children). Intersex people have long faced misunderstanding, stigma, and prejudice. This is, in part, because they can represent a clear challenge to our culture's obsession with sex/gender binaries. As it turns out, nature is not nearly so simplistic! To learn more, check out the work of organizations such as Bodies Like Ours, Organisation Intersex International, Intersex Initiative, and the Intersex Society of North America.

BODY IMAGE AND CULTURE

Our feelings about our bodies are socially constructed, meaning they have been taught to us and shaped by our cultures. Media—including television, movies, magazines, commercials, and social media—play a significant role in how we view and understand our bodies. In many cultures—particularly Western ones—we're exposed to fatphobic messages within a larger diet culture. We're taught repeatedly that thinner is better and healthier and that bodies should look like those glorified in the movies. As it turns out, though, health and size are independent variables.[36] These negative and inaccurate sociocultural messages around thinness are often internalized and may become individual-level barriers to libido.[37] Many of us have judgmental thoughts and feelings about our own and others' bodies, sometimes on a daily basis. We compare ourselves to others and often think of our bodies as lacking or not good enough. Media images of what's considered to be sexy tend to show mostly cisgender, heterosexual, white, thin, nondisabled young people. Those who don't fit into these identities—which is most of us—are often left feeling insecure, self-conscious, or less-than.

Since sexual activity often involves touch and our bodies, it's difficult for many people to isolate negative feelings about their bodies when they're being sexual, especially with a partner. Many folks can get stuck *spectatoring*: *observing* their bodies being sexual instead of *experiencing* their bodies being sexual.[38] When spectatoring, we're not fully present and we lose the ability to enjoy the physical experience of touch and intimacy. This is where many folks struggle with sex and where body image can negatively impact libido. It's difficult to experience pleasure when your mind is critiquing every movement or body part. Why would we want to be sexual when the experience highlights all that negative self-talk and self-consciousness? It's like signing up to be criticized, but instead of someone else doing it, we're doing it to ourselves.

For People of Color, there are additional discriminatory systems that can add to body image concerns. Two of these are *colorism*—viewing darker skin tones as undesirable—and *texturism*—viewing textured hair as undesirable. There exists a centuries-long history of racism in North American and European beauty standards that exist at the sociocultural level and impacts us at the relational and individual levels.[39] For many people—women and femmes in particular—racist beauty standards contribute to the idea that sexiness only looks one particular way: light-skinned, smooth-haired, thin, young, nondisabled. These cultural messages can leave many people feeling inadequate, like they must take great steps to achieve or perform sexiness.[40] And when our attention is on how we look, it's quite challenging to experience pleasure and be present in the moment, placing people at greater risk of spectatoring and sexual desire disruption.

So what can we do when we realize that negative body image is impacting our sex lives? We discuss this in detail in chapters 5 and 7, but to start, we can become more aware of the media we consume, and we can intentionally seek out more body-neutral messages. Follow a diverse representation of bodies on social media, including fat bodies, disabled bodies, older bodies, queer bodies, and racially diverse bodies. Consider limiting your intake of pop culture magazines that depict unrealistic, airbrushed bodies. Practice mindfully observing when negative self-talk about your body intrudes into your mind and redirecting your thoughts to the sensations in the moment. Given that, in many ways, we cannot escape the culture or media surrounding us, cultivating a more neutral or even positive body image is often a lifelong journey. It takes intentional practice and awareness to challenge the messages we receive on a daily basis and to protect ourselves from how these influences negatively impact us.

THE SEXUAL STAIRCASE: SHIFTING OUR THOUGHTS

The dominant sexual script many people have internalized is a goal-oriented model of partnered sex. For better or worse, this is how most of us were taught that sex is "supposed to be." We refer to this as the Sexual Staircase (see figure 4) because of its hierarchical and ascending nature, starting at the bottom with what's commonly called *foreplay*. Not all partners will visit every single stair on the Sexual Staircase—for example, not everyone loves or chooses to engage in oral sex—but the one-way arrow represents that the (often unspoken) goal is to get to the top: to achieve penile-vaginal penetration and orgasms. There are a *lot* of problems with this way of thinking about partnered sex that, in turn, set us up for problems during sex. First, the Sexual Staircase is deeply heteronormative in nature, built on stereotypical sexual scripts for heterosexual cisgender men. Heteronormativity presumes penile-vaginal penetration, even though there are many folks for whom this is not their favorite type of sexual activity. This presumption reflects a broader issue: penetrative sex tends to be a favorite sexual activity for people with penises, since for them, this style of stimulation is typically a reliable pathway to orgasm (hence, why orgasm appears at the very tip-top of the Staircase). Penetrative sex is less commonly favored, however, by people with vulvas, who typically require direct clitoral stimulation for optimal pleasure and orgasms. Clitoral stimulation is much more likely to occur during foreplay activities—the lower steps on the Staircase that, quite frankly, often get skipped in favor of penile-vaginal penetration. When non-penetrative sex is downplayed or not seen as "real" sex, people who enjoy and benefit from this type of stimulation often don't get their needs met. The Sexual Staircase unfortunately reinforces this approach. A related

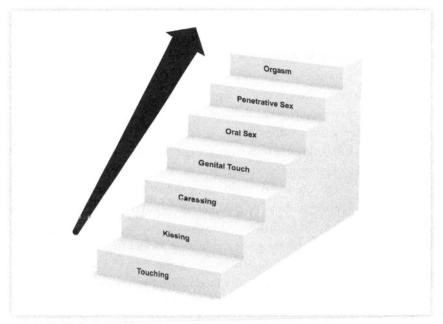

FIGURE 4. The Sexual Staircase. Inspired by Robert T. Francoeur, *Becoming a Sexual Person*, 2nd ed. (New York: Macmillan, 1991).

issue is that, over time in long-term relationships, the Sexual Staircase often gets shorter—we begin to skip steps and some partners lose the things that are most pleasurable for them. As you might guess, this is not a helpful approach for maintaining libido!

Another clear problem with the Sexual Staircase is that for many people, including cisgender heterosexual folks, penile-vaginal penetration is not always possible. This can be due to a variety of reasons, which can be either temporary or long term: for example, needed rest after childbirth or a surgery, erectile difficulties, or pain with penetrative sex. The Sexual Staircase feeds a strong "all-or-nothing" approach to sex: penile-vaginal intercourse, or it didn't happen. This is a common relationship trap—if penetrative intercourse isn't happening (for whatever reason), partners are often neglecting all sexual intimacy. Over time, as you may imagine, such partnerships tend to feel increasingly disconnected, commonly creating relationship strain that further negatively impacts the sexual dynamic.

Finally, this model is obviously not a great fit for many folks who are queer, transgender, or nonbinary. The heteronormativity of the Sexual

Staircase blatantly assumes that there's one penis and one vagina involved in sex. Even though this clearly doesn't align for many people, Staircase thinking can still influence us in complex ways, given that it's a cultural norm. For example, queer folks may still find that they have a rigidity in their sexual scripts or that they tend to prioritize penetration over other aspects of sex. They may have internalized the Staircase notion that if sex doesn't include penetration or orgasms, it doesn't feel like "real sex." While this, of course, is not true, such internalized heteronormativity can commonly lead to feelings of shame, self-consciousness, anxiety, and guilt around sexual experiences.

Let's turn to a different way of thinking about partnered sex—one that is much more open-ended and flexible. We've found that this Wheel Model is a much more helpful, realistic, and inclusive way of approaching sexual activity. In looking at the image of the Wheel Model (figure 5), you'll see that the sexual activities listed are the same as those on the Sexual Staircase (plus some extras, since there's more space!). What you should immediately notice about this model is that the sexual activities are not organized hierarchically, and therefore all have equal value.

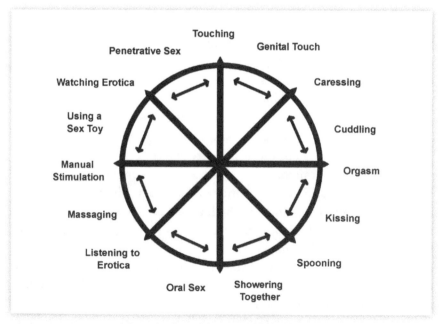

FIGURE 5. The Wheel Model. Inspired by Robert T. Francoeur, *Becoming a Sexual Person*, 2nd ed. (New York: Macmillan, 1991).

But wait! Many folks stop us here in disbelief—"Are you saying that intercourse is the same as kissing?!" Well . . . yes and no. At base value, no one type of sexual activity is better or worse than another. That's not to say there aren't personal preferences though—often there are very strong ones. For example, penile-vaginal intercourse is some people's favorite and most preferred sexual activity. For other people, their favorite sexual activity is a really good make out session. The important takeaway here is that although you may prefer some sexual activities over others, this doesn't mean that your favorites are inherently better or worse than any other type of sex. Remember, one of the main problems with the Sexual Staircase is an inherent assumption that everyone's sexual script, preferences, and desires are the same. The Wheel Model, in contrast, helps us to move away from these cultural assumptions into a healthier, more nuanced view of sex.

It's extremely common—perhaps inevitable—for partners to have different sexual preferences. The multidirectional arrows of the Wheel Model indicate that there does not need to be a linear order to partnered sexual activities (unlike the Staircase model, where the script is predetermined for us). It's sort of like those awesome Choose Your Own Adventure children's books from the 1980s and '90s where there are multiple possibilities for the story line. Choosing your own *sexual* adventure with the Wheel Model means that no two sexual experiences have to be the same (though, of course, they can be if you like that). For example, you could start with oral sex and then move into kissing. Or you can have a heavy make out session with no genital touch or contact. Of course, if the traditional Staircase script works for you and your partner(s), you can certainly still enjoy that in an open-ended way by communicating your preferences rather than assuming that they're understood. Again, the main problem with the Sexual Staircase is that it's based on an assumed path and doesn't take into account individual desires or differences.

Often, after discussing the Sexual Staircase and Wheel Model with clients, we're asked an excellent question: why do we continue to rely on rigid and unhelpful Staircase thinking in our culture? After all, when partners make assumptions about sex—as seen in the Sexual Staircase—all sorts of negative outcomes can result, especially low sexual satisfaction (which, as we've discussed, is an important variable for libido). We suspect that the Sexual Staircase continues to reign supreme because our culture makes it easy to do so. It's easy *not* to discuss sexual preferences with a partner, as this can be a tremendously vulnerable topic. And certainly, we live in a culture that doesn't typically educate us about healthy sexual communication or encourage us to discuss sex (even with our partners and healthcare providers). At its very core, the open-ended Wheel Model of partnered sex requires thoughtful communication—before, during, and after sexual experiences.

Without question, there needs to be a broader cultural shift away from the Sexual Staircase. That said, moving toward the Wheel Model is something you can absolutely work on individually and with partners, and we'll be discussing this at length throughout this book. At the end of the day, there's no way that we know of to improve your sexual relationship without talking about it (or learning to talk about it!) . . . and we realize that this can be challenging.

chapter 3

INTERPERSONAL
FACTORS

I n the last chapter, we reviewed a number of big picture factors at the social and cultural level that can impact our libido. We turn now to the interpersonal level of the ecological model, which concerns relationships between people. Interpersonal factors—especially between sexual partners—play an enormous role in libido, yet most of us are never really taught much about healthy communication. Many of us didn't witness healthy communication growing up, a pattern that can repeat in our own relationships (sexual or otherwise). None of us are born just knowing how to be an effective communicator, and that's especially true when it comes to the topic of sex. Healthy interpersonal communication is a skill, and just like any other skill, it can be learned and practiced. In this chapter, we'll review several key ways that interpersonal interactions and communication can break down and negatively impact sexual desire.

WHO'S "THE PROBLEM"?

Before we discuss interpersonal barriers to libido, it's important to address how we approach libido differences. Many folks tend to view the lower-libido partner as "the problem." This common framing of sexual concerns is strongly influenced by the heteronormative narratives and cultural assumptions that we reviewed in chapter 2. As a result, individuals come to see us with a complaint of "low" libido when the issue is more often about navigating a desire discrepancy in their relationship. Differences in desire are not problems that are specific to any one partner. They are *relationship issues* and need to be approached as such. We find that it's tremendously helpful for partners to address sexual desire discrepancies together, reinforcing that they are a team and that there is a role for all partners involved. This dance of desire requires navigating the three parts of a sexual relationship: you, me, and us.

A NOTE ABOUT RELATIONSHIP ISSUES

Libido differences can be challenging to navigate even when a relationship is going well. These differences can be much harder to manage when there are other significant problems within a relationship. Problems with trust, infidelity, resentment, jealousy, and other such concerns can all impact sexual desire, and understandably so. It can be difficult and sometimes ineffective to work on multiple relationship issues at the same time. As sex therapists, we often recommend that partners address some of these other relationship difficulties—depending on how significant they are—before trying to work on the sexual desire discrepancy. That's not to say that things need to be perfect in a relationship, as that's not a realistic goal, but if there is a high level of conflict between partners, it can be difficult to work on the sexual relationship. In these cases, the initial focus often must be de-escalating conflict and distress. As such, focusing on overarching relational issues with a skilled therapist may be a necessary place to start versus focusing specifically on sex. We'll discuss more about relationship and interpersonal issues throughout this chapter and in chapter 6. In chapter 9, we discuss how to find the right therapist.

SEXUAL COMMUNICATION: ASSUMPTIONS AND EXPECTATIONS

Something that we hear a lot from people who have lower desire than their partner(s) is that over time, they start to avoid touching—even to hug or kiss—out of a worry that it might arouse their partner(s) and trigger pressure to have sex. We've met many individuals who will even avoid changing clothes around their partner(s) due to fear of frustrating them, disappointing them, or reminding them about the desire discrepancy. This pattern of thinking—that any and all arousal or touching will automatically lead to (usually penetrative) sex—is a direct result of the Sexual Staircase thinking that we discussed in chapter 2. When we operate according to the Sexual Staircase, sex with a partner becomes very all or nothing. Either all touch leads to sexual activity and orgasms, or there's no touch at all. Over time, this mindset often feeds emotional and physical disconnection between partners, and a pattern of intimacy avoidance is unintentionally established. It's common, for example, to hear partners with higher libido talk about missing general affectionate touch in their relationships, regardless of whether sex is involved. This difficult dynamic develops in large part because the Sexual Staircase is all about assumptions and a predetermined sexual script. Assumptions about sex, as it turns out, often create problems.

Recall that one of the big problems with the goal-oriented Sexual Staircase model is its heavy focus on penile-vaginal intercourse to the exclusion of many other sexual activities. Because this is quite a limited way to think about partnered sex, we often lose sight of the many other activities that can create intimacy and pleasure, and we can start to feel a lot of pressure around having intercourse. We get trapped in the all-or-nothing thought pattern, which can look something like: "Well, if we aren't going to have penetrative intercourse (or I don't want to), why would we bother to kiss?" However, even if a partner feels disappointed that touch doesn't lead to sexual activity, they'll likely still prefer *some* physical touch to *none* at all. Staircase thinking is where many relationships get stuck.

Can you recall a time where you were asked about your sexual preferences, or about what brings you pleasure? Many of us are not taught to name or notice our sexual interests, let alone to develop our own or to think outside of the Sexual Staircase script. This, then, means that we often hold private assumptions about what sex is supposed to look like, or what a partner may want from us. Assumptions can be a huge setup for sexual disappointment or disconnection. Here are a few examples of common sexual assumptions:

- "If we start touching, it will lead to intercourse."
- "If my partner gets aroused and it doesn't end in an orgasm, they'll be upset/frustrated/disappointed."
- "Penetration is the most enjoyable (or most important) sexual activity."

- "If it doesn't involve penetration or an orgasm, it doesn't count as sex."
- "If I don't have sex with my partner every [insert assumption about frequency], I'm not being a good wife/husband/spouse/partner."
- "If my partner doesn't orgasm, it means I didn't do a good job (or I'm bad in bed)."
- "If I don't have spontaneous desire for sex, something is wrong with me, something's wrong in the relationship, or my partner will be disappointed."

These assumptions can be really problematic, often leading to resentment and/or feelings of pressure. Of course, such feelings can then further aggravate desire discrepancies between partners. The best way to combat the negative effects of sexual assumptions (or really, assumptions of any kind) is to talk about them as openly and honestly as possible. Sound challenging? It definitely can be. Most of us weren't taught healthy communication strategies, particularly around such a vulnerable topic. These are skills that require education and practice. We'll review some key concepts here. Our Resources section lists books and other tools for practicing good communication.

THE GOTTMANS' FOUR HORSEMEN

Dr. John Gottman and Dr. Julie Schwartz Gottman, a married couple, are two of the foremost relationship therapists and researchers in the field. Their therapeutic approach—the Gottman Method—is based on forty-plus years of research. They have famously noted four corrosive patterns of partner communication—which they call the Four Horsemen of the Apocalypse—that, if continued over time, highly predict the end of a relationship.[1] Routine use of the Four Horsemen leaves folks struggling to feel heard and understood in their relationships. Perhaps unsurprisingly, such feelings can absolutely contribute to, or worsen, sexual desire differences.

The first Horseman is *criticism*. Criticism is when we attack or blame a partner. The focus of the communication is on the other person and often targets a perceived deficit in their character. For example: "You never initiate sex with me. What's wrong with you?" Or, "You're always hounding me for sex. You have a problem." As you can imagine, being on the receiving end of this type of communication is challenging and certainly doesn't foster closeness. Criticism most often results in defensive and guarded reactions (more on this below). The antidote to criticism is to use what the Gottmans refer to as a gentle start-up. This essentially means to approach the subject more softly. For example, using statements that start with "I feel" and stating something like: "I feel undesired when we don't both initiate sex," or, "I feel overwhelmed when you ask to have sex multiple times per week."

The second Horseman is *defensiveness*. Defensiveness is when we cast ourselves in the victimized role and avoid taking responsibility for our part in the dynamic. This strategy often derails the speaker's original message and instead centers the listener. This can sound like: "Well, you don't initiate sex either," or, "If you spent more time with me, I would initiate more." The antidote to defensiveness is to take some responsibility and to validate the other person's feelings. It's about owning your part in the dynamic. This can sound like: "You're right, I don't initiate sex very often," or, "It makes sense that you're upset about the imbalance in who initiates sex."

The third Horseman is *contempt*. The Gottmans discovered that contempt is the most psychologically and emotionally harmful of the Four Horsemen. If left unchanged over time, it's the greatest predictor that a relationship will end.[2] Contempt is a bit like criticism on steroids and refers to when we approach our partner(s) or relationship(s) from a place of superiority. It can involve mockery, eye-rolling, name-calling, condescension, and disrespect. For example: "You're such a prude, you're never in the mood for sex," or, "You're a lousy lover." The antidote to contempt is to talk about your own feelings and needs, rather than focusing on the other person and their perceived shortcomings. For example, this can sound like: "I feel frustrated about our sexual desire discrepancy," or, "I need us to spend more time kissing during sex."

The fourth Horseman is *stonewalling*. Stonewalling is when we stop responding to our partner(s) and turn away from them, either emotionally or physically. This might look like avoiding eye contact, looking away, becoming verbally unresponsive, or leaving the room. This is often a result of *flooding*, which occurs when your body goes into survival mode, also known as the stress response. Signs of flooding can include an accelerated resting heart rate (around one hundred beats per minute, or eighty-five beats for folks who are more athletic), clammy hands, increased breathing rate, difficulty concentrating or thinking clearly, or feeling like you want to run away. The antidote to stonewalling is to practice physiological self-soothing.

This can be anything that helps your nervous system to calm down and de-escalate from the situation—for example, going for a walk, meditating, taking a shower or bath, listening to music, or lifting weights. When one or more partners are flooded, taking a break for at least twenty to thirty minutes can be helpful to calm the nervous system. Then, revisit the dialogue when everyone is in a more regulated state.

ABUSE OR INTERPERSONAL VIOLENCE

We mentioned contempt as one of the Four Horsemen. While occasional contemptuous behaviors can occur within generally healthy relationships, it becomes a different issue when these behaviors are a more consistent pattern. Name-calling, mockery, and disrespect are signs of abuse. Additional warning signs, as outlined by the National Domestic Violence Hotline, include being demeaned by a partner, being denied control of finances, threats or intimidation, being prevented from seeing friends or family, and pressure to perform sex acts. Abuse also includes a partner expressing extreme jealousy, destroying property, and being physically violent. If some of these signs sound familiar, we strongly encourage you to seek support. If you live in the United States, you can text START to 88788 from a mobile phone to be connected to the National Domestic Violence Hotline, or call 1-800-799-7233. You can also contact a mental healthcare provider in your area for help.

SHARING SEXUAL INTERESTS: DON'T YUCK SOMEONE'S YUM

Communicating about sex with partners can be a major challenge, but it is critically important for navigating sexual desire differences. A well-known saying in the sexual health community is "don't yuck someone's yum." This means we can respect the sexual interests of others, even if we ourselves don't have the same interests. It's so important to be aware of this approach as a sexual partner. When you're listening to a partner share (in general or about sex), it's critically important to place yourself in a position of *curiosity*, listening to better understand their inner world and postponing your own agenda. If we respond to someone's sexual interests with judgment, disgust, or criticism, they can shut down and understandably feel like it's unsafe to share. In some partnerships, we have seen such criticism shut down sexual activity altogether.

Let's look at Xiang and Imani's relationship. Early on in their relationship, Xiang told Imani that she thought giving oral sex was "gross." Imani clearly remembers this moment—it stood out as pivotal to her, especially because one of her favorite sexual activities is giving and receiving oral stimulation. When she heard Xiang refer to oral sex in such a negative way, she felt a part of her own sexuality shut down. Instead of talking about this with Xiang, however, Imani kept her feelings to herself. She drew the conclusion that oral sex was simply off the table in their relationship. Over time, she began to lose interest in sex as she started to generalize Xiang's comment, coming to believe that Xiang was also not open to other sexual activities and had an overall feeling that sex was mostly "gross."

Whether or not Imani's assumptions about Xiang were actually true became secondary to her very real libido change. Imani internalized feelings of shame related to negative and judgmental comments about her favorite sexual activity. Imani and Xiang's desire discrepancy reminds us that it's important to be thoughtful with our words, particularly around a subject as vulnerable as sex. This doesn't mean we can't share sexual dislikes or our true feelings, but we need to do so in a non-shaming way. As you'll see, throughout this chapter, we come back to the role of effective and healthy communication techniques again and again.

FAKING ORGASM

Faking orgasm is a common relational issue most typically seen in cisgender heterosexual partnerships. At its foundation, this is a communication difficulty in which one partner pretends to experience pleasure and climax, either to end the sexual experience more quickly or to make their partner(s) feel good. Some may choose to fake orgasm because they know that their partner wants the experience to be mutually satisfying and they're trying to give that impression. Alternatively, they may be trying to avoid their partner feeling disappointed or unsatisfied. Faking orgasms is problematic when it comes to libido, as it's a misrepresentation of your actual experience. It also reinforces a sexual routine that shortchanges your pleasure. At a larger level, faking orgasm is typically an avoidance strategy—an attempt to sidestep what may be a challenging conversation about one's sexual desires and needs. In these situations, the person faking orgasm may not be having the sexual experiences that they want, which lessens their incentive for partnered sex (aka desire). As partners begin to communicate more openly about sex, optimizing pleasure is a critically important topic. In short, faking orgasm is doing you no favors when it comes to libido.

PERPETUAL PROBLEMS VERSUS SOLVABLE PROBLEMS

Did you know that about 69 percent of relationship problems are considered perpetual?[3] Drawing on their forty-plus years of research, the Gottmans highlight the difference between perpetual problems and solvable problems. They found that a majority of relationship problems persist over time due to intrinsic differences between partners. These perpetual problems rarely have a definitive solution and tend to come up again and again. Conversely, solvable problems are those that actually can be resolved and tend to be situational in nature, such as disagreements over what color to paint a room or which apartment to rent.

A sexual desire discrepancy can be either a solvable problem or a perpetual problem, depending on the partnership. Maybe one partner prefers morning sex while another prefers sex in the evening. Or one partner prefers sex several times per week and the other prefers sex once per month or less. One partner may be kinky and the other not so much, and so on. While the idea that a desire discrepancy may be a perpetual problem can sound like a gloomy prospect, some may find this to be comforting. It means that rather than trying to change the other person or trying to resolve an unresolvable problem, the goal becomes more about *managing* this difference in a healthy way over time: finding ways to honor each person while also respecting boundaries. This is where partners practice reasonable compromise, give and take. We cover these strategies in chapter 6.

NEW RELATIONSHIP ENERGY

In chapter 1, we discussed the so-called honeymoon phase of relationships, otherwise known as a time of new relationship energy (NRE).[4] In the NRE stage of a partnership, things feel new and exciting. Many people experience a surge in spontaneous desire for sex and the frequency of partnered sexual activity is often highest at this point. Depending on the relationship and factors such as distance, this stage may last anywhere from a few months to a few years. Ultimately, as relationships continue and perhaps shift into stability, NRE often fades. For some, as partnerships become more committed and comfortable, their spontaneous desire shifts into responsive desire. It's important to recognize that this is not only common, it's also a predictable aspect of long-term relationships. Our bodies must return to that pre-honeymoon phase at some point—they simply can't maintain the flood of hormones and neurotransmitters that occur during NRE. People often ask us, "Why can't it be like it was at the beginning of my relationship?" We get it . . . NRE is often a powerful and lovely feeling! Unfortunately, though, the one thing a long-term partner cannot be is new again. Alas, we get used to each other and that tends to decrease the sense of novelty or excitement. That said, however, there are certainly ways to create freshness and enthusiasm in long-term partnerships. This often involves seeing each other in new spaces and engaging with each other in new and different ways.

Some ways to create novelty and excitement in a relationship include:

- Spending time with other people and getting to watch your partner(s) interact with them
- Taking a class together to learn a new skill, like cooking or dance
- Doing something adventurous together, like going to an amusement park, zip-lining, visiting a haunted house, or hiking a new trail
- Visiting a restaurant that's different from your typical spot
- Going on a walk or drive together without a destination in mind
- Doing something playful together, like mini golfing, ice skating, air hockey, or playing pool

Maintaining a sense of novelty or excitement in long-term relationships requires intentional effort. Many popular magazines, TV, movies, and social media promote the concept of novelty in relationships as a prime ingredient for maintaining sexual desire. While this may be very helpful for some, recall that sexual satisfaction and pleasure are typically what's most important for cultivating desire—either spontaneous or responsive. For some partnerships, sharing more fun or novel experiences can positively impact desire, whereas for others, this may not translate to a boost in libido and additional factors may need to be addressed. Remember, sexual desire is complex and pleasure is key.

THE PURSUE-WITHDRAW PATTERN

In relationships, a common dynamic that emerges between partners is called the *pursue-withdraw pattern*. This pattern of interaction has been described by many therapists—most notably Dr. Sue Johnson, who developed emotionally focused couple therapy—and can be useful to understand. In the pursue-withdraw pattern, the pursuer tends to approach their partner for connection or with a relational need: for example, physical touch for comfort, or talking through feelings of insecurity. However, the pursuit is done in a negative way—for example, with blame, criticism, or harshness. As a result, the withdrawing partner responds by distancing themselves. They pull away from the negative pursuit either to self-soothe or in an effort to minimize conflict. They also might not realize the pursuer's underlying "reach" or need, which can get lost or missed due to the way their partner approaches them. Withdrawers may also struggle to reach out for connection themselves, either emotionally or sexually. Thus, we get one partner moving toward and another partner moving away. This dance can occur both in the general relationship and the sexual relationship.

Let's look at an example: Rosario and Sam have been dating for a year and a half. They don't live together but see each other a few times a week. Sam got divorced three years ago after twenty years of marriage. His tendency throughout that marriage was to shut down and pull away from his ex-wife when she would express her relational needs, which she often did by criticizing him (e.g., saying "you never ask me about my day" when she needed connection). There was little sexual intimacy in his marriage and Sam was mostly sexual through masturbation. Additionally, as he's gotten older, Sam has experienced some difficulty getting erections. Although he takes medication that helps him have more reliable erections, he finds this embarrassing and shameful. In the current relationship, Rosario feels most desired by Sam when there is frequent—for her, multiple times per week—penetrative sex. When Sam has difficulty getting an erection or when intercourse occurs less than weekly, she internally questions Sam's love for her and outwardly criticizes him, similar to his ex-wife's behavior. Additionally, when Rosario perceives a lack of sexual interest from Sam, she becomes upset and questions his commitment to their relationship. Sam shuts down by becoming less verbally responsive, engaging in less physical touch, avoiding eye contact, or leaving the room. Rosario generally expects to be sexual on nights that she and Sam spend time together. Sam is aware of this expectation and finds it pressuring and stressful. There are many times that he intentionally doesn't take his erectile medication on date nights with Rosario, due to this feeling of pressure. It's his attempt to avoid disappointing her or causing conflict. Sex essentially becomes "off the table," since Rosario won't pursue sex unless intercourse is the central focus. Rather than reassure Rosario of his love and desire for her, Sam retreats, reinforcing her fear that he is disinterested.

The pursue-withdraw pattern is not just about who is initiating sex: it tends to be a larger, ineffective dynamic between partners that leads to further disconnection and, over time, tension and resentment. In the case of Rosario and Sam, we see a couple of problems related to the pursue-withdraw pattern. First, Rosario has internalized rigid gender roles and demonstrates notable heteronormative bias: she expects men to initiate sex, sees erections as a necessary sign of sexual interest, and views frequent sex as a measure of love. When her expectations around these beliefs aren't met, she feels insecure. Her way of managing that insecurity is to question the relationship and her partner's commitment, hoping that she will be heard and validated. Sam meanwhile experiences shame around his erection problems due to gendered messages he has internalized about what it means to be a man. Given the dynamics of his past marriage, he is especially sensitive to criticism and has developed a habit of withdrawing when feeling pressured. Rosario was single prior to meeting Sam and had built up some specific expectations and fantasies about what sexual relationships "should" be like. As their relationship continues, they become increasingly entrenched in these roles and feel helpless to change the pattern.

It is possible to pursue a partner in a healthy way, creating a positive sense of emotional connection. When this is done effectively, closeness and a sense of relational security can result. In the pursue-withdraw pattern, however, the opposite happens: both the pursuer's ineffective attempts at closeness and the withdrawer's avoidance create relational distress. Both partners perpetuate this cycle and, as such, both partners must adjust their behavior. For the dynamic between Rosario and Sam to change, both need to try something different. For example, Rosario needs to communicate her needs more effectively. This means recognizing that Sam is not the sole "problem" (which is how she currently views the situation, whether she realizes it or not). It also means identifying her internalized expectations and focusing more on expressing what she longs for and how she feels—the deeper needs behind her criticism. Sam needs to be more engaged with and responsive to Rosario. He can do this by verbally reassuring her of his love and commitment, by initiating more general physical touch, or perhaps by offering alternative ways to be sexual with Rosario when intercourse is not of interest or accessible for him. This case is an important reminder that it's not one person who is the "problem" when it comes to libido; rather, the difficulty lies in the relational dynamic and how partners either healthfully manage or ineffectively mismanage their differences. We'll discuss this further in chapter 6.

DIFFERENCES BETWEEN PARTNERS

Partners don't have to share all the same sexual interests, fantasies, and desires. In fact, they usually don't! As with other aspects of a relationship, differences in sexual likes and dislikes are the norm, not the exception. These differences may not be limited to preferences about sexual frequency—they also often extend to different interests in sexual activities. The goal is not to eliminate these sexual differences—that's not always possible—but to effectively manage them over time. One exercise that can help partners negotiate a compromise around sexual differences is from the Gottman Method and is called the Art of Compromise.

To practice the Art of Compromise exercise, you and a partner will each draw two concentric ovals: a small one in the middle of a piece of paper, and a larger one surrounding it. In the smaller oval, you'll identify what your core needs are with respect to the issue you're discussing—whether it's to feel loved or desired or to have physical touch. This should be a short list. Some common core needs include connection, closeness, pleasure, comfort, and affection. Whatever core needs you include in the smaller oval represent your non-negotiables: the things that must be kept as you work toward compromise. In the larger oval, you'll want to list all of the ways in which you might be flexible around the issue without compromising your core needs. These are your negotiables. Oftentimes, the list of ways in which you can be flexible will outnumber the inflexibilities or non-negotiables. There are often multiple ways to get our needs met. Let's look at an example of this exercise in action.

Patrick and David have differences around their sexual interests and preferences. Patrick's favorite partnered sexual activity is oral sex and David's favorite is penetration. Patrick doesn't mind penetrative sex, but he prefers it less frequently than David. David's preference would be to have penetrative sex each time they're sexual together. Historically, when they've tried to talk about this difference, both partners feel stuck, the conversation becomes heated, and the issue remains unresolved. Figure 6 shows Patrick and David's compromise ovals.

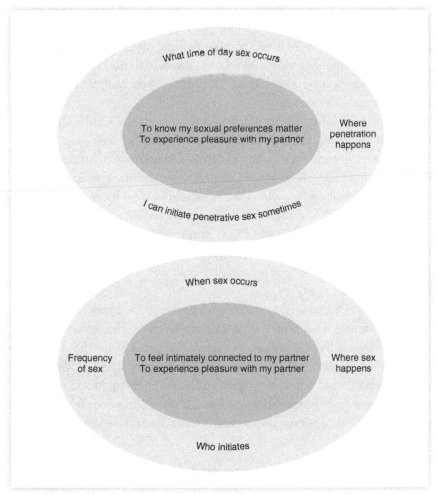

FIGURE 6. Compromise Ovals for Patrick and David. Adapted from John M. Gottman and Nan Silver, *The Seven Principles for Making Marriage Work: A Practical Guide from the Country's Foremost Relationship Expert* (New York: Harmony Books, 2015).

Patrick's core needs—written in the smaller oval—are to know that his sexual preferences matter (this helps him to feel cared for and valued) and to experience pleasure with his partner. As part of this exercise, Patrick gave more thought to his areas of flexibility—written in the larger oval—and came up with the following: where penetrative sex happens and what time of day sex occurs. He is also open to initiating penetrative sex more often— he knows this is important to David, and it's something he's comfortable doing some of the time. Meanwhile, David identifies one of his core needs as feeling intimately connected to his partner, and he finds that this best occurs for him via penetrative sex. Like Patrick, his other core need is to experience pleasure with his partner. David's areas of flexibility are also when and where sex occurs, who initiates, and how often their sexual activity includes penetrative sex.

As they were doing the Art of Compromise exercise, David realized that talking more openly about their relationship *in and of itself* led to feeling more intimately connected to Patrick, thus fulfilling one of his core needs. Both Patrick and David also realized that there are other sexual activities that they both enjoy and could be incorporated into sex more often. Sometimes, they realized, sex might not include penetrative activities but rather other mutually pleasurable acts. This compromise respects both partners' core needs to experience pleasure together. Like David, Patrick also found that the process of talking more openly about core needs helped him feel valued and understood.

The Art of Compromise exercise may not work for every relationship's sexual differences. However, the exercise can teach us a lot about ourselves and our partners by identifying core needs and areas of flexibility. Often, partners find solutions that they did not anticipate or consider. Something to also keep in mind is that compromises should be revisited and revised as needed, based on subsequent experiences. If something doesn't work, you can come back to this exercise and consider an alternative compromise.

SEXUAL INCOMPATIBILITIES

So, you've started having hard conversations with your partner about sexual desires. Congratulations on tackling this important skill! What happens, however, if you discover that your partner's desires are drastically different from and potentially incompatible with your own? Let's take a look at an example.

Antonia and Grace have been in a monogamous relationship for thirteen years and have long struggled with a difference in sexual interests. Grace considers herself to be more vanilla around sex, whereas Antonia has always been interested in kink and BDSM. Antonia has suppressed many of these interests because she knows that they just aren't Grace's thing. Over time, though, exploring kink has come to feel more important to Antonia and is something that she really wants to pursue. Antonia has brought up her interest in kink and BDSM more often lately and both partners feel very stuck in how to move forward. Antonia is having a hard time imagining never getting to explore this part of her sexuality. Grace, however, feels like participating in kink and BDSM is too much of a stretch for her without feeling like she's compromising her own needs.

In general, partners with sexual incompatibilities have five potential options:

1. Continue to try changing each other and stay stuck in gridlock. For Antonia and Grace, this means that nothing really changes and that perhaps frustration and resentment in the relationship grows.
2. Work together to find areas of compromise and flexibility. For Antonia and Grace, this may look like completing the Art of Compromise exercise (covered in the previous section) to find areas of overlapping interest that were perhaps not previously realized.
3. Radically accept (without resentment) sexual differences and learn to live with them as they are. For Antonia, this might involve exploring her interest in kink and BDSM without Grace— for example, watching kinky erotica, fantasizing about BDSM, and using masturbation.
4. Open up the relationship to include other sexual partners. For Antonia and Grace, this may mean exploring a non-monogamous arrangement that would allow Antonia to engage in kink and BDSM activities with another partner. Grace could also explore the vanilla types of sex that appeal to her with other sexual

partners. (Ethical non-monogamy may be a new concept for many readers and one that raises complex emotions. We'll address it in much more detail in the following section.)

5. End the relationship. This certainly may be a less than ideal option, but it's important to note that it is an option. For Antonia and Grace, this may mean deciding to part ways if they are unable to find a mutually satisfying compromise or accept their differences.

RELATIONSHIP STRUCTURES: MONOGAMY AND ETHICAL NON-MONOGAMY

Though we don't often stop to think about it, relationships have structures. In most cultures, monogamy is the default relationship structure, with two partners exclusively paired together both sexually and romantically. Because of these cultural norms, humans tend to be serial monogamists, becoming involved in back-to-back monogamous relationships with one person at a time. Other relationship structures exist, however, and are important to acknowledge in the context of desire differences.

Ethical non-monogamy (ENM) is a type of relationship structure in which partners agree that they can have sexual and/or romantic relationships with others.[5] Also referred to as consensual non-monogamy, ENM itself can take many forms, including polyamory and swinging. In general, polyamory involves romantic/sexual relationships with more than one person at a time, often with emotional connections prioritized. Swinging involves partners being sexual with others, either separately or together—the focus tends to be less on emotional connection and more on physical experiences. Though ENM relationship structures are not our societal default, such partnerships are not exactly rare either. Population estimates in the United States and Canada suggest that about 4 percent of adults are currently engaging in some form of ENM, with an up to 21 percent lifetime prevalence rate.[6] You may also be surprised to learn that people in ENM relationships come from quite diverse backgrounds, including a range of ages, faith traditions, education levels, income levels, political affiliations, genders, sexual orientations, races, and ethnicities.

ENM is a big topic, and we certainly won't cover it all here (many great books have been written on this subject—see the Resources section for more information). With regard to libido, however, exploring relationship structures outside of the traditional monogamous default can be useful in managing sexual desire differences for some people. However, a major change in relationship structure should not be undertaken lightly and never without significant preparation and communication. In order to explore ENM in an effective and healthy way, we highly recommend reading and learning more about these relationships and perhaps working with a sex or relationship therapist who is knowledgeable about these types of relationship structures.

THE MENTAL LOAD

The balance of give and take in a relationship will naturally fluctuate between partners as you move through life together. Maybe your partner tends to be in charge of cooking meals while you handle household cleaning duties, or perhaps one person tackles financial planning and the other does yard work. The constant effort, thought, and energy that goes into running a household or managing a family is known as the *mental load.*[7] The mental load may include things like:

- Decorating for the holidays
- Planning meals
- Tidying up before guests arrive
- Running errands for an aging parent
- Prepping children's lunches
- Making and keeping track of medical appointments
- Cleaning out the fridge
- Arranging date nights
- Keeping track of friends' and family members' birthdays
- Initiating quality time together
- Planning trips or vacations

All of these tasks are simply part of our daily lives, yet they can leave many of us feeling overwhelmed and stressed. Part of the reason these tasks are so exhausting is that they are typically not just a one-step process. Each can involve a whole set of smaller steps that often go unnoticed or underappreciated. These actions take up a lot of mental, emotional, and physical energy. And because the demands of daily life never let up, it's no wonder we are so tired!

How partners manage the mental load in their relationship can create a balance or imbalance of power and responsibility. Sometimes one person will give more than the other. Other times, it will switch. Research shows that in cisgender heterosexual relationships, women statistically carry much more of the mental load than men.[8] Of course, this isn't true for all relationships, and those roles can certainly be reversed. And while traditional gender roles may not determine who carries more of the mental load in relationships between LGBTQ+ folks, it's still common for one partner to take on more than the other.

What's most important here is that the mental load isn't unbalanced in one direction *most of the time*. It's a setup for resentment if one person feels like the household or family management tasks predominantly fall to them. This dynamic can make a relationship feel difficult to sustain and, as we'll see, can impact sexual desire. When the mental load feels unfair, it can breed resentment, disconnectedness, and sometimes parentification (feeling like a parent to a significant other), which—understandably—is not very sexy.[9] Imagine how that could translate to a lack of interest in sex or even just a lack of energy to be sexual. If the mental load feels unbalanced in your relationship, one thing you can do is write out a list (really!) of all the various household chores and responsibilities—big and small—that need to be done. Use the list to start a discussion about who is currently doing what and how all parties would like it to be handled in the future. Importantly, the list is not meant to be a criticism of one partner to another (e.g., "Look at everything I do that you're not doing!"), but rather an accounting of relationship tasks that can be approached as a team and revisited as needed. Renegotiating relationship roles and responsibilities can help create a stronger feeling of equity between partners and lift some of the barriers to sexual desire related to a lack of time or energy.

A final note about the mental load is that tasks don't have to be exactly equal between partners. It's definitely not about 50/50, tit for tat, or quid pro quo. Rather, the division of labor just needs to feel fair for everyone involved. Since fairness is subjective, this will be different in every partnership. It's important that relationship roles be discussed and negotiated clearly and openly so that resentment and emotional disconnection can be minimized.

The mental load is not just a problem between partners—it exists as a greater social, cultural, and economic problem. If you're interested in reading more about the mental load, please see the Resources section at the back of this book for recommendations.

TRYING TO GET PREGNANT OR ADOPT

Trying to have children—whether through pregnancy, surrogacy, or adoption—can have a negative impact on libido for many people. In trying to conceive, it's perhaps unsurprising that when there's a sense of pressure to have sex at a particular time, in a particular way, and at a particular frequency, anxiety and stress can result. It's not uncommon for partners in this situation to develop problems with sexual function, including difficulty with arousal (i.e., lubrication, erections), decreased libido, trouble with orgasm/ejaculation, and sometimes even sexual pain. In our therapy practices, we commonly meet partners who have developed low libido while trying to conceive. It highlights an important and foundational concept: Pressure is a libido killer!

For folks who are trying to get pregnant, a sense of pressure may be unavoidable to some degree. However, it's important to note that this process can affect your desire for sex both during the time frame of trying to conceive and sometimes long afterward. For some, sex becomes a chore. For a period of time, pleasure and fun may be placed on the back burner and partners may rely heavily on the Sexual Staircase, with penetrative intercourse and ejaculation becoming the only goal.

As we've discussed, goal-oriented sex—via the Sexual Staircase—often leads to a host of problems. So what can you do to help your libido when you're also trying to conceive? An important strategy is trying to maintain a balance of pleasure-focused, non-goal-oriented sex to prevent sex from becoming too strongly linked to pressure. If you're able, you can try to conceive some months and not others, mixing it up to ensure that pleasure doesn't get forgotten.

For some partners, another option is to talk to your medical provider about an at-home insemination kit for intravaginal insemination (IVI) or intracervical insemination (ICI). This strategy may be helpful, especially if there are difficulties with sexual functioning, as it takes the pressure off of intercourse. At-home insemination involves a partner ejaculating into a specimen cup and then using a syringe to place the semen into the vagina. This might help to take pressured sex out of the equation altogether, allowing partners to focus exclusively on building pleasure and intimacy during sexual experiences.

A third option is to practice mindful touch to help you focus on the present moment, get out of your head, and potentially reduce the sense of pressure. We'll discuss a specific type of exercise for this in chapter 7.

The process of surrogacy or adoption can also be stressful and even potentially traumatic. For partners who had hoped to be able to conceive but were unable to do so, sexual activity may trigger a sense of loss or grief that can subsequently disrupt libido. Among LGBTQ+ partners, adoption is a much more common pathway for having children. Over 21 percent of LGBTQ+ couples are raising adopted children, compared with just 3 percent of heterosexual couples.[10] Those who pursue agency adoption may encounter stigma, prejudice, or discrimination during the process—an all-too-common experience. For example, in many states, adoption and child services agencies are allowed to deny placements with LGBTQ+ partners. Implicit discrimination—such as beliefs by adoption agency employees that LGBTQ+ parents are less desirable—can create enormous emotional, financial, and legal barriers to growing families. Stress related to these difficult and discriminatory adoption processes can certainly have a negative impact on libido and overall sexual and relationship health (recall our prior discussion of minority stress in chapter 2).

Whether through pregnancy, surrogacy, or adoption, the transition to parenthood is commonly a stressful time for partnerships. There's typically less time to spend together to nurture the relationship as there are now more responsibilities, likely less sleep, and more demands on time.[11] It can be challenging to make date nights happen or to have the energy for sex during this transition. We encourage you to be gentle with yourselves during this time. It may take a while to get into a rhythm of nurturing both your partnership and a new child at the same time. One exercise we often recommend during such transitions is the intimacy date exercise, which we discuss in chapter 6.

When partners experience infertility, pregnancy loss, or learn that they cannot conceive the way they intended, they often go through a host of emotions, including grief. Importantly, grief is not a linear experience. For some people, sex can be a way to work through grief. For others, sex may be the last thing they want to engage in while grieving. As noted, sex itself may stir up feelings of loss and grief. It may take time to work through these emotions. While some folks may try to conceive again right away, others may not. Some may decide to try another method for growing their family. There is no one way to be or start a family and every partnership may experience these processes differently, including the ways in which libido is impacted.

chapter 4

INDIVIDUAL FACTORS

In the last chapter we reviewed interpersonal (that is, relational) factors that can impact libido. We now move into the final level of the ecological model, which is the individual level. As you might imagine, there are a ton of individual-level factors that can affect our sexual desire. These range from medical and health-related issues to psychological variables to personal experiences and life events. As the name implies, the factors at the individual level are person-specific and will depend on your own life history. A common theme, however, is that these individual-level factors tend to affect sexual *satisfaction* in some way. As you'll recall, one's degree of sexual satisfaction is one of the most important predictors of libido level. While it's impossible to name every single individual-level factor related to sexual desire, in this chapter we'll explore some of the most common ones.

HORMONES

Often, one of the first individual-level factors that folks with libido concerns consider—particularly if they are hoping to increase their sexual desire—is hormone levels. Typically, discussion centers around what are known as our *sex* or *reproductive hormones*: estrogens, androgens, and progesterone. (Though, as we've seen, there's speculation that hormones associated with chronic stress, like cortisol, also play an important role in libido.) There's a great deal of misunderstanding and oversimplification in our culture when it comes to sex and hormones. For example, while our culture commonly references "male" versus "female" sex hormones, in fact we all have some combination of these major hormones and there is actually a great deal more commonality in these levels across sex and gender than most people realize. This means that cultural references to "male" and "female" hormones are not only cisnormative but also inaccurate. Let's take a closer look at hormones, their role in sexual desire, and some other common misconceptions.

Androgens are a class of hormones released from the testes, ovaries, and adrenal glands (endocrine glands located just above the kidneys). As mentioned, we all have androgens, regardless of sex or gender, but at different levels depending on a number of biological and environmental factors. *Testosterone*, a type of androgen, has been a major focus of the medical community when it comes to libido. Testosterone is widely believed to both impact libido and have the ability to "fix" low or decreased sexual desire. This belief seems related to an assumption that because cisgender men tend to report higher levels of libido than cisgender women *and* on average tend to have more testosterone, this particular hormone must be the key to sexual desire.[1] Current science, however, does not support these deeply embedded cultural assumptions about testosterone and gender. Without a doubt, testosterone is linked to sexual desire . . . somehow. This involves a lot of nuance (and chemistry!) and is not the simple "higher testosterone equals higher libido" equation that we're often led to believe it is.[2] For example, some studies show that higher testosterone in cisgender women is associated with increased solitary desire—that is, the desire to engage in self-stimulation—but not increased desire for partnered sex, especially when perceived stress and cortisol levels were accounted for. In cisgender men, masturbation frequency—rather than testosterone level—appears to be more strongly linked to libido levels. These are just a few examples of the ways in which the level of testosterone in and of itself does not account for reported gender differences in libido.[3]

Estrogen has also been considered in efforts to increase libido—typically for cisgender heterosexual women. The helpfulness of this class of hormones appears to be most directly related to physiological arousal. That is, estrogen can improve vulvovaginal tissue health and lubrication (and is commonly prescribed for this reason, especially through menopause), often making sexual arousal more satisfying and pleasurable. Of course, as we've discussed, many people experience increased libido in response to their own physical arousal. Thus, if physical arousal is improved, increased libido can sometimes result (or at least more satisfying sexual experiences!).

As with so many things when it comes to our sexuality, hormones are complicated! Certainly we know that shifts in someone's hormone levels can impact their sexual function. This has been clearly observed in people on hormone therapy (e.g., for gender-affirming care or menopause) and in those who have experienced hormone fluctuations related to any number of factors (e.g., puberty, use of contraception, pregnancy, aging). Throughout this book, we'll continue to touch on the ways that hormone shifts may change aspects of our sexual health. The important message here, however, is that hormones are rarely the magic cure-all for libido that we are commonly led to believe. Some folks have certainly found that hormone prescriptions have improved their sexual health, but many others have not. These are important considerations and should always be discussed with your medical provider. We say more about this in chapter 9 when we cover strategies for seeking additional sexual healthcare.

SEXUAL PAIN

Painful sex is a major underlying cause of low libido. We simply aren't going to feel excited to do something that hurts! This is a normal and rational response to pain. However, we tend to treat sexual pain very differently than other types of pain. Consider this: You accidently touch a hot stove and burn your hand. Sometime later, your partner asks you to touch the hot stove again. There's probably no way you would do this, much less feel excited about placing your hand on that stove. Again, this is a healthy and adaptive response. Many people who experience sexual pain, however, continue to engage in the same painful activities over and over. There's often an attitude of pushing through the pain in order to avoid disappointing a partner. As we'll see below, this pattern is not only incredibly damaging to sexual desire but, in some cases, can actually make the pain much worse. Before we dive into the complicated cycle of sexual pain, let's take a look at some of the many reasons why a person might experience pain during sexual activity:

- Pelvic floor muscle tension
- Lack of trust or safety with a partner, potentially leading to pelvic tension
- Endometriosis, a condition where tissue that usually grows inside the uterus (called the endometrium) also grows outside of the uterus

- Gastrointestinal issues (e.g., irritable bowel syndrome)
- Swelling and irritation of the penile glans, known as balanitis
- Peyronie's disease (significant curvature of the penis due to scar tissue)
- Infections (e.g., bacterial vaginosis, yeast infections, urinary tract infections, and some sexually transmitted infections)
- Genitourinary syndrome (changes to the vulvovaginal and urethral areas) of menopause
- Inadequate physical arousal or lubrication
- A pinched nerve
- Phimosis, a condition in which the foreskin of the penis is too tight and difficult to retract
- Hormone changes (e.g., related to contraception or other medications, aging, thyroid issues)
- Arthritis
- Recovery from surgery
- Pregnancy
- Recovery from childbirth
- Dermatological (skin) issues, such as lichen sclerosus or lichen planus

We'll look at a few of these causes in more detail. However, it's important to say up front that sex—especially vaginal or anal penetration—is not supposed to be painful! We live in a culture that has long reinforced the myth that sexual activity is "supposed to be" uncomfortable or even painful, and we meet many people who believe this. This is simply not the case. Remember: sexual pain should not be pushed through. While we'll talk more about the role of sexual medicine providers and how to find one in chapter 9, suffice to say that sexual or genital pain means that a medical evaluation with a sexual health specialist is needed.

WHEN PAIN IS INTENTIONAL

An important caveat to any discussion of sexual pain is that, for some folks, pain is a source of pleasure. Specifically, those in kink and BDSM communities may explore, experiment, and play with lots of different physical sensations. At times, this might include some level of pain—for example, spanking. The important difference is that this form of sexual pain is intentional, consensual, and has been discussed and agreed upon ahead of time between sexual partners. When we talk about the sexual pain cycle in this chapter, we're referring to unwanted, unintentional pain that can disrupt pleasure and libido.

Factors that contribute to sexual pain fall broadly into three categories: *physical, psychological,* and *relational.* Oftentimes, these categories overlap and can reinforce one another in difficult ways. Let's look at an example:

Margo and Elliot enjoyed a pleasurable and satisfying sex life for many years. Starting around age fifty-five, Margo noticed that she had more vulvovaginal dryness and discomfort with intercourse. Using a store-bought lubricant helped for a short period of time. However, Margo's discomfort slowly worsened into pain both at the start of penile-vaginal penetration and with deeper penetration. Gradually, she became less and less interested in sex. Not only did intercourse with Elliot hurt each time, but the pain also was so distracting it disrupted any potential pleasure and her ability to orgasm. Because she didn't want to alarm Elliot or hurt his feelings, Margo never told him about the increased pain. She gradually stopped initiating sex and would also decline Elliot's initiations. Because they had never previously had to deal with sexual health concerns, the couple avoided discussing this new and difficult dynamic. This led, over time, to hurt feelings, resentment, and increased avoidance of sex and physical touch.

Unfortunately, Margo and Elliot's story is a very common one. It illustrates how what started as a medical issue evolved into both psychological and relationship problems due to discomfort with talking about sex and a lack of information about typical sexuality and aging concerns. In this case, Margo had started to develop symptoms of genitourinary syndrome of menopause (GSM), a common condition in which menopausal changes in the body's hormones can lead to dryness, thinning, and atrophy of the genital tissues. GSM reduces the overall health of our genitals and can create a number of problems for people with vulvas, including sexual discomfort, pain, and decreased sensation, leading to delayed or absent orgasm. Because the vulvovaginal tissues also serve a protective function for the urethral tract, unhealthy tissues due to GSM can additionally lead to irritation of the urethra, increased urinary urges and frequency of urination, and even an increased risk of urinary tract infections (UTIs).[4]

GSM is very treatable. The problem is that most people have never heard about it (including some physicians!) and thus they don't understand this common cause of sexual pain. In Margo's case, she was unaware that GSM could start to develop as menstrual cycles become less regular (a time before menopause, referred to as perimenopause). She attributed vulvovaginal dryness and sexual discomfort to getting older without realizing that treatment was available (something we'll talk more about in chapter 9). Because she didn't want to upset or worry Elliot, Margo continued to have painful sex with him for quite some time, kicking off what's known as the *sexual pain cycle*.

The sexual pain cycle is easily activated and can actually make pain much worse over time. We often meet patients who have been told by healthcare providers that, especially for penetrative sexual pain, they "just need to relax." While relaxation is certainly an important component, this dismissive (and inaccurate!) advice sends the message that sexual pain is all in your head and that a person can simply think their way out of the pain. As you can see in figure 7, the sexual pain cycle includes physical, psychological, and relational aspects of pain. Typically, all three of these overlapping components need to be addressed in order for pain to improve. Simply put, sexual pain involves more than just our minds.

The sexual pain cycle starts with *anticipatory anxiety* (link 1) about pain. Such anxiety—oftentimes based on past experience—tends to create tension in the body.* This is usually an automatic, *involuntary reaction* (link 2) to anxiety. It's also a protective function of our nervous systems, which are wired to minimize our experiences of pain. We're often unaware of our bodies tightening or clenching in this anticipatory way. Body tension related to anticipatory anxiety about pain can, of course, affect all of our body's muscle groups. Of particular concern, however, are the pelvic floor muscles.

Did you know that there are more than twenty different muscles in your pelvis? These muscles each have individual names and specific functions but

---

*Anticipatory anxiety about pain with sex can exist even for folks with no prior sexual history. For example, we commonly hear from sex therapy clients, especially those assigned female at birth, that they were taught from a young age that penile-vaginal penetration hurts or perhaps is even supposed to hurt, especially the first time. As you can imagine, this expectation—an outcome of poor sexual health education and cultural misinformation—can easily create anticipatory anxiety around sexual activity and place people at risk of kicking off the sexual pain cycle.

FIGURE 7. The Sexual Pain Cycle. Adapted from
https://www.vaginismus.com/causes-of-vaginismus.

collectively are referred to as the *pelvic floor* or *pelvic floor muscles*. All people, regardless of gender, have pelvic floor muscles. This group of muscles acts almost like a hammock or floor (hence the name) for our body and does a lot of important work for us day to day, including stabilizing the lower back and hips, contributing to bowel and bladder function, and supporting the pelvic organs (e.g., bladder, intestines, uterus). Pelvic floor muscles operate just like any other muscle of the body: they can be weak and require strengthening, or they can be overly tight and require stretching and relaxation. Potential signs of pelvic floor muscle *weakness* include bowel or bladder incontinence or vaginal prolapse, whereas folks with pelvic floor muscle *tension* often struggle with constipation, lower back or hip pain, and pain with sexual activity. Because there are so many muscles that comprise the pelvic floor, it's not uncommon for folks to have some areas with muscle weakness and other areas with muscle tension. It's very important that these concerns be assessed and treated by a specialist in pelvic floor health and/or sexual medicine.

PELVIC FLOOR POINTS

Pelvic floor muscles are somewhat less obvious than the other muscles in our bodies—certainly they are harder to see and access than, say, a bicep or abdominal muscle. The pelvis also tends to be a forgotten (or avoided) area of the body due to sexual shame. Thus, someone may not realize how tense their pelvic floor muscles really are until they experience sexual, genital, or pelvic pain. Pelvic floor muscle tension is one of the most common contributors to sexual pain, lower back and hip pain, and even constipation. It can also negatively impact erectile function and orgasms. The gold standard treatment for difficulties with this muscle group is pelvic floor physical therapy, a specialized form of physical therapy that involves specific techniques to improve pelvic floor muscle health. You can search for a pelvic floor physical therapist in your area by visiting https://hermanwallace .com/ or https://aptapelvichealth.org/ptlocator. We talk more about this important type of sexual healthcare provider in chapter 9.

Getting back to the sexual pain cycle, when someone experiences anticipatory anxiety about a sexual encounter—whether that's a fear of pain or even nervousness about how the encounter will go—it's likely that their body will have an automatic, often unnoticed, clenching response. Sometimes folks will notice this type of stress response in other areas of their bodies—for example, a tightening of the neck and shoulders. The pelvis, however, tends to be an overlooked area of the body. Most people don't realize how many muscles are there and how tense these muscles can get. This is where the sexual pain cycle can really start to ramp up. Because of the way the pelvic floor muscles surround the vaginal and anal openings, attempts at penetration when the muscles are clenched very commonly result in *painful sex* (link 3).

Sexual pain quickly becomes *reinforced* (link 4) in both physical and psychological ways. Physically, the pelvic floor muscles "learn" that sexual activity will cause pain, and these muscles often become progressively more tense in response. That is, rather than just clenching up in reaction to penetration, the muscles start to become more chronically tense. This is referred to as *bracing* or *guarding* (link 5) and is a conditioned response in which the pelvic floor muscles remain in a constant state of vigilance. Guarding of these muscles can actually make sex even *more* painful. From a psychological standpoint, sexual pain can quickly reinforce a lack of interest in sexual activity. Avoiding pain is a strong motivator when it comes to human behavior and, as we stated earlier, it's both a normal and predictable reaction to experience disinterest in behaviors that cause us pain. When it comes to painful sex, this typically means *avoiding physical intimacy* (link 6) and a notable decline in libido.

The more often we engage in painful sexual activity, the stronger the links of the sexual pain cycle become. In terms of sexual desire, it's common to see a lack of interest become generalized to non-painful sexual activities. As we saw in our example with Margo and Elliot, Margo's pain occurred specifically during penetrative intercourse. Over time, she began to lose interest in other intimate activities—such as kissing, touching, and oral sex—that were not painful. Sometimes this is related to Sexual Staircase thinking—the assumption that any sexual activity will lead to (painful) intercourse. Other times, however, it simply reflects a conditioned response to pain that has become more generalized so that even non-painful encounters with a partner are psychologically linked to the experience of pain. In Margo and Elliot's case, what began as sexual pain related to a medical condition—GSM—quickly developed into pelvic floor muscle tension as well. From there, pain became physically and psychologically reinforced, leading to reduced libido and Margo's withdrawal from the sexual relationship. This is an unfortunately common pattern underlying sexual desire discrepancies, making it especially important to address any discomfort or pain that occurs with sexual activity. Rather than pushing through pain and continuing to reinforce the sexual pain cycle, we must learn to initiate and reinforce a cycle of sexual pleasure.

THE IMPORTANCE OF LUBRICANTS

Use of store-bought lubricants can be very important during sexual activities, whether they include external genital stimulation or penetration of some kind. Adding a store-bought lubricant can reduce friction and sexual pain. It can also provide pleasurable sensations. Picking the best store-bought lubricant for your needs can be tough, given how many options exist. And, believe it or not, it's actually pretty important to be an informed shopper when it comes to lubricants, as not all products are created equally. Many contain potentially harmful ingredients, which can lead to genital irritation and discomfort.

There are four general types of store-bought lubricants:

1. Water-based (including aloe-based):
   - Compatible with all sex toys and safer-sex barriers (e.g., condoms)
   - Dries out more quickly than other types of lubricants because it gets absorbed by the skin, so may require more frequent application
   - Often contains preservatives, which may cause irritation for those with sensitive skin or sensitive immune systems

2. Silicone-based:
   - Doesn't absorb into the skin, so it lasts the longest of any lubricant type
   - Hypoallergenic for most because it doesn't absorb into the skin and does not require preservatives
   - Compatible with safer-sex barriers (e.g., condoms)
   - Not always compatible with silicone toys, as it can compromise the toy's integrity (the silicone in the lubricant can bind to the silicone in the toy—it's not necessarily unsafe, but may change the toy's feel, look, and shape)

3. Oil-based:
   - Lasts longer than water-based, but not as long as silicone-based lubricants
   - Compatible with most sex toys
   - Only plant oil–based lubricants are recommended; avoid petroleum-based products, which can foster bacteria
   - *Not compatible* with safer-sex barriers (e.g., condoms) made of latex or polyisoprene
   - If used internally, will take longer to clean out of the body, so it's not recommended for folks who experience chronic infections

4. Hybrid (silicone and water):
   - Lasts longer than water-based, but not as long as silicone-based lubricants
   - Less likely to cause irritation than water-based, but not entirely hypoallergenic

> • Compatible with all sex toy materials and safer-sex barrier methods (e.g., condoms)
> • The newest type of personal lubricant, so there is less information about it
>
> Choosing a store-bought lubricant can feel overwhelming, given all the options, but there is good information available. To learn more, you can visit the website of Smitten Kitten, a trusted and inclusive sexual health shop: www.smittenkittenonline.com.

Before we move to the next section, take a moment to reflect on the topic of sexual pain in your **sexual health journal**: Have you ever experienced discomfort or pain during sex? How did you handle those experiences? Did you feel pressure (from yourself or a partner) to push through the pain? Have you ever talked about sexual pain experiences with a partner? If yes, how did that go, and, if no, what do you feel prevented the communication? If you sought medical care for sexual pain, were your concerns addressed or dismissed?

LACK OF PLEASURE

Remember the incentive-motivation system of libido that we discussed in chapter 1? If you aren't enjoying the sex that you're having, it follows that you probably won't feel very motivated to pursue it, making responsive desire difficult to experience. This is certainly true if sexual activity is uncomfortable or painful. Even if sex doesn't hurt though, that doesn't necessarily mean it feels good! For some people, a neutral sexual experience—the absence of sexual pleasure or satisfaction—is a major contributing factor to sexual disinterest. This may be due to trouble reaching orgasm or not knowing what feels good for our bodies. For some people, it's about the Sexual Staircase and not feeling excited by the activities at the top of that hierarchy, such as penetrative sex. That is, they may find non-penetrative activities much more arousing and pleasurable but, for whatever reason, those activities aren't happening. For some folks, going a week without an orgasm is unimaginable—they find this aspect of pleasure to be highly motivating in their pursuit of partnered sex. Others may go months, years, or their whole lifetimes without an orgasm and feel completely unbothered.

As we mentioned in chapter 1, it's important to identify your sexual accelerators: what feels good and motivates you so that sex is pleasurable, not just a neutral activity. And it's perfectly okay if your accelerators aren't penetration or orgasms! If your motivators for sexual activity are about closeness, then there may be physically intimate—but not necessarily genitally focused—ways to experience that, such as massaging, caressing, or cuddling. This is where it's important to have flexibility about what sex and intimacy look like. If you're struggling to identify what feels sexually pleasurable for you, further exploration is almost always helpful. (We'll discuss this more in part II, where we cover strategies for building stronger connections to both ourselves and our partners.) As previously discussed, having difficulty understanding our own sexual pleasure is often related to multiple factors, such as a lack of accurate sexual health education, trouble discussing what we enjoy sexually, or even internalized guilt and shame related to our bodies and sex. Remember, however, that sexual satisfaction and pleasure are predictors and critical components of libido. Thus, it's important to consider what helps (or harms) these aspects of our sex lives.

MORE ABOUT LUBRICANTS AND TOYS

Sexual aids (toys or devices) and lubricants can be essential in exploring and increasing sexual pleasure for many people. However, not all products are created equally. Sexual aids should be made of medical- or food-grade materials. They should not have a chemical smell and they should be nonporous, meaning that they cannot harbor bacteria or viruses. Examples of nonporous materials include 100 percent silicone, surgical steel, sealed ceramic, and medical-grade plastics. Sexual aids should be made by reputable companies and designed for actual sexual use, not just for novelty purposes. Some lubricants and sex toys contain ingredients that can cause irritation, allergic reactions, or infections, so it's important to read labels and know exactly what you're getting—particularly if the product is being used inside your body! Some ingredients that may cause irritation include:

- Glycerin(e)
- Propylene glycol

> - Sugars, like glucose, maltodextrin, and other flavors added to products
> - Parabens
>
> To learn more about sexual aid safety, we recommend visiting the website www.badvibes.org.

Let's take a moment to address lack of sexual pleasure in your **sexual health journal**. Thinking about your past sexual experiences, has anything been missing that you feel would make sex more pleasurable for you? Have you noticed a tendency to ignore your own pleasure during sex, perhaps to prioritize a partner's pleasure instead? Is it challenging to ask for what you want or to provide feedback to sexual partners in order to increase your pleasure? If yes, what makes it challenging to communicate about this? If no, how did the experience go?

SHAME

Many people struggle with feelings of shame about sex, gender, and sexuality. As we discussed in chapter 2, feelings of sexual shame can impact libido in major ways. Shame involves feelings of inadequacy or of not being good enough. It centers on where we perceive ourselves as lacking. Some people may feel shame about their sexual interests and fantasies. Others may experience shame about their sexual orientation or gender due to cultural or family messages that being anything other than heterosexual and cisgender is unacceptable. People can have shame for experiencing libido that they perceive to be too low or too high. Shame can come up around body image and judgment about how we look.

Feelings of shame can absolutely disrupt sexual desire, whether it's spontaneous or responsive. Sex and shame are incompatible for most people (except in the case of some specific kinks), yet sexual shame is highly prevalent. The *lack of open communication* in our society about sex and gender often contributes to the explicitly *negative messages* we receive around these topics, and both of these factors can create sexual shame. For example, what's considered attractive and sexy in Western media is not reflective of how most of us look and is based on racist, heterosexist, and cisnormative cultural scripts. Some people have received the message that sex in general is "bad," whereas others have been taught that certain sexual activities—for example, using a vibrator—are "dirty" or shameful. Adding to this complicated mix, we also simultaneously receive many social messages that pressure us to be "good in bed," even as our society fails to teach us about sex or communication skills. Confusing, right? The antidote to sexual shame involves both empathy—for self and others—and education. As the old saying goes, "Knowledge is power."

So, how do we work through feelings of sexual shame? How do we build both empathy and knowledge around sex, gender, and sexuality? First, we want you to know that these feelings of shame are incredibly common. Remember that accurate and inclusive sexual health education plays a huge role in reducing feelings of shame. For example, reading more about sex, gender, and sexuality (just like you're doing now!) is one way to increase knowledge, reduce shame, and normalize your sexual experiences. Another great strategy is to talk more openly about sex-related topics with a close friend or an emotionally safe sexual partner, as this may help to reduce some of the stigma around sex. You can also follow more sex-positive content on social media, to learn more and potentially dive deeper into sexual health conversations that normalize the incredible diversity of sexual experiences. We can receive empathy from others as we share more about our sexual experiences, and we can offer ourselves more empathy through self-compassion.

MENTAL HEALTH

While there are many ways that mental health can impact libido, there are specific concerns, such as mood and anxiety symptoms, that tend to appear more frequently in our sex therapy practices. Additionally, difficulties related to past trauma can be a major barrier to libido. We'll talk here about some of these general mental health concerns before addressing trauma in the next section. First, we want to start with an explanation of the nervous system and how it plays an important role in our overall mental health and sexual experiences. (This is an expansion of information about the stress response that we first introduced in chapter 1, so feel free to revisit that section if needed.)

Understandably, various mental health concerns can contribute to changes in libido. For many people, when feeling depressed, anxious, experiencing the effects of trauma, and so on, it's challenging to experience spontaneous or responsive desire. For others, this can work in the opposite direction. Some folks experience *heightened* libido alongside mental health concerns, such as with mania, anxiety, and low self-esteem, to name a few. In these cases, sexual activity can be a way to self-soothe or co-regulate. *Co-regulation* is when the calm and safe presence of another person helps to bring us from a stress response (*dysregulation*) back to a *regulated* (safe and calm) state. If sexual activity feels regulating, it can become a resource for some people when mental health symptoms arise. This is another example of the dual control model at work: the same variables will affect each person's sexual accelerators and brakes in unique ways. The impact of the stress response on our sexual functioning is helpful to understand, particularly in the context of mental health. We'll provide a more detailed overview here.

Our nervous system has two main branches: the *central nervous system* (CNS) and the *peripheral nervous system* (PNS). The CNS is made up of the brain and the spinal cord. The PNS is made up of nerves that branch off of the spinal cord; its job is to connect the brain and spinal cord to the rest of the body. The PNS further divides into the *autonomic nervous system* (ANS) and the *somatic nervous system* (SNS). We'll focus on the ANS, which controls our automatic bodily functions, including heart rate, breathing, digestion, and sexual function. This is also the system that has primary control over the stress response.

The ANS has two main branches: the *sympathetic* and the *parasympathetic*. The sympathetic branch operates our fight-or-flight response. When activated, it mobilizes us to run or fight for our lives. Our lungs expand to allow for more oxygen; we may experience a faster heart rate, higher blood pressure, sweat, and other physiological changes. We may also experience a sense of anxiety, anger, agitation, or panic because of these physiological changes. The sympathetic branch of the ANS allows our bodies to orgasm and ejaculate, but it is separate from the system that operates our initial sexual arousal (more on that in a moment).

The parasympathetic branch of the ANS operates our rest-and-digest response, so called because digestion processes in our gut tend to occur when it's activated. This is representative of the state of calm that the parasympathetic branch can create when our system perceives safety. This calm state may also be accompanied by a slowed heart rate, lower blood pressure, and other physiological changes. When this occurs, we tend to experience more optimal sexual function. In fact, the parasympathetic branch of the ANS must be activated to initiate sexual arousal, such as genital swelling, lubrication, and erections. In addition to its rest-and-digest function, a second job of the parasympathetic branch is to trigger an immobilization response when a threat is perceived: bodily shutdown as a survival tactic. In the wild, this often looks like an animal playing dead in the face of danger. In this state, we humans can experience depressed mood, dissociation, numbness, or a sense of isolation.

For better or worse, the way our nervous system impacts sexual functioning is a product of our physiology. Let's go back in time to our cave dwelling days for a brief example. Say you're having sex while lying by the fire in your cozy cave when suddenly a bear shows up. Danger alert! How do you imagine your body might react? This is a stress-response moment in which the sympathetic nervous system takes charge. Blood flow will quickly be redirected from your genitals and toward your hands, feet, and lungs so you can run, fight, or otherwise try to survive the threat. In these moments, genital lubrication, swelling, and other sexual arousal responses are deemed by your nervous system to be nonessential functions. Sexual arousal will not save you from that bear!

What does this all have to do with sexual desire? Even though most of us are not experiencing the same dangers as our ancestors—facing predators, battling the natural elements day in and day out—our bodies are still primed to respond in the same way to threats. Modern-day dangers that activate the ANS can result from sociocultural and interpersonal factors such as minority stress, violence, war, financial insecurity, and other threats to our livelihood and well-being, as discussed in chapters 2 and 3. At the individual level, we can also experience *perceived* threats, whether internal (from our thoughts and emotions) or external (from our environment or social situations). At times, we can perceive danger where there isn't any due to our *negativity bias*—an instinctive survival strategy that holds that we're more likely to stay alive by erring on the side of assuming danger rather than safety. This is why we sometimes experience a stress response when the situation doesn't seem to warrant it—like a positive sexual encounter. Let's look at an example.

Mario has been casually dating. He has a new partner and had been looking forward to having sex with her for the first time. Whenever they kissed and touched, he easily got aroused and had an erection, as he felt excited and turned on. When they moved into penetrative intercourse for the first time, however, he was surprised to find that it was difficult to maintain his erection. Mario was left feeling frustrated and insecure. The experience was especially confusing as he felt very attracted to his new partner and couldn't understand his loss of arousal. In talking about the encounter with a friend, Mario realized that he had experienced several negative thoughts about his sexual abilities and fears about what would happen if sex didn't go well. These common thoughts—"What if I can't stay hard?" or "What if I disappoint her?"—had crept in during their sexual experience.

Physiologically, at the beginning of the sexual encounter, the parasympathetic branch of Mario's ANS activated and allowed arousal and an erection to occur. Unfortunately, his negative thoughts interrupted the process and triggered the sympathetic branch of his ANS. This stress response created a flood of adrenaline, which caused genital blood flow loss and disrupted Mario's erection. In the world of sexual medicine, this common scenario is referred to as a *hyperadrenergic response* and—(not so) fun fact—it's sometimes even able to overpower erectile medications. Our nervous system is incredibly powerful! Even though Mario felt excited about having sex with his new partner, his internal stressor—negative thoughts—interfered with his sexual functioning on a physiological level.

Sexual challenges like these can commonly lead to low libido. This is often because the stress response becomes linked——both psychologically and physiologically—to sexual activity and, over time, we become much less inclined to do things that feel overwhelming or lead to negative outcomes. Mental health challenges can also be associated with the stress response. Let's examine some specific mental health concerns and how they relate to libido.

Depression often involves low interest or pleasure in doing things we typically enjoy, feeling down or hopeless, low self-esteem or feelings of worthlessness, low energy, sleep disruptions, changes in appetite, restlessness, and, sometimes, suicidal thoughts. Depression may lead to negative thoughts about ourselves and others, such as, "I'm not good enough for my partner," or "My friends don't really care about me." There can be a tendency to isolate, which may be a form of self-protection from overwhelming feelings or a result of low energy. There can be heightened sensitivity to feeling rejected or a general feeling of disconnection from others. Depression can also negatively impact sexual desire because the energy required to initiate sex or respond to a partner's initiation may just not be there.

Anxiety is often associated with experiencing a lot of worries, feeling on edge, difficulty relaxing, irritability, muscle tension, stomachaches, restlessness, and a fear of something awful happening. We may have anxious thoughts such as, "What if something bad happens?" or "What if I disappoint my partner?" When we experience anxiety, sexual desire may increase or decrease, depending on the person. Some people, when anxious, may tend to want more sex to help with co-regulation, while others may want less sex to focus on self-soothing. Additionally, the physical signs of sexual arousal often mirror the physical signs of anxiety: both can lead to increased heart rate, shallow breathing, and sweating, to name a few. This overlap of signals can trigger some people to become anxious about sex, as they may misinterpret these bodily sensations as signs of anxiety rather than arousal. If your anxiety increases during sexual encounters, it's helpful to redirect your attention to what's happening in the present moment. When we focus on something sensory—touch, taste, smell, sight, or sound—it can help to get us out of our heads. Anxious thoughts often focus on what will or won't happen in the future—even over the next few moments—so giving ourselves something else to concentrate on can help interrupt this process. We'll address these strategies more in chapter 5.

For many people, medication is a vital aspect of mental healthcare—alone or in conjunction with therapy. This may include medications used to help stabilize anxiety or improve mood. When working with your healthcare team, it's important to be aware that one class of mental health medications, known as selective serotonin reuptake inhibitors or *SSRIs*, has a particular reputation for sexual side effects.

SSRIs are commonly prescribed as antidepressants, but may also be used to help with anxiety symptoms. They work by increasing serotonin, a common neurotransmitter that helps brain cells (aka neurons) communicate. More serotonin available in the brain is associated with improved transmission between neurons. SSRIs are generally quite safe but, like all medications, come with side effect profiles and may not be the best fit for everyone. As for sexual side effects, we tend to see two issues with SSRIs: (1) decreased libido, and/or (2) delayed arousal and orgasm. The slowing of arousal and orgasm is one reason that SSRIs are occasionally prescribed off-label to help with early ejaculation concerns.

It's tricky to predict who might experience SSRI-related sexual side effects. Some people take such medications for months or years without any concerns, whereas others very quickly experience sexual side effects. Not everyone experiences both problems either: for some, SSRIs impact libido and for others the main concern is delayed or absent orgasm. For many folks, SSRI-related sexual side effects are quite dose-dependent, and small adjustments in dosage can alleviate any sexual concerns. There is also emerging evidence that adding the medication bupropion to an SSRI regimen can be effective in both boosting the antidepressant response and reducing or eliminating sexual side effects, although bupropion is not yet federally approved for such use in the United States.[5] Reducing mental health symptoms and optimizing sexual function while using mental health medications can require some trial and error. It's a balancing act that requires conversations with one's healthcare providers.

ANTSY OR ANXIOUS?

Some people experience anxiety that is specific to sexual situations because they're worried about "performance" or have previously experienced pain with sex. Other folks may struggle to relax during sex because they're worried about nonsexual things or generally experience worry that's difficult to control as part of their day-to-day life. Such folks may also have a "busy brain," where the mind often feels like it's racing or that it's hard to slow down thoughts. These may be signs of more generalized anxiety—that is, anxiety that's not just limited to sexual experiences. If you're noticing these signs of anxiety, seeking general mental healthcare might be helpful. We'll talk more about referrals and when to consider seeing a mental health provider about anxiety in part III.

Consider reflecting on the following prompts in your **sexual health journal:** How has mental health impacted your sexual experiences? Has your sexual functioning changed as a result of taking mental health medication or seeking other types of mental health treatment? Is mental health a topic that you've felt comfortable discussing with sexual partners? Why or why not?

TRAUMA

In the previous section, we discussed how our autonomic nervous system (ANS) works. This is also relevant when addressing trauma, whether of a sexual or nonsexual nature. To survive a traumatic situation, many people's bodies activate a stress response involving the sympathetic (fight-or-flight) or parasympathetic (shutdown) branches of the ANS. In some circumstances, we can get stuck in a more chronic stress response. Some people will go on to experience symptoms of posttraumatic stress disorder (PTSD) after traumatic experiences, and some won't. Part of what can be so challenging about trauma is that when our nervous systems try to protect us from further threat or danger, we can become wired to respond defensively to people, places, and things that resemble past trauma(s). Remember Hebb's law (discussed in chapter 2) that "what fires together, wires together"? People, places, and things associated with trauma can trigger a stress response within us. For some, these triggers can include sexual activity or a situation focusing on body parts that may or may not be sexual (for example, during a pelvic exam at the doctor's office).

Because sex is vulnerable, we often need cues of safety for the experience to be satisfying and motivating. If we're in a stress response, sexual activity may feel frightening, anxiety provoking, and impossible to go through with. Here are some signs that sex may be triggering a stress response:

- Recoiling from touch with a safe partner
- Dissociating (when your mind disconnects from your body) during physical touch or sexual intimacy with a safe partner
- Crying with sex (though note that this can also occur with pleasure and the release of tension)
- Bracing (involuntarily tensing the body) with sexual touch or activity
- Avoiding sexual content, discussion, touch, and/or physical intimacy

Recall that libido is a spectrum and that a lack of interest in sex in and of itself is not necessarily related to past trauma. As we've discussed, someone's disinterest in sex may be due to asexuality, the sexual pain cycle, or several other variables. People occasionally ask us if lifelong disinterest in sex or decreases in libido are related to repressed trauma—that is, trauma from something they can't remember. Given the immense number of factors that can negatively impact libido, in our experience, this is unlikely to be the case.

Sometimes people can identify the specific situation that taught them to react to sexual cues with a stress- or shame-based response. Other times, people can't identify why or where this comes from. In either case, we can address trauma or stress-response triggers most effectively with what therapists call *graded exposure*. Since trauma is what happens when something overwhelms us and we get stuck in a stress response, working through those triggers and situations requires safety, slowness, and gradual exposure, armed with resources and strong support. It's dipping a toe into the stressful situation and then coming back to calm and safety. Then we dip two toes in, then three, and so on and so forth. This is how both anxiety and trauma are best treated. Let's look at an example.

From a young age, Aiko was taught that sex outside of marriage is a sin. Though they are nonbinary, they were raised as a girl and taught that girls and women don't engage in self-pleasure, nor do they really experience much pleasure from sex at all. In fact, they recall a family member telling them that sex is really about pleasing your partner and "just waiting for it to be over." In response to these repeated negative messages about sex, Aiko eventually learned to shut off their sexuality. For example, when they noticed that they were feeling sexual attraction to others during their teen years, they would become fearful and pray until the sexual arousal and thoughts went away. Fast-forward many years, and now, when Aiko attempts to be sexual with their safe and loving partner, Finley, their body braces and they often have intrusive thoughts that what they're doing is wrong or bad. In nonsexual moments, Aiko finds this confusing, as they love and feel attracted to Finley. However, when Finley tries to initiate hugs and affectionate touch, Aiko physically pulls away. Finley feels frustrated and rejected, as he interprets Aiko's behavior as dismissive when he reaches for connection and affection.

After several conflicts around this, Aiko and Finley decided to try sex therapy. They learned about how Aiko's nervous system had become wired over time to interpret sex as threatening. This helped Finley better understand that Aiko's response was not a rejection of him, but rather a stress response based on years of traumatic messages, guilt, and sexual shame. Rather than approaching Aiko from behind to initiate a hug, for example, Finley began trying to directly ask for a hug and verbally letting Aiko know when he wanted a moment of connection. This technique helped ease Aiko's stress response, allowing them to communicate to Finley if they aren't in a place to receive touch. With sexual activity, Aiko and Finley practiced slowing things down, incorporating more non-genital touch, and using a lot of verbal communication to check in along the way. This helped dial back Aiko's stress response so that they could be more mentally and emotionally present in their body. In chapter 7 we'll introduce and guide you through an exercise to apply this process of graded exposure in a more structured way.

Trauma comes in many forms and can impact people in vastly different ways. Aiko's story reflects the often traumatic impact of negative messages about sex. A traumatic stress response may also be related to a history of sexual pain; past physical, sexual, emotional, or verbal violence; or any number of other harmful experiences. Though experiences of trauma certainly vary, in each case, addressing the impact of the trauma—especially any stress response that may have developed—is a critical aspect of sexual health.

PREGNANCY AND POSTPARTUM

Being pregnant obviously brings many life changes, including sexual ones. Not only does pregnancy involve physical discomfort and hormonal shifts; one's mental focus also may change, focusing more on imminent parenthood or an expanding family. Some folks experience an increase in sexual desire during certain times of their pregnancies, whereas others may experience a decrease. Some worry that they may cause harm to themselves or the fetus if they have sex during pregnancy—which is safe in most cases, though you should always talk with your medical provider about your concerns. The research on how pregnancy affects sexual desire and satisfaction shows mixed results, and it is based almost entirely on the experiences of cisgender women.[6] It's important to note, however, that cisgender women are not the only people who can become pregnant. Transgender men and nonbinary people also get pregnant, though unfortunately, there is limited research about these experiences.[7]

Overall, current research suggests that sexual desire and frequency of sex decrease over the course of a pregnancy.[8] This is often related to physical symptoms (not feeling well), negative body image, physical limitations as the pregnancy progresses, and hormonal changes. There can also be less clitoral sensation for some people during pregnancy, which can make orgasm more difficult and subsequently decrease libido and sexual satisfaction.[9] Perhaps unsurprisingly, relationship problems during pregnancy can also negatively impact sexual desire and satisfaction. Evidence is mixed, however, and there are some reports of *increased* libido during pregnancy. For example, the second trimester can bring an increase in blood flow to the pelvis and genitals, which in turn can increase physical arousal and thus, for some, increase sexual desire.

Research on the pregnancy experiences of men and nonbinary people is finally starting to emerge.[10] Unfortunately, this work has not yet addressed their sexual experiences and needs during pregnancy. We may be able to draw some parallels, however, from the existing research with pregnant cisgender women. Two important variables that repeatedly emerge in this research are, firstly, the state of one's sexual life and relationship *prior* to pregnancy, and, secondly, the way one feels (physically and emotionally) during pregnancy. Both of these variables impact sexual satisfaction. We clearly need more research on the sexual experiences of pregnant trans and nonbinary people, although given the major importance of sexual satisfaction to overall libido, we suspect these variables may be similar across genders.

Partners of pregnant people can experience both increases and decreases in libido, like the mixed experiences of pregnant folks. Some partners experience an increase in desire as they feel attracted to their partner's changing body or feel emotionally closer as they prepare for parenthood. Concerns about sex harming the fetus may ultimately lead to discovering new and different ways of being sexual, which can increase libido. Conversely, such concerns may interfere with desire, lowering libido. Folks may also start to see their pregnant partner as more of a parent and less of a sexual partner, which can challenge typical arousal patterns. Overall, the impact of pregnancy on sex seems to have some trends, as well as a lot of individual differences.

Sexual desire during the postpartum period, often referred to as the fourth trimester or fourth stage of labor, can also be a challenge. There are three distinct postpartum phases; the first occurs within six to twelve hours after delivery.[11] During this acute phase, the birthing parent is typically being medically monitored for any immediate medical crisis, such as postpartum hemorrhage, embolism, or eclampsia. The second postpartum phase, ranging from two to six weeks long, is a time of major physical and emotional change. There are cardiovascular, metabolic, and genitourinary shifts as the birthing parent's body continues to recover from the delivery and as they may engage in breastfeeding or chestfeeding.* This is also the

---

* *Chestfeeding*, sometimes referred to as *bodyfeeding*, is the process of providing milk to a baby from a person's chest. It's an inclusive term that can be used by anyone. *Chestfeeding* is often the term preferred by trans and nonbinary folks as a gender-neutral alternative to *breastfeeding* or *nursing*, especially when such traditional cisnormative terms do not apply or contribute to gender dysphoria.

time when postpartum depression and/or anxiety symptoms may emerge and require support.

It's common for medical providers to recommend that birthing parents abstain from penetrative sexual activity for six weeks after delivery—essentially until the end of the second postpartum phase. However, the six-week mark is often too soon for many folks to resume sexual activity, despite having medical clearance. Lack of sleep, residual pain, and less quality time with their partner(s) are common reasons for needing more recovery time. The third postpartum phase can last many months. Ideally, it's a time in which muscle tone, connective tissue, and pelvic floor functioning are restored—though for some, changes can last years and recovery may never fully align with one's prepregnancy experience. Much of this depends, of course, on variables like the delivery type, baby's size, and degree of physical trauma during birth.

It can take several months to several years to return to a prepregnancy state of libido. Breast- or chestfeeding can often prolong this period, due to the hormonal influences. For cisgender women, decreased estrogen and increased prolactin in the postpartum period is associated with a reduction in spontaneous sexual desire as the body prepares for milk production. Cessation of breast- or chestfeeding and a subsequent return to prepregnancy hormone levels has been associated with improved energy, mood, and spontaneous sexual desire.[12] Additionally, emotional exhaustion and the psychological demands of the transition to parenthood may impede libido for quite some time. As we discussed in chapters 2 and 3, this is where an imbalance in the mental load (often along gendered lines) can emerge in some partnerships—an example of how personal, interpersonal, and cultural factors can overlap to impact libido. There are many reasons why sex might take a back seat during both pregnancy and the postpartum period. In part II of the book, we'll discuss strategies that can help ensure that you are optimizing both your connection to yourself and your partner(s) during these important life transitions.

GRIEF AND LOSS

Grief can affect us in unique and complex ways. Some of us may find sexual activity life-affirming and feel drawn to sex for emotional comfort; others are unable to imagine being sexual during the depths of grief. Grief can pull us into a stress response, where we can feel stuck for months, even years. For some of us, grief triggers depression, anxiety, and/or trauma symptoms. Everyone has their own experience of grief and their own time line for grieving; it's not a linear or universal experience. It's understandable, then, that those of us who think of sex as unimaginable during grief would experience decreased libido. This can either be generalized toward all sexual activity, or it can be situational—such as lowered desire for partnered sex but maintenance of solo sexual activity while grieving.

After loss, some people may feel guilty experiencing pleasure, engaging in sexual activity, or forming new relationships. For example, we may feel bad that we are still able to experience pleasure when our loved one is no longer able to do so. For some, joining a grief support group can be helpful. For others, what's most helpful, at least for a period of time, is distracting oneself from the emotional pain and just getting through each day without intentionally processing the grief.

For people who have experienced the loss of a pregnancy or a child, sex can feel additionally challenging if it reminds them of this loss. Grief and loss can distract us from being mindful and present during sex, which can decrease arousal and pleasure and thus negatively impact libido. When sex becomes a reminder of our loss, it may also trigger a stress response, which, as we've discussed, can inhibit both libido and arousal.

Grief is not only something experienced in the wake of a death—it can result from other types of loss as well. Examples include a breakup or divorce, loss of independence, bodily changes associated with aging or illness, or major life transitions. For those who experience a decline in sexual desire from grief or loss, it often takes time for desire to reemerge and for healing to occur, not unlike healing from trauma. What's important here is to honor your needs, be patient with yourself and your partner(s), and to pace your sexual activity accordingly.

DESIRE AND AGING

As we've noted, we live in a culture that doesn't encourage us to talk openly and honestly about sexual health. This is especially true when it comes to sex and aging, given a long (ageist) history of treating older adults as asexual or uninterested in sexual intimacy. Research is quite clear, however, that most older adults not only feel sex is important but also want to optimize their partnered sexual experiences in the face of age-related barriers to sexual activity.[13] It's common for people to report having lower libido as they age, though we often find that this is a secondary issue to other sexual challenges (such as sexual pain, or inconsistent arousal or orgasm) that may or may not be age-related. Sexual challenges with aging are related to a variety of factors including health status, changes in physical ability, and relational challenges. Here are some of the other sex-related changes we may experience as we get older:

- Reduced blood flow to the genitals
- Decreased genital sensitivity
- Hormone changes
- Thinning and reduced elasticity of vulvovaginal tissue
- Less intense orgasms and/or ejaculation
- Needing more time or greater stimulation for arousal and orgasm
- Challenges obtaining or maintaining arousal, including erections
- Changes in partner's health that impact sex
- Becoming more of a caregiver for a partner
- Loss of a partner[14]

If we are lucky to live long enough, we will absolutely experience fluctuations in our sexual function. For better or worse, none of us stay the same across time! Some people may find these age-related changes distressing, but that's certainly not true of everyone. Sometimes the distress is related to a lack of preparation for or knowledge about sexual changes that occur with age. Again, these are not topics that our culture does a good job of educating people about, leading to a lack of understanding about normal, predictable changes to sexual health over time.

Thankfully, some people find that, in older adulthood, they are having the best sex of their lives. This is a time when folks may be retiring or winding down their careers, when children are grown, and there may be more time to spend with one's partner(s) as a result. Less overall busyness and stress can also make it easier to relax into sexual experiences—for example, spending more time building up arousal and not feeling rushed by our to-do lists. A more open schedule can also become a huge benefit. For example, partners may have more opportunity to have sex when they have the most energy— perhaps midday—rather than at night when they are tired, or early in the morning before a busy day. Menopause, while commonly associated with a hormone-related decline in spontaneous libido, can also create an increase in sexual desire due to no longer having to worry or feel distracted about a potential pregnancy.

Other aspects of physical aging can also impact us sexually. Our bodies may have less flexibility, less mobility, and more aches and pains. To successfully address these changes, we must embrace behavioral flexibility, creativity, and open-mindedness. For example, for sex to be more comfortable and enjoyable as we age, sexual aids are often essential. Store-bought lubricants, vibrators, pillows, or furniture designed to improve sexual comfort can all make sex more accessible. Overall, it's important to know that, with some added support and flexibility, we can be sexual and satisfied throughout our life span.

CANCER

Medical professionals rarely discuss sexual well-being with cancer patients or their partners given that, for most, treatment understandably becomes the priority after diagnosis. However, the importance of sexual health isn't diminished by a cancer diagnosis (or any other medical condition, for that matter!). Many cancer patients, cancer survivors, and their partners report sexual concerns that are often related to treatment itself.[15] Sexual health difficulties related to cancer can happen before, during, and after treatment as patients become survivors. In the list below are just some of the common concerns that we see around sexual health throughout cancer care:

- Decreased sexual desire
- Vulvovaginal dryness and/or atrophy
- Erectile difficulties
- Changes in physical sensation
- Changes in orgasmic and/or ejaculatory functioning
- Genital pain and/or pain that occurs during sexual activity
- Surgical or medication-induced menopause
- Body image concerns related to physical changes

The vulvovaginal changes that can happen with cancer treatment include dryness, thinning, and changes in the vaginal structure (e.g., shortening and/or narrowing of the vaginal canal). These changes can be caused by chemotherapy, radiation, and certain surgical procedures. Oftentimes they can lead to discomfort or pain with sexual activity—especially with vaginal penetration—and can even cause problems during nonsexual activities (for example, pain during a pelvic exam). As we know, sexual or genital pain does not bode well for our libido! It's important to keep your cancer team aware of vulvovaginal changes because excellent treatment options exist. These might include over-the-counter lubricants (see our previous discussion about choosing a lubricant), vaginal moisturizers, vaginal estrogen, or pelvic floor physical therapy. It's critical to ask your medical team which options are right for you, given your specific medical history.

Penile changes during cancer can be significant. Treatments such as chemotherapy, radiation, and surgical procedures like prostatectomy may result in notable changes to erectile, orgasmic, and ejaculatory function. There may also be changes in penile size and shape, as well as overall genital sensation. As with vulvovaginal changes related to cancer, some excellent treatment options are available for people with penises. These might include using a penile constriction ring, a vacuum device, or taking PDE5 inhibitor medications (known commercially as Viagra, Cialis, Levitra, and Stendra), all of which may help with arousal and erections. Other options include injection therapy (sounds rough, we know, but it can be very effective for erectile difficulties!) or surgical placement of a penile prosthesis. Here too, pelvic floor physical therapy can be enormously beneficial in treating cancer-related changes to the pelvic and genital areas. As always, it's critically important to discuss treatment options with your oncology team to determine what's best for you.

Sensory changes—both in the genitals and in other areas of the body—are common with cancer treatment, including radiation and chemotherapy. A number of potential treatment options exist for sensation changes, including sexual aids (e.g., vibrators), body mapping techniques (alone or with a partner) to rediscover what sensations currently exist, and mindfulness training. We'll discuss these common sex therapy approaches in more detail in part II.

In addition to the direct effects on sexual function noted above, cancer treatment may also indirectly affect sexual health via fatigue, nausea, incontinence, and overall stress. These side effects can have a detrimental impact on overall well-being, sexual self-esteem, and body image.[16] Unfortunately, sexual desire is quite often negatively impacted by cancer treatment. Desire changes may be directly related to treatment procedures (e.g., recovery from a surgery) or can result from a complex combination of factors, such as the development of sexual pain, orgasmic difficulties, fatigue, and so on.[17]

For those who are partnered, it's also important to recognize that cancer treatment can change relational dynamics, sometimes in profound and unexpected ways. How you and your partner(s) navigate sex during cancer treatment is an important topic for discussion. For partners who become caregivers, sex during cancer care can be a unique and somewhat stressful experience. Partners may avoid physical intimacy or struggle to talk about sexual health, especially when surviving cancer has, understandably, become a major focus of the relationship. This is often compounded by a general lack of sexual health education and, unfortunately, a common feeling that we can't talk with our medical providers about sexual concerns.

CANCER, SEX, AND SAFETY

Several sexual safety concerns can arise during cancer treatment. These are important to be aware of and to discuss with your sexual partner(s) and your oncology team. First, even if your periods have stopped or you think cancer treatment has impacted your fertility, you still may be able to become pregnant or to get someone else pregnant. It's important to talk with your medical provider about reliable birth control options or, if you want to get pregnant, when it will be safe to try and what that process may look like for you.

Other safety concerns revolve around chemotherapy and cancer-fighting medications. Some of these medications can appear in bodily fluids for up to forty-eight hours following the treatment, making it important to be cautious during sexual activity. Consider barrier methods, like condoms and dental dams, to protect yourself and your partners. Last but certainly not least: because cancer treatment can create enormous physical changes, it's common for sexual activities to become uncomfortable or even painful. This is particularly true with chemotherapy and radiation to certain areas of the body. If sexual activity becomes painful at any point, it's very important to stop! (Really, this is true regardless of whether you're undergoing cancer treatment.) Resist the temptation to just grit your teeth and push through it. Instead, consult with your medical team about appropriate treatment options. Sexual pain is treatable, but we need to make sure that our care team knows what's happening so they can help.

For many people, the sexual concerns that emerge during cancer treatment tend to persist, and even worsen, in survivorship. Embarrassment and shame often create reluctance to disclose sexual health concerns. Though studies have shown that patients prefer that their healthcare providers initiate sexual health conversations, few oncologists routinely do so.[18] The hard truth is that you, as the patient, may need to start these conversations about sexual concerns and cancer. We've included some materials that might help with these conversations in the Resources section.

DISABILITY

Disabilities include a wide range of conditions, some of which may create challenges around sex. When it comes to libido, disability can be a contributing factor—one of many—that involves individual, relational, and sociocultural levels of experience. While we can't cover the full, diverse range of disabilities here, let's look at a few common examples of how a disability can impact sex:

- Loss of sensation (for example, due to spinal cord injury, paralysis, cancer treatment)
- Mobility challenges (for example, due to arthritis, multiple sclerosis, loss of limb, stroke, back injury, or pain)
- Sensory sensitivity: discomfort or dysregulation that occurs with specific sensations (for example, due to autism or sensory processing disorder)
- Chronic pain or fatigue (for example, due to fibromyalgia, rheumatoid arthritis, back pain)

Note that these challenges often overlap. That is, a disability may cause one or all of the above impacts, often requiring creativity, flexibility, and adaptability to optimize sexual pleasure and health.

Some disabled people prepare for sex with the help of an advocate—someone who specializes in assisting them. An advocate may help their client set up for sex, change positions, or clean up afterward. This may require the disabled person to engage in a lot more detailed, logistically focused communication about sex than nondisabled people typically do. There is also a certain lack of privacy that comes with having an advocate assist with sex. Privacy concerns are also common for folks who live with family members, in a group home, or in an assisted care setting. These variables often negatively impact sexual desire, as it can feel overwhelming to manage all of these factors. We are pleased to note, however, that more and more sexual aids are being created to help make sex more accessible for disabled folks—for example, sexual toys designed for people who have challenges with grip and wedge pillows to help with positioning or in which a vibrator can be inserted for a hands-free experience. We list some of these great tools in the Resources section. Unfortunately, cost and availability of these products can still be a barrier for many.

Despite many cultural narratives to the contrary, disabled people certainly can and do enjoy satisfying sex—solo or partnered. We've found that what's most helpful in navigating disability-related challenges—like so many challenges around sex—is breaking free of the Sexual Staircase and moving toward a more open-ended, flexible approach. The Sexual Staircase is built on cultural ableism, presuming that everybody wants and can engage in the same sexual script. In our experience, folks who never found a fit in the Sexual Staircase—for example, due to a lifelong disability—may have already explored flexible alternatives. It is key for us to normalize diverse sexual experiences—otherwise, folks can feel stuck trying to uphold the Sexual Staircase. Over time, this can lead to frustration, guilt, or shame, all of which negatively impact libido.

It's also critical to recognize that disabled people are likely contending with minority stress experiences, such as prejudice and discrimination. It can be immensely challenging to get through the day in a world that's often not built for you. Being a disabled person in an ableist world can leave many people fatigued or emotionally drained. As discussed, this can be an indirect but profound barrier to sexual desire. We've included some materials for navigating sex and disability in the Resources section at the back of the book.

GENDER DYSPHORIA AND EUPHORIA/PLEASURE

As we discussed in chapter 2, cultural values like cisnormativity can negatively impact our individual lives and sexual health through minority stressors like discrimination or internalized transphobia. The experience of *gender* or *anatomical dysphoria* may also play a role in libido. Broadly speaking, *gender dysphoria* refers to the distress experienced when a person's gender identity is incongruent with the gender they were assigned at birth. Dysphoria can be experienced in many ways, including a sense of misalignment, sadness, or anxiety related to gender. It may also arise in relation to specific body parts, often referred to as *anatomical dysphoria*. Folks who experience dysphoria may identify as transgender or nonbinary, or they may not. It's also important to note that not all trans and nonbinary people experience dysphoria. For those who do, dysphoric experiences can be quite variable depending on the person and even the day. For example, one person may feel dysphoria related to their voice while feeling quite comfortable about their body. Other folks may experience significant distress related to any number of body parts. Of note, cisgender people often assume that trans and nonbinary folks harbor deep distress around their genitals, which may or may not be true depending on the individual. It's important to recognize the potentially objectifying nature of such an assumption.

Gender and anatomical dysphoria can negatively impact sexual desire, particularly if being touched (by self or partners) triggers feelings of distress. Sex may be avoided, may provoke anxiety, or may be disaffirming with regard to gender. Let's look at an example.

Zander and Sutton are newly dating and share a strong desire for partnered sexual activity. Zander was assigned female at birth and has been transitioning for the past two years to align with a more masculine gender identity. He started testosterone about a year ago, as hormone therapy aligns with his transition goals. Though he has experienced genital changes, Zander is not yet where he wants to be with his physical transition. Focusing on his genitals still triggers dysphoria, making it challenging to be sexual in the way he and Sutton both want. When Zander experiences this anatomical dysphoria, anxiety and distress distract him from being present and feeling connected during sex. Sutton, meanwhile, is nonbinary and is not medically transitioning, as this is not part of their goals. Sutton does not experience dysphoria around their body or sexuality. They are trying to be as supportive of Zander as possible, though they notice that Zander pulls away when things start to get physical. This can feel hurtful for Sutton. Zander, despite experiencing sexual desire, finds that his dysphoria has started to create an avoidance cycle around sex with Sutton.

With slow and safe exploration, Zander learned that his anatomical dysphoria typically only occurred with direct genital touch. This realization allowed him to adapt—avoiding direct genital touch for the time being—and explore his sexuality, both solo and with Sutton. He ultimately discovered a way to have orgasms by rubbing his body against Sutton's, without either of them touching his genitals. This felt more comfortable and less dysphoric, and Zander found sex to be much more pleasurable this way. (In the next chapter, we review such strategies—like mindfulness and pleasure mapping—in detail.)

Gender transition itself can result in various sexual health changes and, of course, impact one's libido. The impact can be very positive, fostering *gender euphoria* and *gender pleasure*—feelings of comfort or joy in relation to one's gender.[19] For example, in our case above, Zander might, as his transition progresses, experience an increase in libido due to greater comfort with his gender expression. Transition can also impact libido in a more direct, physiological way. For example, for many people, hormone therapy can change their level of spontaneous sexual desire: there might be an increase or decrease, depending on the hormone type and dosage. It's important to remember, however, that not all trans and nonbinary people want or pursue gender-affirming medical interventions.

KIDS, PETS, AND OTHER DISTRACTIONS

Recall that one of the requirements for responsive desire is the ability to focus on the moment, particularly on our physical sensations. Many of us, however, don't exactly live in quiet and calm environments—our homes can be hectic! From children who need our care to cleaning tasks, loud roommates, and cute but clingy pets, we've heard about many, many different types of home distractions in our work as sex therapists.

Kids, especially young ones, naturally require a lot of our attention and can make it difficult to find privacy. Many parents find the presence of kids at home distracting when it comes to sex. Between hearing them stir in the other room or even them blatantly walking into your bedroom without knocking, it can be tough to focus on connecting with a partner. We've found that even simple things like getting a lock for your bedroom door or teaching kids to knock before entering (these are great teachable moments for setting boundaries, after all!) can be helpful strategies for managing some of these distractions. For some folks, a lock on the door is all they need to feel more at ease, while others may feel a broader anxiety about having sex while kids are in the house. In part II, we'll focus more on reconnecting to yourself and with a partner, which we hope will help to address some of this anxiety.

It may surprise you to learn that distracting pets come up a lot in sex therapy. Though our pets are special to us, they can easily draw our attention away from sex due to things like barking or crying at the door, scratching, or nipping at our toes. A noisy pet, or one that sleeps between partners and won't move out of the way, can definitely dampen the mood. We have had multiple conversations with folks about getting their pets trained or out of the bedroom so as not to create yet another possible distraction during sex. Chapter 7 contains an in-depth exercise to practice focusing amid distractions—whether from kids, pets, or anything else.

Part II

chapter 5

CONNECTION
WITH SELF

I n the first section of the book, we covered a lot of information and theory related to sexual desire and libido differences in relationships. Now, in part II, we'll focus on behavioral skills and interventions, putting your knowledge about libido into practice! Chapter 5 will focus on you, the reader, and on creating a healthy connection with yourself and your body. Chapter 6 will focus on relational strategies and interventions. Finally, we dedicate an entire chapter—chapter 7—to a very important sex therapy technique known as *sensate focus*.

BELIEFS ABOUT SEX

Our beliefs about sex come from larger social systems such as our culture, faith tradition, family of origin, media, and friends. It's impossible to live in this world and not pick up messages about sex. Some of these messages are explicitly taught to us, and some are implicit, unspoken values and rules. Often, the sociocultural messages we receive about sex, sexuality, and gender can result in feelings of shame, guilt, and general negativity (recall our discussions about hetero- and cisnormativity, for example, in chapter 2). These messages strongly reinforce the rigid Sexual Staircase and can leave us struggling with negative automatic thoughts about sex. These are thoughts we have about ourselves, others, and the world that have become deeply internalized over time. Here are some examples of common automatic thoughts about sex:

- "I should be able to orgasm from penetrative sex."
- "My desire for sex should be spontaneous and frequent."
- "I should have an erection every time I want to."
- "I don't desire sex very often—something must be wrong with me."
- "If my partner doesn't have an orgasm, the sexual encounter was a failure."

Do any of those thoughts resonate? They're quite common and tend to result from getting stuck—mentally and emotionally—on the Sexual Staircase. These thoughts involve patterns known in the world of psychology as *thought biases* or *thought distortions*. In table 3 are some common thought biases and how they apply to sex.

TABLE 3. COMMON THOUGHT BIASES	
Thought Bias	**Description and Examples**
Polarized thinking	Thinking of things as all-or-none, rather than with nuance or shades of gray; also known as black-and-white thinking. **E.g.,** "If my partner doesn't orgasm, then sex was a failure." "Sex either includes penetrative intercourse or doesn't happen at all."
"Should," "must," or "ought" statements	Telling ourselves the way things should, must, or ought to be. **E.g.,** "I *should* be able to orgasm from penetration." "There *must* be something wrong with me if I don't orgasm from penetration."
Catastrophizing	Focusing on the worst-case scenario. **E.g.,** "If I can't get an erection, I'll never be able to have sex again."

Thought Bias	Description and Examples
Mind reading	Assuming what others are thinking. **E.g.,** "My partner is only kissing me because they want to have sex."
Fortune-telling	Predicting (usually inaccurately!) what will happen in the future. **E.g.,** "If I don't increase my desire, my partner will cheat on me or leave me."
Labeling	Assigning a label (usually negative or disparaging) to ourselves or other people. **E.g.,** "I'm sexually broken because I have low desire."
Mental filter	Only focusing on the negative and discounting the positive. **E.g.,** "Even though sex felt good, I didn't have an orgasm, so it wasn't successful."

Noticing and naming our thought biases is often the first step in changing these mental patterns. In table 4 are some alternatives to try when encountering thought biases related to sex:

TABLE 4. COMMON THOUGHT BIASES AND ALTERNATIVES

Thought Bias	Alternative
Polarized thinking **E.g.,** "If my partner doesn't orgasm, then sex was a failure"; "Sex either includes penetrative intercourse or it doesn't happen at all."	"Sex can be enjoyable with or without orgasms." Or, "Just because there wasn't an orgasm doesn't mean it was a bad experience." "Sex can involve many different types of pleasurable activities, not just intercourse."

continues

Thought Bias	Alternative
"Should," "must," or "ought" statements **E.g.,** "I *should* be able to orgasm from penetration"; "There *must* be something wrong with me if I don't orgasm from penetration."	"There are other ways for me to orgasm that feel just as good." Or, "Many people don't orgasm from penetration alone. There's nothing wrong with me."
Catastrophizing **E.g.,** "If I can't get an erection, I'll never be able to have sex again."	"One sexual event doesn't determine the rest of my experiences."
Mind reading **E.g.,** "My partner is only kissing me because they want to have sex."	"My partner may be kissing me for different reasons. I won't know what their intention is without asking."
Fortune-telling **E.g.,** "If I don't increase my desire, my partner will cheat on me or leave me."	"I don't actually know what will happen in the future. If I'm concerned, I can check in with my partner and discuss it."
Labeling **E.g.,** "I'm sexually broken because I have low desire for sex."	"Labeling myself, while understandable, is not helpful and may actually keep me stuck."
Mental filter **E.g.,** "Even though sex felt good, I didn't have an orgasm, so it wasn't successful."	"Sex was pleasurable for me, and my partner said they had a good time. That matters and is important for me to focus on."

Learning to adopt these more balanced thoughts takes time and practice, so it's totally okay if the shift doesn't happen quickly or easily for you at first. These thoughts are often deeply ingrained over many years and strongly reinforced by sociocultural messages, so it takes practice for the alternative thought processes to take root. Remember Hebb's law that "what fires together, wires together"? If automatic negative thoughts have accompanied your sexual experiences, it will take frequent repetition of more balanced thought processes for this to change. Just noticing and naming these negative thought patterns is a great place to start! Increasing our awareness of thought biases and subsequently challenging them is an important technique that many mental health providers use in therapy. As discussed in part I, increasing your exposure to sex-positive messaging is critical to challenging negative beliefs and thought processes related to sex, sexuality, and gender.[1]

Before moving forward, spend some time with your **sexual health journal** considering the following:

- Do any of the thought biases in the charts resonate for you? If so, which one(s)? Jot down some of the automatic negative thoughts you've had about sex, your partner(s), and yourself. See if you can come up with some balanced thought alternatives. Feel free to use our examples as a guide to find what fits best for you.
- Where do some of your beliefs about sex come from? Were the messages you received about sex, gender, or sexuality explicit or implicit? Do the messages you were taught align with your current values and needs? If there is a discrepancy between the messages you were taught and your current values, write down some of your sexual values. Some examples of sexual values include: connection, pleasure, curiosity, safety, self-expression.

MINDFULNESS AND SEX

You may have come across the term *mindfulness*, given its current popularity. Many people think of it as interchangeable with meditation, but meditation is just one way to practice mindfulness. Though it may feel like a new fad, mindfulness is rooted in Buddhist philosophy. It involves three general principles: *presence*, *awareness*, and *non-judgment*. The first principle, *presence*, means being fully conscious of ourselves and our surroundings. This can be a difficult task, as our brains generally don't like to stay present for extended periods of time. Our neurons (aka brain cells) are constantly firing and taking us in many different directions—this is normal and to be expected! Our brains tend to go in two directions: either *past-focused* or *future-focused* thoughts. While it's important for us to recall the past (to remember important events or things we've learned) as well as to think about the future (for planning purposes), many people tend to get stuck in either past-focused or future-focused thinking. When we spend a great deal of mental energy and time focused on either the past or future (sometimes known as rumination), we may actually be at risk for depression and anxiety. Importantly, the emphasis on present-moment thinking found in mindfulness is not an attempt to erase past- or future-focused thoughts. Rather, the practice of mindfulness is intended to help us shift the ratio of these thoughts—to come back to the present and our current surroundings just a bit more often.

Awareness, the second principle of mindfulness, is intricately linked to being present. Specifically, in being mindful, we're working to become more aware of the present moment. There are two general strategies for bringing awareness to the present moment: (1) attending to mental sensations and (2) attending to physical sensations. Mental sensations—that is, thoughts and emotions—are perhaps the less effective way to practice present-moment focus. Certainly, if cued, you could tell us a thought or an emotion that you're currently having (hopefully not bored!) in a way that would be present-focused. Mental sensations, however, are abstract by their very nature. This makes them . . . slippery. Even if you focus on a feeling of being bored in the present moment, your awareness of that emotion is likely to quickly lead to another thought: a related emotion, perhaps a memory of something you forgot to do, and on and on until we're definitely no longer present! Suffice to say, then, that mental sensations may not be the easiest way to stay aware of the present moment. That leads us to physical sensations. A good way to remember this strategy for present-moment awareness is keeping the five senses in mind. You probably learned about these as a kid—remember taste, touch, sight, smell, sound? Compared to those slippery mental sensations, our five senses are concrete. You can literally touch or hear things, for example, and this makes it much easier to stay present. (We should note that some folks, such as disabled folks, may not have all five of these senses available to them. In these cases, the other senses can be useful focal points.) Turns out, this is especially helpful when it comes to sex, as sexual experiences are filled with physical sensations (more on that in a minute)!

The third principle of mindfulness is *non-judgment*. This refers to accepting our sensations—mental or physical—as they are, rather than focusing on how they "should be" or how we wish them to be, and rather than assigning them a negative or positive value. It's useful to recognize that our judgments can actually be positive or negative. For example, you may judge a piece of artwork to be visually beautiful (positive visual sensation) or a chair to be uncomfortable (negative tactile sensation). Traditional mindfulness practice encourages us to be curious, neutral observers of our experiences in the present moment. In some ways, as sex therapists, we're less concerned about whether you have positive judgments. After all, pleasure and positivity are important for our sexual health. When it comes to libido, we find that it's typically the negative judgments that create barriers and act as brakes to desire. Consider, for example, some of the thought biases you read about in the last section.

It's challenging for most of us to stay present in the moment. Our thoughts are constantly pulling us in different directions. Again, this is what brains do and is not necessarily cause for alarm. It's why, however, you may often hear mindfulness described as a practice. Recall the saying: "What fires together, wires together." This is how mindfulness operates. With repeated practice over time, being present in the moment—without judgment—becomes easier for us to do.

Let's look at an example of the difference between mind*less*ness and mind*full*ness. Have you ever driven somewhere, arrived at your destination, and then realized you don't recall the journey? The whole drive may have felt like a blur, or you were so lost in thoughts that you weren't taking in your surroundings. That's an example of a more mindless drive. By getting lost in our thoughts, we're much less aware of our physical sensations and our environment. Now think about a more memorable drive: maybe a scenic ride through the countryside, or driving through a place that was new to you. Imagine being in awe throughout the drive, visually taking in your surroundings, the smells in the air, the sounds in the background. That's an example of a mindful drive. That's what it feels like to be fully aware and present, engaged primarily with our physical (versus mental) sensations.

Another great example is taking a shower. How many of us shower mindlessly, engaged in past- or future-focused thoughts? For example, if you shower in the morning, your attention is likely to be pulled into future-focused thinking about the day ahead and things that need to get done. If you shower in the evening, perhaps your attention is pulled to the past, replaying things that happened earlier that same day. Consider for a moment the many physical sensations that we tend to miss in favor of those mental sensations. A mindful shower might involve attending to the scent of soap or shampoo, the pressure and temperature of the water as it hits your skin, the humidity of the steam, the sight of the suds building up as you wash your body, and the sound of the water hitting the shower floor. Now that's a more mindful experience!

You might be thinking, "This is great, but what's it got to do with sex and libido?" When people describe their most satisfying sexual experiences, research shows us that mindfulness is a key component.[2] As you'll recall, sexual satisfaction is one of the most important predictors of sexual desire (solo or partnered), and it's most likely to occur when we set aside other distractions and feel present in the moment. When we think about the past, we disconnect from our bodies and can get stuck in our mental sensations. The same thing happens when we think about the future—even just the next few moments ahead. Both experiences can trigger a sense of anxiety and turn on that ol' unhelpful stress response. Mindfulness—nonjudgmental present-moment awareness—helps us better experience pleasure and a sense of connection.

Even outside of sexual experiences, research suggests that a general mindfulness practice can have positive benefits for libido.[3] Here are some opportunities to incorporate mindfulness into your daily life:

- During a shower or bath
- During a walk or other types of exercise
- While eating
- While completing household tasks (e.g., laundry, dishes)
- Listening to a guided meditation
- While gardening or mowing the lawn

Remember, when practicing mindfulness, it's natural for our thoughts to shift back and forth between the past, present, and future. The objective here—which gets easier with practice—is to notice when your awareness has moved away from the present and to then non-judgmentally return your focus back to present-moment sensations. In chapter 7, we'll explore an important mindfulness practice for partners that can be particularly helpful with libido.

BREATHING AND GROUNDING EXERCISES

Grounding is any resource or practice that helps us become aware of our surroundings and the present moment. For some people, grounding literally involves placing their bare feet on the ground. In general, though, it's about orienting our minds toward our physical sensations via some combination of sight, smell, touch, sound, and taste. This is an effort to activate our parasympathetic nervous system (PNS)—the rest-and-digest branch—to create a sense of calm and presence. (For a refresher on the important branches of our nervous system, revisit chapter 4.)

One of the most direct ways to stimulate the PNS is to notice our breathing. When we inhale, we activate our sympathetic nervous system. When we exhale, we activate our parasympathetic nervous system. When our inhale and exhale are balanced, a sense of regulation and calm results. Extending our exhalation can stimulate the PNS response. Breathing deeply from the diaphragm is a commonly used strategy. The diaphragm is located just below our lungs and is the muscle associated with respiration. In deep, diaphragmatic breathing, your shoulders and chest will remain still while your stomach will visibly inflate like a balloon with each inhale and completely deflate with each exhale. Note that the stomach goes in the opposite direction of your breath (the stomach goes out when breathing in and in when breathing out). You can try this exercise standing up, sitting, or lying down. If standing or sitting, you can place your hand on your stomach and feel the inflation and deflation happen as you breathe. If lying down, you can place your hand or a light object on your stomach, like a paperback book, and watch as it rises and falls with each inhale and exhale.

Another way to practice intentional breathing with a prolonged exhale is the 4–7–8 technique. As you slowly inhale, you'll count to four, then hold your breath for a count of seven, and then exhale over eight counts. A third breathing technique is box breathing, which involves inhaling for a count of four, holding the breath for a count of four, exhaling as you count to four, and then holding it again for a count of four. You can repeat this a few times and then check in with your body.

As with anything, please only do what works for you. Some people experience *more* agitation or anxiety with mindful breathing, rather than less. In that case, it can help to practice grounding in other ways, such as focusing on your environment and surroundings. An example of this is the 5–4–3–2–1 technique: this is a grounding exercise that involves looking around you and naming five things you can see, four things you can touch, three things you can hear, two things you can smell, and one thing you can taste. This can help us get out of our heads and focus on what's surrounding us in the moment. As you try some of the exercises and suggestions throughout this book, it can be helpful to have a breathing or grounding technique to come back to if you find yourself in a stress response.

Consider reflecting on the following prompts in your **sexual health journal**: What's your breathing like when you're sexual? Are you holding your breath? Is your breathing deeper or shallower? What happens if you spend a moment practicing an intentional breathing technique—like diaphragmatic breathing—before, during, or after sexual experiences? Do these breathing exercises change your experience with self-stimulation? How about with partnered sex?

MINORITY STRESS AS A BARRIER TO SELF-CONNECTION

As we discussed in chapter 2, minority stress is a significant sociocultural problem that can impact us in many ways. When we internalize our culture's oppressive messages related to our various identities—as with internalized racism, homophobia, binegativity, transphobia, ableism, and sexism, among others—it can create a major barrier for our own connection to self. Being taught that there is something inherently wrong with us can have significant negative consequences for our overall health and well-being. Sex, of course, commonly falls into that mix.

Addressing these barriers can feel overwhelming, given that overcoming oppression requires broad societal change at the level of cultural norms, public policy, healthcare, and many other systems. That said, we also want to consider ways that minority stress might be addressed or disrupted at the individual level. Some scholars, healthcare providers, and activists have started to explore such strategies—tools that can help individuals address minority stress and cultivate a better connection to self.[4] We include information about some of these approaches—such as a link to Dr. Candice Nicole Hargons's Black Lives Matter Meditation for Healing Racial Trauma—in the Resources section.

THE IMPORTANCE OF PLEASURE

Given that you're reading a book about libido, the word *pleasure* very likely brings to mind a sexual situation. However, we want to take a moment to broaden the conversation about pleasure. Pleasure can encompass a constellation of emotions, including joy and satisfaction. It can involve sensations or experiences, both by yourself and with others. Humans are designed to seek pleasure, and pleasure can be mental, emotional, relational, spiritual, and physical. Oftentimes these different forms of pleasure can overlap. Importantly, pleasure varies considerably and can be different for each individual. That is, what feels good to you depends on your own experiences, preferences, and bodily sensations. Let's consider some examples. Here are some things that may bring a sense of *physical pleasure*:

- The taste of something delicious
- The feeling of the sun on your body
- Swimming in cool water on a hot day
- Physical touch with someone who feels both physically and emotionally safe
- Lying under a fuzzy blanket
- The sound and smell of a campfire
- Playing with a fidget toy
- Feeling sand beneath your toes
- Getting a massage
- A hot shower
- The feel and smell of freshly washed sheets

Do any of these examples ring true for you? What other physical sensations do you find pleasurable? Take a moment to note these nonsexual physical pleasures in your **sexual health journal.**

Remember that pleasure can also extend beyond the physical. For example, the following experiences may be a source of *emotional pleasure*:

- Having a connected conversation
- Looking forward to an event
- Watching your child learn something new
- Being recognized for something you did
- Seeing your plants grow and thrive

- Recognizing that you made a positive impact in someone's life
- Being seen and accepted as your true self

Here are some examples of *spiritual pleasure*:

- Feeling connected to something greater than yourself
- Feeling connected to the Earth or nature
- Gazing at the stars
- Following the moon's cycles
- Practicing family or religious traditions

Here are some examples of *mental pleasure*:

- Reading a good book
- Studying something you feel passionate about
- Learning a new skill and feeling a sense of mastery
- Finishing a particularly difficult puzzle

Here are some potential examples of *relational pleasure*:

- Having a deep conversation with someone (also listed under emotional pleasure)
- Feeling loved by someone
- Physical touch with someone who feels safe (also listed under physical pleasure)
- Doing a fun activity with someone you enjoy spending time with
- Sharing a meal with a loved one
- Petting an animal

An informal (not scientific, but definitely informational!) poll of our social media followers revealed these other nonsexual examples of pleasure:

- Watching the leaves change colors in autumn
- Having your pet sit and stay on your lap
- Someone playing with your hair
- Having a quiet cup of coffee
- Fresh, warm bread with butter and cheese

- Spooning with your partner early in the morning before getting up
- Soaking in a bubble bath
- Uninhibited laughter
- Sitting on the beach
- Listening to the rain
- Sleeping in

Take a moment to journal about what you were feeling in your body while you were reading these lists of pleasurable activities. Did it bring up any particular thoughts or emotions? What other types of physical, emotional, spiritual, mental, and relational pleasure can you identify in your own life? Are there experiences from your past that have impacted your general relationship with pleasure (across all of these categories)?

Many people have actively worked throughout their lives to shut down experiences of pleasure. First, there is a general societal message—that we may pick up from culture, faith traditions, or family—that pleasure and immorality are intertwined. In the extreme, this view holds that pleasure is bad or even sinful, and that to openly engage with any sort of pleasurable sensation is to place oneself in a position of questionable morality. As discussed in chapter 2, such belief systems are often at the root of sexual guilt and shame, both of which can go on to disrupt our sexual health in a variety of ways (from difficulties with libido to sexual pain to problems with orgasm). A perhaps less intense but still deeply problematic view of pleasure is that pleasure is unimportant. From this perspective, any type of pleasure is often seen as unnecessary, selfish, or taking time away from more "productive" activities. Cultural, religious, or family messages may focus on being selfless and in service to others, which can erase the importance (especially when it comes to health!) of taking time for yourself to engage in play, rest, and pleasurable activities. In Western—and particularly American—culture, we have a tendency to glorify the hustle or grind; we equate our level of busyness to our overall worth as humans. The saying "work hard, play hard" suggests the idea of balance, but the "play hard" part is often neglected in how we talk about ourselves and others. Of the folks we work with in sex therapy, few were taught that pleasure is a right—something to make time for and of equal importance to other life experiences.

We also tend to internalize specific cultural messages about the "right" types of sexual pleasure. Perhaps unsurprisingly, these messages are often related to the rigid script of the Sexual Staircase. For example, some folks believe that solo sexual pleasure is less valid than sexual pleasure with a partner. We meet many people who think their orgasms aren't "real" or are somehow not good enough if they require the use of a sexual aid or vibrator. In line with Sexual Staircase thinking, people with penises are told that pleasure relies solely on their ability to get hard, stay hard, and penetrate for as long as possible. People with vulvas, on the other hand, often receive conflicting information about pleasure, with a heavy (and often unhelpful) emphasis on penetrative sex. For older adults, LGBTQ+ individuals, disabled people, and many others who don't fit into the narrow boxes that society creates around sex and pleasure, there is often an assumption that sexual pleasure just doesn't occur at all. That couldn't be further from the truth, and it's important to be careful about the ways we police our own pleasure and the pleasure of others.

PLEASURE AS A RIGHT

The World Health Organization, alongside many sexual health organizations, has been addressing sexual and reproductive rights for decades. But did you know that the World Association for Sexual Health (WAS) specifically considers sexual pleasure "a fundamental part of sexual rights as a matter of human rights"? In 2019, WAS released the groundbreaking "Declaration on Sexual Pleasure," a research-based statement that defines sexual pleasure as the "physical and/or psychological satisfaction and enjoyment derived from shared or solitary erotic experiences, including thoughts, fantasies, dreams, emotions, and feelings."[5] This international declaration identifies key factors for cultivating sexual pleasure, including "self-determination, consent, safety, privacy, confidence and the ability to communicate and negotiate sexual relations," as well as "safe sexual experiences free of discrimination, coercion, and violence."

It's important here to note that pleasure is not the best or only goal for sexual expression (some researchers refer to this as the *pleasure imperative* and equate it to some degree with toxic positivity).[6] Recall that what motivates us to be sexual—solo or with partners—is wide ranging and not always physical in nature. That said, learning to appreciate more general types of nonsexual pleasure can be a useful way to counter negative, shame-based messages and to begin connecting (or reconnecting) with yourself. Many people have had negative experiences with their bodies that can make even nonsexual physical pleasure tough to notice. This might be related to appearance anxiety, gender or anatomical dysphoria, trauma, or a host of other factors that can create a strained relationship with our physical selves. We invite you to start broadly—gently noticing and identifying nonsexual physical, emotional, spiritual, mental, and relational forms of pleasure—before moving into the more sexual realm.

BODY MAPPING AND PLEASURE MAPPING

Learning (or relearning) how to connect with ourselves is a mindful, embodied process. This can include noticing our physical sensations in general, and our pleasurable sensations in particular. Being open to noticing and engaging with these physical experiences can be new for many people, especially if you've previously been discouraged from doing so. For example, as sex therapists, we often see clients who focus on their partner's sexual pleasure to the exclusion of noticing and cultivating their own. To optimize sexual relationships, it's critical to develop and practice a balance between self-focus and partner-focus.

We recommend practicing a body scan as part of your self-exploration. If you do an internet search for "body scan," you'll find plenty of audio and video guides with instructions. Several sexual health apps also include body scans. Find one that you like and practice it a few times before moving on to the next section. This is a mindfulness exercise—an effort to become more globally aware of your body. Body mapping gives us the opportunity to do just that: to map out sensations from head to toe and decide whether they are positive, negative, or neutral.

Pleasure mapping is a more focused type of body mapping in which—you guessed it—we turn our attention to identifying areas of pleasure across our bodies. Pleasurable areas of the body may be traditional erogenous zones—like the chest or genitals—but often folks are surprised to find other areas of pleasure. We'll go through a pleasure mapping exercise below.

WHEN THE GROUND ISN'T STEADY

For people who have trauma symptoms or chronic dysregulation (e.g., dissociation, hypervigilance, panic attacks, trauma flashbacks), there are times when mindfulness exercises might worsen these symptoms. If you're in a dysregulated

state, paying close attention to your body can sometimes lead to *more* dysregulation. If this is the case for you, we strongly recommend working with a trauma
therapist, particularly one who uses somatic (body-based) interventions.

Before starting this exercise, find a private and comfortable environment.[7] Some folks prefer to explore pleasure mapping in the bath or shower,
others while lying down in bed. Regardless of the location you choose, try
to minimize distractions as much as possible (e.g., silence your phone, lock
the door). You can be fully or partially unclothed, whatever feels most comfortable for you. If you start with some clothing on, as you return to this
exercise over time and develop increased comfort, you can slowly remove
articles of clothing. Feel free to apply lotion or body oil, if that provides
a pleasurable sensation. For folks who experience gender or anatomical
dysphoria, you might choose to skip or modify any part of the exercise that
triggers dysphoria, depending on your needs and what feels best for you.

To start, touch your arms and hands, focusing your attention on the
physical sensation. Notice what feels good. The purpose of this exercise is *not*
to focus on arousal or orgasm, though those experiences may happen along
the way. Our focus is on the broader experience of pleasure. Use different
types of touch by exploring pressure, speed, and various strokes on your
arms. Your eyes may be open or closed, whichever helps you to best focus
on the physical sensations. When you're ready, touch your legs and feet,
continuing to explore physical sensation and what feels good. If something
feels pleasurable, you can linger there for a moment, taking note of this.
Next, let your hands touch your neck, shoulders, chest, abdomen, and inner
thighs. Take your time and remember to focus on pleasure, broadly defined.
You may notice your mind wandering or judging your experience. It's natural
for your mind to do this; try to refocus on physical sensation when this
occurs. If comfortable and ready, you can include genital touch using either
one or both hands. Here, too, explore different types of pressure, rhythm,
and intensity of touch to create various sensory experiences. Get curious
about what feels good. Remember, you aren't trying to orgasm—you're just
noticing what types of touch and areas of the body are pleasurable. If you
notice tension in any parts of your body, you can choose to rub or massage
those areas. Pleasure mapping exercises can take as much or as little time as
you need; there is no set rule. When you're ready to conclude the exercise,

take a few deep breaths—inhaling through your nose and exhaling through your mouth. Wrap up by taking a few moments to reflect on the experience in your **sexual health journal:**

- What part of your body was most pleasurable to touch?
- What type of touch felt best for you? Lighter strokes? Deeper pressure? Using your whole hand? Using just your fingertips?
- What positive emotions came up for you? What negative emotions came up for you? Was there a particular part of your body connected to those feelings?
- Did you notice any automatic thoughts arise during the exercise? What were the thoughts? Were they connected to a particular area or part of your body?

Body and pleasure mapping often work best when practiced repeatedly over time. We encourage you to try these exercises more than once and revisit them, as useful, in working on connecting (or reconnecting) to yourself.

THE WINDOW OF TOLERANCE

When we try something new, or approach something that has been associated with trauma in the past, we may leave what's referred to as our *window of tolerance* (see figure 8). This term, coined by Dr. Daniel Siegel, describes our nervous system's zone of optimal functioning: that is, the state where we feel most regulated, are able to think most clearly, and can best process information.[8] It's a framework for understanding our behavior and experience, though note that the window of tolerance refers to nervous system arousal or activation, not sexual arousal.

When we're within our window of tolerance, we're able to engage in problem-solving and regulate our emotions (as opposed to reacting from a stress response). This is also an optimal state for sexual experiences, as we're better able to notice and enjoy pleasure. When we're outside of our window of tolerance, we're either above the window, in a state of hyperarousal, or below our window, in a state of hypoarousal. *Hyperarousal* is when the sympathetic branch of our nervous system is activated, whereas *hypoarousal* is when the parasympathetic branch of our nervous system is activated (if you need a nervous system refresher, feel free to revisit chapter 4). Both of

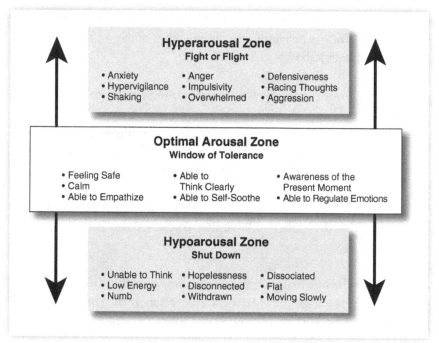

FIGURE 8. The Window of Tolerance. Adapted from Daniel J. Siegel, *Mindsight: The New Science of Personal Transformation* (New York: Bantam Books, 2010).

these states involve a stress response. Every individual's window of tolerance is a bit different and can be wide or narrow, based on our traits and past experiences. For example, those with a history of trauma may find that they have a narrow window of tolerance—they may more easily move above or below their personal window into a stress response. It's also useful to note that our window of tolerance can widen or narrow depending on the internal or external context of the situation. For example, the presence of supportive loved ones can help widen our window of tolerance, making it feel less overwhelming and more manageable to approach a challenging task or situation. Without support, that same challenge might more easily push us outside of our window of tolerance.

Fortunately, we can intentionally widen our window of tolerance in slow and gradual ways. This is often the goal of therapeutic work, both in general psychotherapy and in more specialized sex therapy. It's important to note, however, that if we stretch too far or too quickly beyond our window of tolerance, we run the risk of provoking that same old stress response. As a visual example, imagine a rubber band that, if pulled too much or too quickly, snaps. However, if a rubber band is stretched slowly and consistently over time, it will gently expand. As Deb Dana, author of the book *Anchored*, states: "Our goal in shaping new patterns is to stretch but not stress our system."[9] The exercises and concepts you've been reading about in part II of this book are designed to help you get into, maintain, and even gently stretch your window of tolerance as you work toward your sexual health goals.

ANXIETY HIERARCHY

Many folks experience anxiety about sex or physical touch in general. This is common and can be caused by a variety of factors, including past trauma, a sexual desire discrepancy that has created an all-or-none mindset around partnered touch, and a lack of good sexual health education, to name a few. To go back to the window of tolerance: in an effort to widen our window and become less dysregulated with touch or sex, we need to move slowly, at a tolerable pace for our nervous system. This is often a slower pace than most people attempt or realize is necessary—folks may go too fast due to self-pressure or pressure from a partner. The idea is to slowly widen our window of tolerance without going so far or so fast that we trigger our stress response. We want to keep ourselves tethered to regulation so that the experience we are attempting feels manageable and safe, even if it's a challenge. This requires breaking up our behaviors into much smaller steps, using what therapists call an *anxiety hierarchy*. Anxiety hierarchies are individualized according to each person's different needs and goals. To create an anxiety hierarchy, think about something you want to work on with regard to touch or sexual health, starting with whatever is most anxiety provoking for you. Some examples may include:

- Being able to look at my genitals more comfortably
- Being able to have a pelvic exam/Pap smear
- Being able to have penetrative sex without my body tensing
- Being able to experience pleasure during nonsexual touch with a partner

To create an anxiety hierarchy, we tend to work backward from what feels *most* anxiety provoking or dysregulating to what feels *least* anxiety provoking. Sometimes it helps to assign a number to each behavior; we often use a scale of 0 (no anxiety or stress response) to 100 (worst anxiety or stress response imaginable). For example, Mo rates using a vibrator to be 100/100, but this is something they wish to work toward in order to potentially increase their sexual pleasure. In Mo's case, we place vibrator use at the top of the anxiety hierarchy and work backward to identify less stressful steps that will help them get there. Here's an example of Mo's anxiety hierarchy:

- 100/100: Use the vibrator directly on my genitals
- 90/100: Use the vibrator on my upper inner thighs
- 80/100: Use the vibrator on my stomach or chest
- 60/100: Use the vibrator on my arms and legs
- 40/100: Turn on the vibrator and use it on my hand
- 35/100: Unbox the vibrator and look at it when it arrives
- 30/100: Look at photos of vibrators online; select a vibrator to purchase
- 20/100: Imagine using a vibrator on myself
- 10/100: Talk about using a vibrator with my therapist or partner

Many people, in working to widen their window of tolerance for a given activity, misstep by trying to do too much way too quickly. We unintentionally overwhelm our nervous systems and end up right back where we started—in a stress response. Often, when that happens, we give up on our goal, perhaps avoiding it altogether. Let's look at a partnered example of an anxiety hierarchy.

Joycelyn is a forty-five-year-old woman in her second marriage. Her ex-husband was verbally and emotionally abusive, called her names, and said sexually shaming things to her. After many years in that relationship, she developed a stress response around physical closeness, especially with men. Unfortunately, this even includes her loving and safe second husband, Jabari. When Jabari tries to hug or hold Joycelyn, her body tenses up and her heart beats more rapidly; she quickly enters a stress response. She knows this is related to past trauma and not because Jabari isn't safe. Unfortunately, however, we typically can't just verbally convince our nervous systems that they're safe. Rather, we have to gradually retrain our bodies to widen the window of tolerance and activate our rest-and-digest parasympathetic response in situations that have become anxiety provoking. Here's Joycelyn's anxiety hierarchy for being able to be comfortably held by her husband:

- 100/100: Holding each other for three minutes while lying on the couch
- 90/100: Holding each other for one minute while lying on the couch
- 80/100: Holding each other for one minute while standing up
- 70/100: Jabari putting two arms around Joycelyn's waist
- 65/100: Joycelyn putting her arms around Jabari's waist
- 50/100: Jabari putting an arm around Joycelyn's shoulders
- 45/100: Joycelyn putting an arm around Jabari's shoulders
- 30/100: Holding Jabari's hand
- 15/100: Sitting next to Jabari on the couch with their thighs touching
- 5/100: Sitting next to Jabari on the couch

These examples can give you a sense of how an anxiety hierarchy works. There are often many small steps required. Again, we want to emphasize the importance of taking things slowly. You might spend quite a bit of time at each level, depending on what you notice about your response. If you notice that your initial hierarchy feels like too much too soon, you can always create smaller steps based on your experience with the hierarchy. Take your time with this, because even though it doesn't seem like it, slower is faster.

SEXUAL AIDS

In this section, we'll guide you through exploring and using sexual aids. In our experience, sexual aids, such as vibrators, can bring up strong emotions. For some folks, these are positive reactions: sexual aids can help to increase sensation, pleasure, and arousal and can also create greater opportunity for sexual exploration. For others, the prospect of using a sexual aid can feel daunting—overwhelming, scary, anxiety provoking, or even potentially threatening. These latter reactions, we've found, are often directly tied to sociocultural messages and the resulting beliefs that use of sexual aids is "unnatural" or represents some sort of sexual failure. Before we talk specifically about how to use sexual aids, let's first review why they can be such an important component of sexual health.

Though sexual aids are not typically regarded as medical devices in our wider culture, they are definitely considered such by sexual health providers. Vibrators in particular are known to provide sexual health benefits, and some are classified by the Food and Drug Administration (FDA) as obstetrical and gynecological therapeutic devices to treat sexual concerns.[10] There is significant evidence that vibrators are effective for addressing delayed or absent orgasmic function as well as pelvic floor muscle tension that may be contributing to arousal difficulties or sexual pain.[11] For folks who have experienced a decrease in sexual or genital sensation—a common development as we age, or with medical conditions like diabetes and multiple sclerosis—use of a vibrator is often critical for reaching the new, higher threshold of stimulation required for pleasure and orgasm. Importantly, this does not represent some sort of sexual failure or lack of effort, but rather the common reality of sensory changes over the course of our lives. It's also perhaps important to know that the use of sexual aids is quite common, regardless of gender or sexual orientation. For example, 53 percent of cisgender women and 45 percent of cisgender men have used a vibrator at some point in their lives.[12] Among lesbian and bisexual cisgender women in the United States and United Kingdom, over 75 percent reported lifetime vibrator use.[13] This research is now ten or more years old, and the numbers have almost certainly grown in the years since these initial prevalence studies were conducted.

In addition to addressing changes in sensation or muscle tension, sexual aids can also help you further discover what's pleasurable for you. We strongly recommend exploring on your own first, as this reduces the distractions inherent (even if unintended) in partnered sexual experiences and overall tends to feel more comfortable. Once you identify how you best experience pleasure with a sexual aid, you can choose whether to share and incorporate it into partnered sex.

Vibrators

Vibrators come in a variety of shapes, sizes, and styles. Some are designed for external stimulation, some for internal stimulation, and some can be used for both. If you've never used a vibrator before, selecting one can be a bit overwhelming, so let's explore some options. Different types of vibrators include:

- External: As the name implies, these are used externally and come in a variety of shapes and sizes.
- Internal: These are designed for penetration, though they can often be used both internally and externally. These vibrators are often shaped like a penis.
- Wands: A type of external vibrator, these are typically larger and look a bit like a microphone in shape. They are generally more intense and offer good pressure for people who enjoy or need a heightened level of stimulation.
- Air pressure: These external vibrators offer a light suction or fluttery sensation and are often specifically used to focus on clitoral or nipple stimulation. They help to gently stimulate blood flow, which can improve arousal and sensitivity.
- Pulsator: A type of internal vibrator, these products are often shaped like a penis and offer a thrusting motion to simulate the sensation of penetrative sex.
- Dual stimulator: These products offer a combination of internal and external stimulation. Some may perhaps be familiar with the Vibratex Rabbit, the dual stimulator made famous by an episode of *Sex and the City.*

For those who are new to using vibrators, we generally recommend beginning with an external or air pressure vibrator. Their vibrations are often not too intense, and because they are used externally, they are good choices for beginners, for folks uninterested in penetrative sex, or for anyone who may have discomfort or pain with penetration. If you find that after some use you need more intense vibration or more pressure, you can consider trying out a wand, pulsator, or a dual stimulator.

Before getting started, read the instructions that come with your vibrator. These might be located on or within the packaging, or perhaps the website from which you purchased the product. Some websites include instructional videos to show you how to best use your product. Prior to using your vibrator directly on your genitals, we suggest easing into it by testing the sensations on your arms or hands. Get to know the different settings and features; it may require a number of sessions to truly build comfort with them all. If you intend to use a lubricant, which we certainly recommend, determine which one is best for your specific vibrator. If you're planning to use the vibrator internally, a store-bought lubricant is essential to help with comfort and can even increase pleasure.

When you're ready for further exploration, find a private space with minimal distractions where you can get comfortable and focus. Start by using your hands to touch different parts of your body wherever it feels good to you. As you get comfortable with this touch, you may want to incorporate genital touch using your hand. This is a good time to apply the lubricant you selected. When you feel ready, turn your vibrator on to the lowest setting. Many products have different vibration patterns to choose from. Find one that feels most comfortable to start off with. Before using the vibrator directly on your genitals, you may want to try using it on other body parts first. Additionally, some people like to use a vibrator through clothes, a towel, or sheets to help adjust to the sensation, particularly if the low setting feels too intense. Some people like to put the vibrator directly on their clitoris or penis, and others find that to be too intense or not enjoyable. Some people like to explore using the vibrator on their labia or scrotum. You can place the vibrator on the base of your penis; it can also be used on the skin between the penis and anus, or the vagina and anus, known as the perineum. This area is highly sensitive, and using a vibrator on it can be very pleasurable.

Most people require direct clitoral or penile stimulation to have an orgasm. For people with clitorises, the most reliable way to have an orgasm is typically with direct clitoral stimulation. The clitoris has far more (and far more sensitive) nerve endings than the internal canal of the vagina. Some people like to stimulate the clitoris while simultaneously experiencing vaginal or anal penetration. Take some time with this and find what feels good to you.

Once you're comfortable using your vibrator, you can try out some of the other features—different vibration patterns, or a higher intensity. Make sure to clean your vibrator after each use (gentle soap and warm water work just fine!) and store it in a cool, dry place. Do not use cleaning products like bleach or disinfectants, as they can irritate your skin and damage your vibrator.

Masturbation Sleeves

Vibrators can be great for folks of all genders and body types. People with penises can also further their self-exploration and pleasure using what's known as a masturbation sleeve. This is typically a silicone sexual aid that comes in a hard plastic tube. Masturbation sleeves have an opening at the top where your penis can be inserted, providing a sensation that's similar to penetrative sex. Masturbation sleeves come in different sizes and price points. As with vibrators, they can be useful for learning more about what type of sensation feels good to you, for further connecting with your body, and for exploring your patterns of arousal.

Before using your sleeve, read through the instructions that come with it, or go to the product's website to learn how to use and care for it. Masturbation sleeves are best used with a store-bought lubricant, so choose one that you like ahead of time. We recommend a water-based lubricant, as it can be used with any type of sleeve material and is easier to clean off after use.

Just like with vibrators, some people like to fantasize while using a masturbation sleeve, whereas others prefer to listen to or watch erotic content. The masturbation sleeve is best used once an erection is present, so find what works for you to help build physical arousal. Start by touching different parts of your body with your hands, noticing what feels good. When you're comfortable, you can use your hand to gently touch the base of your penis, the head of your penis, your scrotum, and your perineum. Once you have an erection, you can place the head of your penis into the sleeve. Pause to notice the physical sensations. As you're comfortable, you can then insert your penis further into the sleeve, noticing the changes in physical sensations. Once your penis is as deep as you would like it to be or feel comfortable with, pause for a moment to notice the sensation of containment within the sleeve. When you're ready, you can incorporate gentle movement of the sleeve, up and down or side to side—whatever direction feels good for you. If you'd like and are able, you can ejaculate directly into the sleeve, or elsewhere. You can also stop stimulation prior to climax. Again, we recommend doing what feels best to you.

After each use, make sure to clean your masturbation sleeve using gentle soap and water. Some companies recommend turning the product inside out (like a sock) for a more thorough wash. Be sure to dry it completely. Some sleeves should be lightly powdered with cornstarch after drying and before your next use. This can keep the material from getting sticky or degrading.

We strongly recommend reading your product's cleaning instructions. As with all sexual aids, there can be significant variability in care instructions depending on the product and materials from which it's made.

GENDER EUPHORIA AND GENDER PLEASURE

The resources available to help folks experience gender euphoria and pleasure during sex have been getting better and better. From sexual aids designed to help reduce genital dysphoria to sexually explicit material created by and for trans and nonbinary folks, there are many options. See the Resources section for some ideas. For folks who have had gender-affirming surgeries, it can be useful to practice reconnecting to yourself and your sexuality after recovery. It's common, for example, for there to be a learning process involved in reaching orgasms again after gender-affirming genital surgeries. The body mapping and pleasure mapping techniques discussed in this chapter can be a useful starting point.

SEXUALLY EXPLICIT MATERIAL

In this section, we'll be discussing sexually explicit material (SEM), broadly defined as any media that's intended to sexually arouse. When asked about SEM, most people—in our experience—tend to think of online video pornography. Importantly, though, SEM encompasses a wide variety of media like audio stories, romance novels, art, magazines, photos, movies, and television, in addition to online porn. SEM can be a polarizing topic, though we've found that folks are often surprised to learn what research has shown about these materials—the data often differ dramatically from the dominant cultural narratives. Let's start with a few questions for your **sexual health journal:**

- What immediate thoughts and emotions come up for you in considering the topic of sexually explicit material? What messages or education might those reactions be rooted in?
- When you think back to the messages you've been exposed to regarding SEM, are they generally positive, negative, or neutral?
- At what age did you first discover sexually explicit material? What was the experience like for you?

SEM can be both empowering and problematic, depending on the content and how it's used. Interestingly, research suggests that SEM can enhance partnered sex by increasing arousal and helping folks to further explore their sexuality. In terms of libido, SEM can be a helpful resource in nurturing or building responsive desire. It's important to note that most of the existing research on the effects of SEM is focused on online video pornography. Across several studies, most people who viewed online pornography disagreed that it negatively affected them.[14] In fact, here are some of the benefits they reported:

- Feeling less repressed about sex
- Feeling more open-minded about sex
- Increased tolerance of other people's sexualities and sexual interests
- Experiencing self-pleasure
- Sustaining sexual interest in long-term relationships
- Increasing attentiveness to a partner's sexual desires
- Finding a community or identity
- Improving sexual communication with partners

SEM is more diverse than most folks realize and—if you know where to look—can provide important positive representation of communities that have historically been marginalized, desexualized, or taught that they are undesirable. SEM that depicts positive, pleasurable sexual experiences for queer, trans, and nonbinary folks, for example, can provide enormously beneficial representation. This, in turn, can be a libido boost for some. That said, we all must be cautious of the content we consume, as there are certainly loads of sexist, racist, transphobic, and otherwise problematic SEM in the world.

Many folks grapple with challenging emotions related to SEM, and this is totally understandable. Particularly when it comes to online and print pornography, there's plenty to be concerned about in terms of unethical and potentially harmful practices. Sex trafficking and forced sexual activity are major problems, and as we've noted, there is also deeply sexist, racist, and transphobic SEM. Ethical porn *does* exist, however, and given the often polarizing nature of this topic, it's important to recognize the nuance. If you choose to explore sexually explicit material, including online porn, we strongly recommend learning more about ethically produced, consent-focused productions.

ETHICAL PORN

Not all porn is the same. While a lot of online porn is certainly produced in harmful and unethical ways, there's an entire genre called *ethical* or *feminist porn* that's created with these concerns in mind. Ethical porn production involves providing performers a safe and respectful work environment. It's consensual, legal, and often involves more diverse performers. In many cases, discussions of sexual consent and negotiation between performers are part of the film, prior to any touching even taking place! Some folks have actually found this a helpful way to see consent discussions modeled so they can then practice with their own partners in real life. Most ethical porn involves a fee or cost. Content that's free often means that the performers weren't compensated fairly or weren't provided with safe and fair working conditions. If you're open to exploring ethical porn further, you can find several sites via an online search. We also include some books on the topic in our Resources section.

In addition to these (appropriate!) ethical concerns, there are many negative messages about SEM in our culture. Purity culture beliefs and messaging are often a culprit here. As we've previously discussed, there's also a common tendency to view pleasure negatively in our culture and to shame individuals—especially women and queer and trans people—who openly enjoy sex and pleasure. The most common concern we hear about SEM by far comes from heterosexual cisgender women who are worried about their male partner's use of porn.[15] This may be a result of gender roles and stereotypes that we have internalized about sexuality in general and SEM specifically; for example, a mistaken belief that a partner's practice of self-stimulation reflects poorly on our own desirability, attractiveness, or the health of a relationship (most times, it doesn't!). We find that many LGBTQ+ folks, by virtue of their own identities, have already spent a great deal of time exploring how these dominant cultural narratives can be harmful and inaccurate.[16] This may be why, as sex therapists, it's rare to see LGBTQ+ folks struggling with SEM to the same extent as cisgender heterosexual individuals.

If the topic of SEM raises strong, challenging emotions for you, it can be helpful to consider different types of sexual content. For example, many folks react more negatively to SEM in video form than to erotic stories in text or audio form. Viewing sex, after all, is often a more explicit experience than reading or listening to a story about it and letting your imagination create its own visual. The preference for written and audio material can also be related to ethical concerns about the SEM. For example, it's easy to know with certainty that no one was hurt or manipulated in any way when listening to or reading an erotic story, as opposed to watching performers in a video. We encourage you to reflect on whether your feelings about SEM may differ by medium and, if so, why that might be. There are no right or wrong answers here—your responses can only help you better understand your relationship to SEM and how it may or may not be useful in exploring libido.

PORN LITERACY?!

A useful concept in the world of sexual health and education is *porn literacy*.[17] This refers to teaching individuals to analyze, evaluate, and think critically about SEM, especially online pornography. Porn literacy involves consideration of how erotic content is created, for whom it's intended, and what biases or messages it may contain. Overall, it's important for folks to recognize that porn and other sexually explicit material is designed to be arousing and entertaining, not educational. Experiences depicted in SEM are often quite unrealistic, have been subject to heavy editing, and may not reflect how many people enjoy being sexual in real life. In the absence of comprehensive sex education, many folks—especially young people—are left learning about sex from SEM. Without porn literacy, this can contribute to several problems, including unsafe sexual practices, feelings of inadequacy, and unrealistic expectations about ourselves and our sexual partners.

chapter 6

CONNECTION
WITH PARTNER(S)

In the last chapter, we focused on important sexual health strategies for connecting or reconnecting with yourself. Here, we move into concepts and exercises that focus on *relational* connection or reconnection. As you'll recall from part I, many folks struggle with libido—as well as other aspects of sex—when feeling emotionally or psychologically disconnected from their sexual partners. And, of course, chronic relationship tension or conflict is often a major barrier to sexual desire! In this chapter, we offer ideas and activities that you can try with partners, including exercises for both emotional and sexual connection. As you read through the different concepts and suggestions, we hope you'll find something that works for you. Please keep in mind that not all exercises will fit for every circumstance. Some activities may be a better fit for your particular relationship(s) than others. Remember, take what works and leave the rest!

SPENDING TIME TOGETHER

For some people, spending time with a partner and connecting with them emotionally is a gateway to sexual intimacy. Others may find the opposite—that sexual connection is a pathway to emotional closeness. Importantly, both of these pathways to connection are valid. However, it can be challenging for partners when their preferred pathways are different—when one partner wants to start with an emotional connection that then leads to sexual connection, while another wants to start with a sexual connection that then leads to emotional connection. For folks who are drawn to starting with emotional connection, it can be helpful to develop intentional *rituals of connection* on a regular basis. Ideally, these rituals reflect a "structured event or routine that you each enjoy and depend on that both reflects and reinforces your sense of togetherness."[1] Here are some examples of rituals of connection:

- Having coffee together in the morning
- Cuddling before bed
- A kiss goodbye
- Eating dinner together
- Game night
- Talking about your day together
- Sunday brunch
- Weekly relationship meetings
- Evening walks together

For folks who are in a long-distance relationship or who don't live with their partner(s), here are some additional examples of rituals of connection:

- Streaming and watching an online movie together
- Cooking together while on a video call
- Doing yoga together online
- Playing an online game together
- Taking a walk together while on a call
- Good morning and good night texts
- Reading a book together on a video call or on the phone

Some of these examples offer active time together, while others are more passive, such as watching a movie. Additionally, many people require not only a shared activity, but also a deeper emotional and mental connection—e.g., talking about feelings and needs, discussing dreams and goals, exploring ideas and personal philosophies—to facilitate interest in sex. One tried-and-true method for developing deeper emotional and mental connections is expressing curiosity via open-ended questions to one another. Here are some examples:

- What are your hopes/plans/dreams for the next five years?
- What's your fondest memory?

- What book has most influenced you and why?
- What scares you the most and what about it feels so scary?
- Who in your family is most challenging for you to get along with and why?
- If you could rewrite an experience in your life, what would it be and what would you change?
- If you won the lottery tomorrow, what would you do with the winnings?
- What do you need most from me lately?
- What's something your parents did that you don't want to repeat?
- What was your best travel experience?

For some partners, having a regularly scheduled date helps to maintain this sense of emotional and mental connection. For others, small rituals throughout the days and weeks are most helpful. For many partnerships, it's both. We recommend experimenting with these ideas to see what works for you.

SPENDING TIME APART

While spending time together is important, many partners also benefit from dedicated time apart. During time apart, partners can nurture their individual interests, friendships, goals, and needs. Additionally, this gives partners room to miss each other, which can help to cultivate sexual desire through longing. If you and your partner(s) don't spend intentional time apart, we encourage you to consider ways that you might explore this option. Before we discuss some examples, however, let's take a moment to address what can often be a strong emotional reaction to this strategy.

The idea of purposefully spending time apart from romantic and sexual partners can bring up difficult emotions for some folks, including anxiety, fear of rejection, and jealousy (a complex combination of many different emotions). We find that such negative reactions tend to stem from some common sociocultural messages. In particular, there's a romanticized idea—often strongly reinforced in the media as well as in purity culture—that sexual and romantic partners are meant to "complete" each other, like interlocking puzzle pieces. This is rooted in complementarianism—the (often cisnormative, gendered) idea that each partner brings the exact complementary needs of the other to the table, which we discussed in chapter 2. It supports the myth that if we've found the "right" partner or "the one," we'll want for nothing more and will live happily ever after. While most adults understand that this fairy-tale ending is just that, they rarely question the corresponding myth that partners who have different interests or take occasional time apart are in a mismatched, "bad," or unhealthy relationship. Many people have deeply internalized the belief that spending brief periods of time apart from their partner signals a relational problem. While it certainly may be true that the desire to spend time apart from a partner could be related to relational conflict, just as often this is not the case. That is, the desire to take some time apart does not, in and of itself, mean a relationship is in jeopardy.

Many of the fears people have about spending time apart from their partners stem from some variation of these concerns:

- If my partner spends time away from me and enjoys themself, they may realize they don't need me or our relationship.
- If my partner spends time with others, they may be at greater risk for infidelity (or they are already cheating on me).
- If my partner wants to spend time away, it must mean they no longer want to be with me or are unhappy in the relationship.

SCARCITY VERSUS ABUNDANCE

By now it's perhaps not surprising to you that the way we think about our relationships has major implications for our behavior. Sex and relationship therapists often talk about the difference between approaching relationships with a mindset of scarcity versus abundance. Much of our culture reinforces the scarcity model of relationships: that love is rare, hard to find, and that there are a limited number of partners for us (many of our cultural messages insist that there's only "the one"!). Approaching relationships from a scarcity mindset often feeds feelings of insecurity, jealousy, self-comparison to others, and a sense of having to compete against other people to find love and connection. An abundance mindset, however, recognizes that there is enough love to go around, that we create and maintain healthy partnerships based on our actions (not whether they're "the one"), and that self-comparison is often a losing game. Many times, when folks struggle with the concept of spending time apart in relationships, we find that their fears are rooted in scarcity thinking.

When we discuss time apart in this context, we're specifically referring to brief periods of time for folks who are living together. This might be a matter of a few hours or a few days. We are not, however, referring to a relational separation in the context of tension or conflict. Here are some examples of taking brief time apart from partners:

- Taking a trip alone
- Spending the weekend separately
- Seeing friends without your partner(s)
- Spending a night of the week doing separate activities
- Spending time in different areas of your home

We invite you to take a moment to consider these points in your **sexual health journal**: What were you taught about togetherness versus separateness in relationships? What reactions come up for you in considering taking some brief time away from your partner(s)? Do you think your reaction would be different if the request was coming from your partner instead of you (e.g., to spend the day alone or to take a weekend trip without you)? If you're in a long-distance relationship or are not living together, do some of these concerns about time apart fit for you? If not, how is time apart considered or approached differently in your relationship?

Research supports the idea that taking time for oneself within a relationship can be helpful for cultivating relational connection. Sound counterintuitive? Dr. Murray Bowen, founder of family systems theory, discussed the importance of *differentiation of self*: the ability to maintain a healthy sense of self while staying in connection with others.[2] Research suggests that differentiation of self plays a significant role in our relationship satisfaction and our ability to manage feelings of jealousy, forgiveness of partners, and conflict resolution.[3] In contrast, being *fused* with a partner—that is, overly emotionally entangled—can result in a loss of our sense of self. Spending time apart allows partners to nurture this important sense of self and can help us to better show up in our relationships.

SHARING SEXUAL INTERESTS AND DESIRES

Sharing your sexual interests and desires with a partner can be quite vulnerable, but it is also very important in our relationships. A helpful practice for exploring these topics is to set up a structured conversation—taking turns intentionally speaking and listening to one another. We recommend doing this outside of sexual activity, perhaps even outside of the bedroom. When you're the listener, it's important to step outside of your own shoes and step into those of your partner. Your goal is to better understand how they experience things. As the listener, it can be helpful to ask open-ended questions (questions that can't simply be answered with a yes or no) to better understand your partner's thoughts and perspective. When it's your turn to speak, your partner will then do the same for you. It's important to keep in mind that just because your partner shares that they're interested in a particular sexual experience or that they fantasize about something, it doesn't mean that you must actually do that thing! Sometimes it's beneficial for partners to simply share their interests, without expectations or judgment—and, of course, fantasy is much different from behavior. Remember, we don't want to yuck someone's yum, as this will leave them feeling less inclined to share in the future. Here are some general recommendations for how to be a good listener when discussing sexual topics:

- Express curiosity
- Ask open-ended questions
- Avoid judgment
- Empathize and validate
- Reflect back what you're hearing

Importantly, you can provide validation without agreement. Validation is about letting your partner know that they make sense or that you can hear their perspective. Here are some examples of validating statements:

- "I hear what you're saying."
- "That definitely makes sense."
- "I understand where you're coming from."
- "I get it."
- "Thanks for trusting me with that."

Sexual communication is a skill and, like any other, requires practice. Discussing sexual interests, desires, and fantasies is a great place to start. It may feel uncomfortable or awkward at first, but as you and your partner(s) practice, you'll likely notice a widening of your window of tolerance and overall comfort.

THE WHEEL OF CONSENT

For many people, exploring sexuality also involves exploring physical touch. How we experience touch can vary widely, from pleasurable and sensual to uncomfortable and perhaps even traumatizing. Past negative experiences with unwanted touch can add barriers to partnered sex, often narrowing our window of tolerance. A useful model called the *Wheel of Consent* (see figure 9)—introduced by Dr. Betty Martin—can help us better understand the complexities of touch.[4] To start, she identifies four roles that we adopt when it comes to touch, split along two factors: (1) Who is doing the touching? and (2) Who is the touch for? The four identified roles are:

- *Serving*: I am doing the touching and the touch is for the other person.
- *Taking*: I am doing the touching and the touch is for me.
- *Allowing*: I am being touched and the touch is for the other person.
- *Accepting*: I am being touched and the touch is for me.

Let's look at some examples of these four roles of touch. When I rub my partner's back to help them feel less stressed, I am doing the touching and the touch is for them (*Serving*). When I run my hands through my partner's hair because I like the way it feels, I am doing the touching and the touch is for me (*Taking*). When my partner comes up and hugs me because they are having a tough day, they are touching and the touch is for them (*Allowing*). When my partner gives me a hug because I'm having a tough day, they are touching and the touch is for me (*Accepting*). Depending on the situation, it may not always be possible to touch for both people's benefit at the same time. Indeed, to optimize sexual functioning, we ideally look for a balance between touch for ourselves and touch for our partners, switching back and forth or taking turns during sexual activity.[5] A common pitfall is when we try to touch our partners intending to prioritize their needs, but actually end up touching them in the way that we (and maybe not they) like. We'll talk more about this dynamic next.

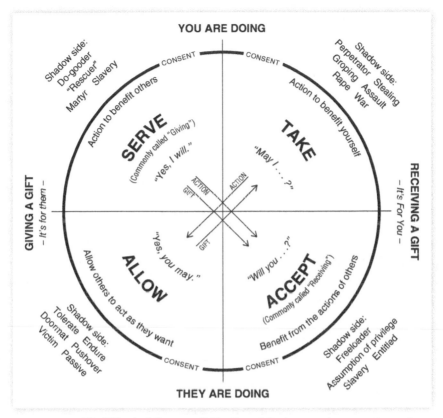

FIGURE 9. The Wheel of Consent.© Dr. Betty Martin. www.bettymartin.org.*

*Note: In any instance of touch, there are two factors: who is doing it and who it's for. Those two factors combine in four ways (quadrants). Each quadrant presents its own challenges, lessons, and joys.

The circle represents consent (your agreement). Inside the circle, there is a gift (touch) given and a gift (touch) received. Outside the circle (without consent), the same action becomes stealing, abusing, etc. (From Dr. Betty Martin, www.bettymartin.org/videos/.)

The Wheel of Consent also outlines a "shadow side" to touch. This involves touch done without consent, or touch that causes harm. It's perhaps obvious to most people that abusive touch and interpersonal violence (both "shadow" aspects of touch) will negatively impact sexual desire. More nuance, however, tends to be in the Allowing role, in which a partner—typically with lower libido—will consent to receiving touch. However, if they are not truly open to receiving this touch—recall our discussion about willingness in chapter 1—they may find themselves just tolerating or enduring it, rather than having a positive experience that cultivates responsive sexual desire.

Over time, touch that is tolerated or endured (as opposed to enjoyed and engaged with) becomes touch that's avoided. This is where many partners with a sexual desire discrepancy land. We have also seen that partners with lower desire, or a more responsive type of desire, often don't know what kind of touch they would like. They tend to be much more practiced in the Serving or Allowing roles and less practiced at Taking or Accepting. Remember, what's important is balance.

Who touch is *for* is a critical concept when it comes to libido. Let's look at an example of how this works. Jonah and Rebekah have had a sexual desire discrepancy for several years. They've learned that Jonah has a more spontaneous style of libido and Rebekah has a more responsive style of libido. Jonah really enjoys penetrative sex. Rebekah enjoys penetrative sex as well, from time to time, but isn't interested in having it quite as often as Jonah. She finds that she best experiences intimacy and pleasure through passionate kissing. When she explains this to Jonah, he often has a difficult time internalizing her feedback because he believes that kissing doesn't "count" as sex—for him, kissing isn't sexual but is rather more romantic. For Rebekah, however, kissing is very sexual. She gets aroused, feels connected, and experiences great pleasure. When Jonah touches Rebekah, it's most often in the way that he likes to touch—the touch is for him. However, though he may not realize it, he operates under the assumption that his touching is for both of them. What Jonah often ends up unintentionally doing is assuming that Rebekah's experiences of sex and preferences for touch are aligned with his. He is not really hearing Rebekah's expressed preference for how she most likes to be touched and be sexual—in this case, through kissing. If Jonah were to use the Wheel of Consent as a guide, he might notice that often, touch has been for him (Taking), and that shifting to touch more for Rebekah (Serving) would likely help her to better enjoy physical intimacy and build more responsive sexual desire. If Jonah is willing to try this, both he and Rebekah are likely to enjoy sexual activity more fully. Including more passionate kissing in their intimacy—even having entire encounters just focused on kissing—would very likely help Rebekah to feel more present in the sexual experience and build responsive sexual desire.

For many of the folks we see in sex therapy, the higher-libido partners tend to touch in a way that's more for them and—intentionally or not—impose their definition of sex onto their partners. Discussing the types of touch—sexual and nonsexual—that each partner prefers and enjoys is an important skill in all sexual partnerships, but it can especially be a game changer for managing sexual desire discrepancies or different styles (spontaneous versus responsive) of libido. To learn more about the Wheel of Consent, you can visit Dr. Martin's website (included in the Resources section at the back of this book) or grab a copy of her book, written with Robyn Dalzen, *The Art of Receiving and Giving: The Wheel of Consent*.

BRIDGING

Many people, especially folks who predominantly experience responsive desire, find it helpful to engage in a certain activity or ritual prior to sex. This strategy is referred to as *bridging*. Bridging can be done alone or with a partner. We find that bridges to sex often fall into three general categories:

RELAXING As the name implies, this type of bridge involves a relaxing activity prior to sex, to help de-stress and become more present. Relaxing bridges may include:

- Meditating
- Walking
- Breathing mindfully
- Bathing or showering
- Sipping tea
- Listening to music
- Massaging each other
- Cuddling together

EMOTIONALLY CONNECTING This type of bridge involves emotionally connecting with a partner prior to sexual activity. Emotional connection bridges may include:

- Playing a game together
- Eating a meal together
- Going for a walk together
- Talking
- Asking each other open-ended questions

AROUSING This type of bridge involves activities that are more explicitly sexual and provoke physical arousal or sexual interest. Arousing bridges may include:

- Listening to a sexy audio story
- Watching an erotic film
- Engaging in kink or BDSM
- Sexting
- Fantasizing
- Role-playing

Bridges can be especially helpful for those who have a predominantly responsive type of sexual desire, as the bridge can provide time to warm up and ease into more of a sexual encounter. For others, the bridges *are* sex and what they enjoy the most. Many folks benefit from experiencing an emotional connection with their partner(s) prior to sexual activity—for them, bridges may be paramount. Additionally, if you find yourself often stuck in a stress response cycle, engaging in a relaxing bridge prior to sexual connection can be transformative. We suggest exploring different types of bridges to see what works best for you and your partnership.

INTIMACY DATES

One of our most commonly recommended exercises for partners is an *intimacy date*, which is designed to foster physical connection. This is not, however, the same as scheduling sex the way our culture often defines it. Typically, when people schedule sex, they are trying to facilitate the Sexual Staircase script, focusing heavily on intercourse and orgasms. We don't often recommend scheduling sex in this way because, for many folks, it unintentionally creates anxiety or pressure rather than positive anticipation. The intimacy date is an important variation of scheduling sex that relies on the open-ended Wheel Model of partnered sex covered in chapter 2. What's different about the intimacy date is the flexible nature of the physical connection, without an assumed script. Intimacy dates are designed to move us away from Staircase thinking by broadening the scope of sexual activities. Please note that if scheduling penetrative sex or orgasm-focused sexual activity works for you, that's great! We recommend continuing whatever works best for your particular partnership(s).

How do we set up an intimacy date? To start, block off a day and time for the date. Most of the time, we recommend not planning any specifics around what will happen during the intimacy date, as this can contribute to pressure or negative anticipation. By keeping plans flexible and open-ended, we can avoid falling into the all-or-nothing approach to sex. We often recommend planning weekly intimacy dates because it's helpful for consistency. Think of it like making a reservation at a restaurant: you choose what day and time you want to go, but you don't order your meal in advance. Once you get to the restaurant, you order what you want depending on how you feel at the time. This approach supports a more open-ended and flexible mindset. It also helps us to practice sexual communication with partners and can be especially useful for people whose sexual desire is more responsive.

At the time of your intimacy date, you and your partner(s) can discuss what you'd each be interested in sexually exploring that particular day. We've included a menu of ideas for you to consider, and you can also revisit the Wheel Model from chapter 2 to brainstorm. Use your **sexual health journal** to start creating your own intimacy date menu.

INTIMACY DATE MENU
- Kissing on the mouth
- Kissing other body parts
- Full-body massage
- Foot massage
- Back massage
- Playing with or touching your partner's hair
- Having your hair touched or caressed
- Showering with a partner
- Laying your head on your partner's chest
- Your partner laying their head on your chest
- Spooning
- Cuddling
- Holding hands
- Penetrative intercourse
- Giving and/or receiving oral sex

- Manual stimulation
- Rubbing genitals together without penetration
- Rubbing your genitals against your partner's body
- Your partner rubbing their genitals against your body
- Using a sex toy together
- Touching, rubbing, biting, or caressing breasts or nipples
- Touching yourself while your partner watches
- Your partner touching themself while you watch
- Mutual masturbation
- Reading or listening to an erotic or romantic story together
- Watching an erotic or romantic video together
- Talking about an erotic or romantic fantasy with your partner
- Sexy talk while touching or caressing your partner
- Sending and/or receiving sexual texts or images
- Talking about sexual activities on the phone
- _____
- _____

You might notice that some of these items were also mentioned as bridging ideas in the previous section. Well spotted! Importantly, it's up to you and your partner(s) to decide if something is a bridge to another type of sexual activity or the main component of an intimacy date, depending on what works best for you in the moment. Sometimes an activity can be a bridge to sexual activity, whereas other times, it may be the activity of choice for that particular intimacy date.

Intimacy dates are a great way to break free of the Sexual Staircase. They offer a space to explore different sexual scripts and ways to experience pleasure and connection. For relationships where there's a desire discrepancy, it can be helpful for the partner whose desire is more responsive to choose from the list for the first few (or more) intimacy dates. This may help that partner better explore touch that's for them, embodying the roles of Taking and Accepting per the Wheel of Consent. This approach also helps to explore what feels pleasurable without pressure—a process that may, in turn, build sexual arousal. Another option is for each partner to choose a few items from the list and use the areas of overlap for further exploration. Either way, it's important for all partners involved to consent to the intimacy date activity.

SEXUAL COERCION

We want to be clear that sexual coercion—trying to convince, pressure, or threaten a partner to have sex—is never okay. If someone is not interested in a sexual experience, we should respect their no and not try to convince them otherwise. Feeling pressured into intimacy date activities (or any physical touch!) is not only unhelpful for addressing sexual desire discrepancies—it is also an unacceptable form of abuse in a relationship.

INITIATING SEX

Take out your **sexual health journal** and write down some reflections about times when you felt good initiating sex. What did that look and feel like? If you have never initiated sex before and typically rely on a partner to do so, why do you think that might be? Next, take some time to write about what it's been like for you to receive a partner's sexual initiation. What style of initiation typically feels good for you to receive? What style of initiation feels good for you to offer? Would you rather sexual initiation be more direct or subtle? Is consent verbal or behavioral?

Shelby and Damien initially came to sex therapy to work on a difference in their sexual desire, though we quickly discovered that libido levels weren't exactly the barrier. Both partners agreed that they were interested in being sexual more often, but Shelby was really struggling with the way that Damien initiated sex. Damien tended to reach out physically, touching Shelby's chest or butt. Rather than turning her on, Damien's actions caused Shelby to feel put on the spot, pressured, and at times even physically violated by what she identified as groping. Damien's method of initiation ended up doing the exact opposite of sparking a positive sexual encounter. Shelby and Damien were able to identify and discuss their different preferences in terms of sexual initiation. Damien preferred for Shelby to convey sexual interest physically, by playfully touching his body, which is why he had been approaching her in this manner. Shelby was happy to initiate in this way with Damien, but she much preferred to receive a verbal sexual initiation herself. She realized that a verbal approach allowed her to better ease into a sexual mindset, especially when she was feeling overly busy or distracted. Shelby also recognized that, physically, she needed time for her arousal to build. This was easier for her when sexual encounters started verbally and gradually led to physical touching.

It's important to remember that what works for you may not work for your partner(s), and vice versa. If you're waiting for a partner to initiate sex with romantic gestures and they initiate verbally with something like, "Hey, let's have sex," you likely need to discuss the effect that this has on you, as well as your preferences for sexual initiation. Have you and your partner(s) ever talked about preferred styles of initiation?

Let's look at some examples of verbal ways to initiate sex:

- "You feel like having sex?"
- "Wanna make out?"
- "Let's make love."
- "Come hop in the shower with me."
- "Let's sleep naked tonight."
- "I want to be with you."
- "Wanna go to bed early tonight?"

Now let's look at some examples of nonverbal ways to initiate sex:

- Caressing
- Kissing your partner's neck
- Massaging
- Hugging
- Spooning or cuddling
- Tickling
- Play fighting

It's important to talk with your partner(s) about these different verbal and nonverbal gestures, because sometimes they may be intended as ways to initiate sexual activity and other times they may just be affectionate gestures that aren't intended to lead to sex. How do you know the difference? We strongly encourage partners to discuss the how and why of sexual initiation so they can best distinguish the intent and impact of different phrases and acts. That way, a gesture like kissing doesn't *always* feel like an all-or-nothing expectation for something sexual. This can also help folks who tend to mind read their partner's intentions, a thought bias discussed in chapter 5.

RESPONDING TO SEXUAL INITIATION

Initiating sex with a partner can be very vulnerable. It means taking a risk to request what you want, knowing that this may not happen. Within a relationship, it's inevitable that partners will have different levels of sexual desire at different times. Sometimes you may want the same thing at the same time, and other times you might have competing or even opposite desires. It's important to be thoughtful in how you tell your partner(s) that you're not interested in sex. To better understand how to respond to sexual initiation from a partner, let's explore another important concept from the work of Drs. John and Julie Gottman (first discussed in chapter 3). These are known as bids for connection.

A *bid for connection* refers to any attempt or gesture to positively connect with a partner. A bid might be made for any number of reasons, including for comfort, affection, attention, affirmation, and humor.[6] We also make bids for sex and intimacy via sexual initiation. Bids for connection are often small and quick—for example, calling your partner over to look at something you found interesting on social media. We can easily miss these cues if we aren't careful. Over time, however, bids for connection (including sexual initiation) add up to form a major part of our relationship patterns. Let's look at bids for connection in action.

There are three ways we can respond to a bid for connection:[7]

1. *Turning away*: When we miss or ignore a bid. This is when we don't hear the bid, don't recognize the bid, or ignore the bid altogether. This may be intentional or unintentional. Repeatedly missing bids for connection creates problems in relationships, as bidding partners often start to feel ignored or invalidated.
2. *Turning against*: When we respond to a bid in a negative way. This is another hurtful way to respond to a bid for connection. It sends a message to the bidder that they are not important.
3. *Turning toward*: When we respond to a bid in a positive way. This doesn't mean that we need to agree to a bid or drop everything and fulfill every bid that comes our way from a partner. Rather, turning toward means that we acknowledge the bid—we communicate to our partner that they matter and that we hear and see their desire for connection.

Here are some different ways someone might *turn away* from a bid:

BID: "WOULD YOU LIKE TO GO UPSTAIRS AND FOOL AROUND?"

- *Disregarding response*: When a bid is either completely ignored or the focus of the response is on a small detail. For example, "I don't like that phrase, *fool around.*"
- *Preoccupied response*: When the respondent is engaged in another activity. For example, scrolling on their phone or watching TV, not really listening or paying attention.
- *Interrupting response*: When the respondent brings up an unrelated matter or offers a counterbid. For example, "Did you see Carmen's new car?"

Here are some different ways to *turn against* a bid:

BID: "DO YOU WANT TO HAVE SEX?"

- *Contemptuous response*: When the respondent makes hurtful or disrespectful comments that may express a sense of superiority. For example, "When's the last time you took a shower?"
- *Belligerent response*: When the respondent is combative and hostile, like they are looking for a fight. For example, "Since when are *you* interested in having sex?"
- *Contradictory response*: When the respondent seems to be looking for a debate. This is less hostile than a belligerent response but still blocks the bid for connection. For example, "You don't really want to have sex with me. You're just offering because you feel like you have to."
- *Domineering response*: When the respondent tries to control the other person. The goal is to get the bidder to withdraw the bid. For example, "I just had sex with you last week, it's never enough for you!"
- *Critical response*: When the respondent attacks the bidder's character. For example, "That's all you ever think about. You're a sex addict!"
- *Defensive response*: When the respondent acts like a victim or denies responsibility for their part. For example, "I'm in the middle of something, can't you see that I'm busy?"

Here are some different ways to *turn toward* a bid:

BID: "WANT TO MAKE LOVE?"

- "Yes, let's go!"
- "I'd love to."
- "I appreciate you asking. I'm not feeling up to it."
- "Definitely, but now isn't a great time. Rain check for later tonight?"
- "I can't today. Can we make some time to be together this weekend?"
- "I'm not feeling up for [insert sexual activity]; how about we cuddle in bed or [name another type of sexual activity]?"
- "I think you're very sexy. Can we plan a date for later?"
- "I'm feeling stressed right now and not open to sex. Is there another way that we can connect?"
- "I'm feeling a bit disconnected at the moment. Can we make some time for emotional connection first?"

Remember that turning toward doesn't mean that you are necessarily saying yes to your partner's exact request. It means that you're answering their bid with kindness, respect, and acknowledgment. Picking up on a partner's bids for connection often requires us to slow down and be a bit more observant. This is an important relationship skill and one that—like so many—gets easier with practice!

RESPECTING A NO TO SEXUAL INITIATION

When you're the person trying to initiate sex and your partner responds with a no, it can contribute to feelings of rejection or hurt, especially if this has become a pattern in the relationship over time. It's vulnerable to ask for what you want, and it can feel quite frustrating and invalidating when your partner repeatedly turns away from or turns against your sexual bids. It's really important to recognize, however, that *how* you respond to your partner's no significantly impacts the relationship dynamic moving forward . . . for better or worse.

A common issue we see in our sex therapy practices involves desire-discrepant partners who are stuck in a pattern of avoidance and/or stress around sexual initiation. It typically looks something like this: Partner A initiates sex and Partner B declines. Partner A feels rejected and maybe makes a snarky comment or becomes frustrated and angry. Perhaps Partner A doesn't talk to Partner B for a while (see the discussion about stonewalling in chapter 3). One of two things then tends to occur. The first is that Partner B will begin to avoid most—if not all—physical contact with Partner A, believing that something as simple as a hug will sexually arouse Partner A and lead to another tense exchange. This is commonly rooted in the all-or-nothing Sexual Staircase thinking that we've previously discussed. Partners stuck in this pattern of avoidance tend to feel increasingly disconnected—physically and emotionally—as time goes on, often leading to resentment and relational distress. In the second common scenario, Partner B will say yes to all of Partner A's sexual advances and go through with sexual activity for fear that rejection will upset Partner A. Recall from our discussion of the Wheel of Consent that this reflects the "shadow" sides of Serving and Allowing—tolerating or enduring touch. This is another way to avoid tension and—though it looks very different—it typically results in the same resentment and relational distress because Partner B feels pressured, even coerced, into sexual activity.

If your response to a partner declining sex is to get mad, turn away and pout, or try to persuade them to be sexual despite their no, this leaves your partner feeling like they can't say no with emotional safety. Responses like these usually lead to less sexual activity, not more. *A person can never truly say yes to sex if their no is not respected.* Let's look at some examples of what *not* to say when your partner declines your sexual initiation:

- "If you loved me, you'd have sex with me."
- "You always say no. I'm so tired of it."
- "Why can't we just do it this one time?"
- "But I did [insert thing] for you. You should do this for me."
- "Something's wrong with you. You never want to have sex."
- "You should see a doctor. Your libido is messed up."

These are examples of coercive statements that are never okay. If you realize that you or your partner have used coercive statements like these in the past, now is a great time to correct and repair by learning new skills. Here are some examples of helpful things to say when your partner declines your sexual initiation:

- "That's okay. Maybe we can make some time for sex another day this week."
- "No problem. Would you be up for doing something else to connect? Like cuddling or spooning?"
- "I miss being intimate with you in that way. Let me know when you're up for it."
- "Thanks for being honest with me."
- "I'd like some physical connection with you. Would you be up for doing something else?"

Remember that respectfully negotiating wants and needs is part of being in a relationship and often takes some practice. If your desire for more physical connection or sexual intimacy is not being met, this is something to discuss thoughtfully—with important consideration given to the timing of these conversations. We don't want to surprise a partner with a discussion that may require emotional preparation. Here's an example of what to say when you want to sit down and discuss this issue further: "I want to talk more about our sex life and find some ways to make sure we're both feeling satisfied. When's a good time to talk?" Then, when you sit down to have this conversation, focus on listening to your partner first. Find out what barriers to yes there may be for them and ask what they need in order to better negotiate and navigate this issue with you. (Hot tip: This is a great place to revisit the suggestions from the section on sharing sexual interests and desires, covered earlier in this chapter.) Consider asking if they have preferences for how you initiate sex or if there's something they need from you—for example, more emotional connection or more equity with the mental load. You also might ask if they would be willing to read this book or see a sex therapist with you to help work on this common relationship challenge.

ADDRESSING THE PURSUE-WITHDRAW PATTERN

Recall the pursue-withdraw pattern from chapter 3. Our roles as a pursuer or withdrawer can be determined in part by our histories, by gender roles or expectations, and by each relationship's particular dynamics. For example, Partner A could be more of a pursuer in a relationship with Partner B, but more of a withdrawer in their relationship with Partner C.

The pursue-withdraw pattern also can show up in the nonsexual parts of our relationships, and our roles are not necessarily consistent across these different contexts. For example, Partner A could be assuming a pursuer role in the nonsexual part of their relationship, but a withdrawer role in their sexual relationship. Remember that changing how we engage with our partners is critical for getting out of this cycle. Let's return to the case of Rosario and Sam from chapter 3 and look at the changes they made to get out of their ineffective pursue-withdraw cycle, creating a more positive, effective dynamic.

Ineffective Cycle

ROSARIO: Did you take your erection pills today?

SAM: No, I haven't had a chance.

ROSARIO: Why not? You knew I was coming over. What are you waiting for? Those pills take time to kick in and you always fall asleep so early. When exactly were you planning to take them?

SAM: I don't know.

ROSARIO: You should have taken them before I got here. I don't understand what the problem is. It's like you don't care about me or if we ever have sex again!

SAM: [eyes looking down, head turned away] I don't know what you want me to say.

ROSARIO: Just forget it. I don't know why I even bother coming over.

Effective Cycle

ROSARIO: I've been looking forward to being with you all day. Did you happen to take your erection pills?

SAM: No, I haven't had a chance.

ROSARIO: Oh. I was hoping you had because I wanted to have sex. It helps me feel loved and desired. What are your thoughts on taking a pill now so that we can have sex later?

SAM: I'm not feeling it today and I worry about disappointing you and getting into a fight. I don't want that, because I really love you and don't want you to feel hurt.

ROSARIO: I can understand that. I don't wanna fight either. Sometimes I just need to know that you want me or that you really do care.

SAM: Of course I care. I want you to know that. I'm still not sure about sex though. I just don't think I can get hard today since I'm pretty tired from work. Would you be up for something else . . . maybe taking a shower together?

ROSARIO: Yes, definitely. Maybe we could make out a little too, if there's no expectation for anything else?

SAM: Yeah. That sounds nice.

These two interactions between Rosario and Sam are vastly different. In the first example, Rosario uses a harsh start-up and criticism to express frustration about Sam not taking his erection medication. He immediately shuts down and responds only with brief sentences and emotional disengagement. Sam doesn't provide any reassurance or respond to Rosario's longing for connection. In the second example, Rosario uses a softer approach to state her hopes and expectations. Sam is better able to hear her desire when it's not couched in criticism. He's also more responsive and engaged in the second dialogue, sharing in a vulnerable way, and affirming his love for Rosario apart from sex. Together, they're able to identify a way to be sexual that can meet both of their needs in the moment.

Sam's desire is affected by the shame he feels around his physical sexual function (in this case, erections), and he has developed a pattern of sexual avoidance out of fear of disappointing his partner or getting into an argument. Because of this dynamic, as well as the pressure he feels from his partner, his libido suffers. Sam becomes less interested in sex with Rosario and withdraws at her pursuit of sexual connection. His disinterest is not because he doesn't love Rosario, however, and when he is able to (a) communicate that to her, (b) express vulnerable feelings about his sexual function, and (c) suggest other types of intimacy, she feels more secure and they become more connected as a couple. Rosario's hurt feelings when Sam doesn't respond to her sexual initiation are understandable and valid. Sam's struggles with erections and his feelings of pressure around sex are also understandable and valid. Neither perspective is wrong, and neither person is the problem—rather, Rosario and Sam's relational dynamic is the point of concern (and intervention). When partners can express their emotions and underlying needs more vulnerably, they are better able to avoid an ineffective pursue-withdraw cycle.

PRACTICE SESSIONS

One way that partners can work on exploring sexual interests and giving each other feedback is through intentional practice sessions: times where you're specifically demonstrating what you like for the purpose of learning and exploration. For example, a practice session focused on kissing could involve taking turns showing each other how you each like to be kissed. Or a practice session might involve trying out different sexual positions with clothing on, at a time when you aren't having sex, to help ease into something new. There are lots of ways to use practice sessions, and they can help shift our mindsets into exploring new experiences without pressure. Here are a few additional ideas for practice sessions:

- Genital touch for the purpose of exploring what feels good, without the goal of orgasm
- Using a new toy together to see what it feels like
- Trying out different oral sex techniques without the goal of orgasm
- Exploring different types of physical sensation together, such as using a feather, an ice cube, a flogger, or massage oil for the purpose of discovering what feels good
- Slowing down penetration to experience what it's like with gentle movement, no movement, and/or faster movement, without the goal of orgasm

The idea with practice sessions is to create an environment for sexual learning, play, and exploration without pressure or goal-oriented outcomes. It's another way of practicing the Wheel Model and taking a step away from Staircase thinking. This is also a great time to practice giving and receiving verbal and physical feedback. Sharing sexual likes and dislikes can be very vulnerable, making practice sessions a unique opportunity to learn from and connect with one another. Remember to treat each other with tenderness.

THE SEXUAL STATE OF THE UNION

Some people enjoy structure, so having a more formal meeting or check-in with your partner(s) to discuss your sexual relationship can be helpful. We recommend planning a specific day and time to check in and making this a regular practice in your relationship. A weekly meeting is ideal to create consistency, though you may need to start with monthly or biweekly. This check-in is best done separately from the previously discussed intimacy date, as these are two distinct practices.

The format of the Sexual State of the Union is inspired by the Gottman Institute's general relationship State of the Union meeting.[8] These meetings provide a dedicated time and place to check in on the relationship or, for our purposes, on sexual health. At the beginning of each Sexual State of the Union, partners start by identifying and sharing what's been going well. Try to focus on a few things that are positive or areas of growth. Here are some examples:

- "We've been communicating more about sex."
- "We've been exploring different ways to experience pleasure together."
- "I really enjoyed our intimacy date this week."
- "We've done a great job practicing sensate focus exercises."*

After acknowledging what's been going well, take turns discussing how you each feel about your sexual relationship, what goals that you would like to work toward, and what specifically you would each like to work on over the next week (or between meetings). End your meeting by asking how you can support the other person in their goals. Here are some examples—by no means an exhaustive list—of topics that might be discussed during a Sexual State of the Union meeting:

- Scheduling an intimacy date for the week
- Scheduling sensate focus sessions for the week
- Asking each other open-ended questions about sexual interests, likes, and dislikes
- Discussing progress toward specific goals you've set, such as reading a book about sexual health, dilator therapy (for people working with a pelvic floor physical therapist), body mapping, or exploring a sexual aid

---

*Sensate focus exercises are discussed in depth in chapter 7.

To review, the general format for the Sexual State of the Union is to:

1. Discuss what's going well sexually, or areas where there's been growth.
2. Discuss sexual health goals for the next week (or between meetings).
3. Ask and discuss how you can help support each other's sexual health goals.

In discussing your goals, it's incredibly useful to state your positive needs (what you do need), rather than negative needs (what you don't need).[9] This is an important communication and relationship health strategy, since we tend to feel emotionally reactive when faced with others' negative needs. As a result, the conversation starts from a defensive and often passive-aggressive position, rather than an open and genuinely curious place. When we share positive needs, on the other hand, our partners are more likely to hear them and effectively engage in discussion. Let's take a look at how some negative needs can be reframed into positive needs:

- *Negative need*: I don't like when you move straight to touching my [insert body part]. *Positive need*: I like my [insert body part] to be stimulated after we've had some time to warm up with other types of touch.
- *Negative need*: I don't like the way you give blow jobs. *Positive need*: I think what would feel good is if we tried [insert positive need] during oral sex.
- *Negative need*: I hate kissing for long periods of time. I completely lose my arousal! *Positive need*: I like kissing but when it lingers, I can get distracted and lose arousal. Maybe we can try [insert positive need]?

As you can see from these examples, part of learning how to restate needs involves knowing what our positive needs actually are. This initial identification can be a challenge for folks who have never been encouraged to think about what they want or enjoy sexually, or for those who know what they like and want but have been discouraged (perhaps culturally) from actually expressing these things. When we either (a) don't know our positive needs or (b) feel bad sharing them, it becomes easy to only communicate negatives—which is what we don't want. Identifying and communicating what you *do* want—a positive need—is much more effective. At the end of the day, you're way more likely to get what you want, need, and like if you're explicitly able to describe and ask for it. In many cases, recognizing what you *don't* like or want can help you identify what it is that you *do* like or want. Negative needs can inform us of our positive needs, which is then what we want to practice communicating.

Take a moment with your **sexual health journal** to consider the following: Do you have a sense of your sexual likes, wants, and needs? If not, how might you do some exploration? If you know your sexual likes, wants, and needs but struggle to vocalize them, what do you think the barriers are to more open communication?

chapter 7

SENSATE FOCUS

Let's revisit the Sexual Staircase from chapter 2 and how it creates a goal-oriented, all-or-nothing approach to sex. Recall that the Staircase model emphasizes penetrative intercourse and downplays the role of other, perhaps more pleasurable, sexual activities. We know that when sex is goal-oriented, without a focus on pleasure and the present moment, anticipatory pressure and anxiety are often quick to follow. This can be due to performance anxiety around what will or won't happen during sex (e.g., "Will I have an orgasm?" or, "Can I keep my erection?"). If you'll recall the sexual pain cycle, those who have previously had painful sex may experience anticipatory anxiety as their nervous system responds in an attempt to protect them from that pain.

In this chapter, we introduce a time- and research-tested sex therapy exercise known as *sensate focus*. Sensate (think "sensation") focus is, at its foundation, a form of mindfulness practice designed to improve sexual functioning and satisfaction by moving us away from goal-oriented, Sexual Staircase–style approaches. These exercises are based on touch sensation and grouped into progressive phases. The famous American sex researchers Masters and Johnson first developed sensate focus exercises in the 1960s and '70s. Over time, other experts have made modifications and updates to the exercises as we've learned more about sexual health. All told, this treatment approach has been a fifty-year sex therapy staple for a reason: it works! Many sexual health books give a nod to sensate focus exercises; however, we find that few offer enough detail to be helpful to readers. For that reason, we want to provide an in-depth set of instructions for each step of sensate focus. We'll also end the chapter with frequently asked questions about these important partnered exercises.

SENSATE FOCUS MODIFICATIONS

Sensate focus exercises have been around for many years. Historically, instructions for these exercises have been focused on cisgender heterosexual couples, but there is no reason sensate focus can't be used by all sexual partners. The instructions included here are based on the 2017 book *Sensate Focus in Sex Therapy: The Illustrated Manual* by Dr. Constance Avery-Clark and Linda Weiner. We have been privileged to learn directly from these authors, who were themselves students of Masters and Johnson. Their book is fabulous, and we both highly recommend it, though we should note that it's written as a guide for therapists rather than for the general public. The inclusive and accessible protocol presented in this chapter has also been modified and adapted from Dr. Jordan Rullo at Sexual Health Solutions (sexualhealthsolutions.com).

Sensate focus is a series of structured exercises based on the idea that we have limited control over certain aspects of the sexual response cycle. Things like becoming lubricated, genital swelling, and erections are part of the autonomic nervous system, like breathing. (If you need a refresher on the nervous system, refer back to chapter 4.) We can't force the process of sexual arousal. When we focus too much on trying to control our physical sexual responses, we often experience difficulties. That's because if we get too focused on controlling our bodies, it often triggers a stress response, not the sexual response.

As you'll recall from chapter 5, mindfulness refers to being more present in the moment with a curious, nonjudgmental attitude. The most effective way to stay present is to focus on our physical sensations, including touch, taste, sound, sight, and smell. Many mindfulness exercises focus on the physical sensations of breathing. Sensate focus exercises invite us to pay particular attention to touch sensations, as that's often the primary sense being engaged during sexual activity. Pleasure, arousal, and connection all exist in the present moment. If we aren't paying attention, we can miss these experiences. If we think about the past or the future, even just to the next moment, we may trigger a stress response, potentially losing our sexual arousal. This is why practicing mindfulness during sex and intimacy can be enormously helpful.

The following exercises are likely different from anything you've tried before. These recommendations might feel strange at first, but with consistent practice, you'll likely see benefits over time. What's nice about sensate focus exercises is that rather than directing you on what *not* to focus on or think about, we provide you with direction about what *to* focus on.

Here are some of the potential benefits of practicing sensate focus exercises:

- Challenging Sexual Staircase–style thinking
- Reducing pressure and anxiety about sexual activity
- Disrupting the sexual pain cycle
- Easing back into partnered touch if it's been a while
- Experiencing touch with mindfulness rather than distraction, anxiety, or fear
- Learning to redirect your attention away from judgmental thoughts about body image
- Gently stretching our window of tolerance around touch

Again, the goal of these exercises is to intentionally focus on sensation, without judgment, during touch with another person. Commonly, during sexual activity, people tend to (a) overfocus on their own thoughts, (b) overfocus on their partner, or (c) disconnect from their own physical sensations. For example, we might think to ourselves, "Am I doing this right?" or "Is my partner close to orgasm?" or "Is this going well?" This type of focus can quickly lead to performance anxiety or a stress response. Sensate focus exercises exist to help address the common *lack* of focus on our individual physical sensations. Optimal sexual experiences involve an ebb and flow of focus on our partner(s) and our own present-moment physical sensations.

Sensate focus is not a sprint—it's a marathon. The amount of time that partners spend on these exercises varies, and we like to remind folks that there is no prize for finishing first. In general, we recommend spending *at least* two to three sessions per phase (more on those in a minute) before moving forward. Treating sensate focus phases like a checklist and moving too quickly leads us right back into goal-oriented thinking and probably isn't much different from what you've already experienced. We also recommend that you practice sensate focus exercises *at least* once per week. If your lifestyle and circumstances allow, we encourage practicing two to three times per week for the best consistency. Often, when starting out, sessions will only last five to ten minutes: you want sufficient time to practice refocusing from distraction, but not so much time that you become bored or overwhelmed. As you become more practiced and comfortable, you can certainly extend the length of each session. Importantly, many instructions for sensate focus direct people to spend anywhere from twenty minutes to an hour on each session. Based on decades of psychological research—which show that efforts to change behavior are much more reliable when approached in smaller, consistent increments—we've modified the instructions we provide to our clients to recommend shorter sessions.

You can think of sensate focus exercises as similar to strengthening a muscle. If you want a stronger bicep, you start with lighter weights and consistent curls, and you gradually build up over time. You wouldn't go to the gym once, do some curls, and expect to see immediate, visible results! Sensate focus operates in the same way: through short, consistent practice sessions over time.

Note that we are very intentional with the language that we use throughout this chapter. We carefully avoid using terms like *giver* and *receiver* of touch, as those labels often create a mindset that is counter to the goal of these exercises. If you are labeled a *giver*, then you likely have expectations and associations attached to that term. If you are labeled the *receiver*, you may think that you are expected to respond to touch in a certain way—perhaps with pleasure or arousal. *Toucher* and *person being touched* are more accurate and aligned with the spirit of sensate focus. Lastly, before we get to the instructions, we also want to clarify what sensate focus is *not*:

- This is *not* foreplay.
- This is *not* about giving and receiving pleasure.
- This is *not* about creating sexual arousal.
- This is *not* a massage exercise.
- This is *not* a romantic exercise.
- This is *not* about focusing on your partner. The focus is on self.

Sensate focus exercises provide a neutral environment. That means if there's arousal, that's fine. If there isn't, that's equally fine. If there's pleasure from the touch, that's fine. If it's not pleasurable, that's equally fine. This is how we create an environment with no pressure or expectations. When the environment is neutral and we operate from a nonjudgmental place of curiosity, we can begin to shift our experience with partners.

Phew, okay! We know that's a lot of background info, but these are important exercises. Next, we'll cover general instructions for sensate focus, followed by specific instructions for when you are the person touching or being touched. This will be followed by a detailed explanation of each phase. We strongly recommend that partners thoroughly read *all three sections* of the general instructions before getting started. When it comes to reading about the sensate focus phases, however, you may choose to review them one at a time or read through them all in advance—your call!

GENERAL INSTRUCTIONS FOR SENSATE FOCUS

- Try to make sessions a priority two to three times per week. We find that scheduling sensate focus sessions—literally adding them to your calendar—works best. This is the way to form a new habit, as practicing less than once per week may result in slow or no progress.
- You don't need to be in the mood for these exercises—you just need to commit to practicing them with frequency. Again, it's like physical exercise: you don't have to feel excited about working out to move your body!
- Sensate focus exercises should be done when sober. Alcohol or recreational drugs don't allow you to be fully present.
- Arrange for complete privacy during the sessions, free from distractions. (We know this can be hard to do, especially if you have kids and/or pets in the home. Do the best that you can.) If you have cell phones, take a moment to turn them on silent or do not disturb mode.
- Remove clothes to whatever extent is comfortable and possible. Nudity is preferred, but if you're not ready for that, then some exposed skin like forearms and legs is a great place to start. You can work your way up to nudity with practice and time.

- Make sure the room temperature is comfortable. If you need a space heater or a fan, try to have those ready for the exercise in advance.
- Have some lighting in the room, but nothing too bright or distracting. That way, if you'd like to have your eyes open, you can see what you're doing.
- Though it may feel counterintuitive, we don't recommend playing music. This is because we are aiming to exclusively focus on the physical sensation of touch.
- Try not to focus on the clock or use a timer. The idea is to allow time to fade into the background by focusing on touch sensations, not on how long the session has lasted. If there is a clock nearby, consider turning it away so you aren't distracted by the display.
- You can keep your eyes open or closed—whichever helps you best focus on touch sensations and is most comfortable for you.
- Sensate focus exercises are nonverbal. If you're talking or listening, then you aren't focusing on sensations! (The exception here is if you experience a stress response and need to verbally communicate. See the FAQs at the end of this chapter for more information.)
- Touch sensations are made up of three components: *temperature*, *pressure*, and *texture* (referred to as TPT). You'll be focusing on TPT during these exercises.
- These exercises often feel sexual for people due to intimate touching with a partner. However, sensate focus is not meant to be "foreplay" and should not lead to sexual activity.
- If one or both partners have a penis and an erection occurs, that's fine—just refocus on TPT. Modification option: If early ejaculation has been a concern for a partner, touch another area of the body until this arousal diminishes. We're trying not to reinforce a focus on arousal or pleasure for these particular exercises.
- If orgasm happens unintentionally during these exercises, it's important to continue with the session, because we don't want to reinforce the goal-oriented mindset.
- Spend as many sessions as you want in each phase of the exercises. Often, the more practice you get with each phase, the more beneficial it will be.

- Only move to the next phase when *all* partners agree. If anyone is feeling anxious about moving forward, spend more time at the current phase, break the next phase into smaller steps, or consult with a sex therapist.

GENERAL INSTRUCTIONS FOR THE TOUCHER

- Decide together who will be the first toucher. We recommend that the person who feels least comfortable starts in this role.
- The toucher uses only hands and fingers for touching.
- Remember that the purpose of the touch is to explore physical sensation. You aren't touching to please or arouse your partner. (If those things happen, that's fine—just remember that it's a by-product of the exercise rather than a goal.)
- Pay attention to the physical sensations of *temperature*, *pressure*, and *texture* (TPT). Here are some things to consider with each sensation:

TEMPERATURE
- What do I notice about temperature? Is my partner's skin hot, cold, somewhere in between? How would I describe it?
- Does the temperature change as I move my hand across my partner's skin?

PRESSURE
- What's it like when I use firm touch?
- What's it like when I use a lighter touch?
- What does it feel like to alter pressure as I move my hands?

TEXTURE
- What do I notice about texture? For example, some areas of the body may have hair, stubble, calluses, bumps, scars, etc.
- Where on my partner's body is the skin smooth? How would I describe it?
- Where on my partner's body is the skin rough? How would I describe it?

- When distracting thoughts drift in (and they will!), gently and nonjudgmentally refocus your awareness to the touch sensations of TPT. You'll find yourself continually refocusing on TPT in this way—this is the practice of mindfulness (returning to our present-moment physical sensations).
- Sexual response is not a goal here. It may happen, and it may not. Either is fine.
- Trust that your partner will prevent you from touching them in a way that's physically or psychologically uncomfortable. They will move your hand to another area of their body if something is uncomfortable to them.
- Touch long enough to get practice refocusing on sensations, but not so long that you become bored or tired.
- When you're ready to switch roles with your partner, say aloud: "Switch," or, if you've both practiced each role, move on to the debriefing portion of the exercise. Otherwise, remember that the touching portion of sensate focus is nonverbal.

GENERAL INSTRUCTIONS
FOR THE PERSON BEING TOUCHED

- While your partner is touching you, you'll also be focusing on *temperature, pressure,* and *texture* (TPT).

TEMPERATURE
- What do I notice about temperature? Are my partner's hands hot, cold, somewhere in between? How would I describe it?
- Does the temperature change as they move their hands across my skin?

PRESSURE
- What's it like when my partner uses firm touch?
- What's it like when my partner uses a lighter touch?
- What does it feel like when my partner alters pressure as they move their hands?

TEXTURE
- What do I notice about texture? For example, some areas of the body may have hair, stubble, calluses, bumps, scars, etc.
- Are my partner's hands smooth or rough? How would I describe their texture?

- Rather than thinking about what your partner may be experiencing, focus on yourself and physical sensations you are experiencing.
- When distracting thoughts arise (and they will!), gently and non-judgmentally refocus on the touch sensations of TPT.
- Remember, there is no goal for sexual response—either it will happen or it won't. Arousal is neither the focus nor the goal of these exercises.
- Sensate focus is nonverbal. If your partner is touching you in a way that makes you physically or psychologically uncomfortable (e.g., makes you ticklish, provokes a stress response), gently move their hand to another part of your body that feels more comfortable. If moving your partner's hand feels overwhelming or there are concerns about hurting their feelings, we recommend that both partners intentionally practice moving each other's hands a few times per session. This can be especially helpful during early phases of sensate focus and may help to neutralize this type of feedback. If you or your partner consistently experience a stress response during sensate focus, please see the FAQ at the end of this chapter for additional guidance.

GENERAL DEBRIEFING QUESTIONS

Once each person has been in the role of touching and being touched, move on to the debriefing portion of the sensate focus session. This is your chance to get out all the talking you didn't do while touching! Lie or sit together and reflect on the following questions:

1. Were you able to focus on yourself?
2. Were you able to focus on physical sensations?
3. How often did you notice distractions? Did they tend to be the same or different?

4. Were you able to bring yourself back from the distractions and refocus on TPT?
5. Did you need to move your partner's hand due to discomfort? If so, what was the discomfort?
6. Is there anything else that you'd like to share about the experience? Remember to keep a nonjudgmental and curious mindset, both with respect to your partner and yourself. Provide a description of your experience, rather than an evaluation. For example, an evaluative observation is, "I'm terrible at focusing," whereas a descriptive observation is, "I had to redirect my attention every few moments."

Now that we've reviewed all the guidelines (we know there are a lot of them!), here are the instructions for each phase. Remember to take your time going through the phases. It's not a race; the benefits are in the process.

PHASE 1: Chest and genitals are off-limits

- The person being touched lies down, either face up or face down, whichever is more comfortable and accessible. The toucher either stands or sits next to them. These exercises are often done on a bed, if that's possible. Otherwise, another comfortable surface is fine.
- At this stage, avoid touching the obvious erogenous zones: chest, nipples, vulva, clitoris, penis, or testicles.
- The toucher will touch their partner all over their body (with exception of chest and genitals). Modification option: If there are body parts that are triggering or uncomfortable, discuss this ahead of time and consider these areas to also be currently off-limits.
- A reminder to focus your attention on the sensations of *temperature, pressure,* and *texture* (TPT).

An important note: At the beginning, it's common for sensate focus to feel somewhat anxiety provoking and for partners to feel nervous or awkward. However, if phase 1 (or really any other phase) feels overwhelming or even terrifying, we strongly recommend meeting either with a sex therapist, to help support you through these phases, or with a somatic- or trauma-focused therapist, who can help add some tools. Please do not force yourself through a stress response in order to complete sensate focus exercises, as this can either reinforce a negative experience or even worsen the reaction. Remember, "What fires together, wires together," and we are trying to change the pattern!

PHASE 2: Chest and genitals are on-limits

- Start with phase 1 to warm up and ease into phase 2.
- For this new phase, you will follow the same instructions as phase 1, except now you can touch the chest and genitals. Though these typical erogenous zones are now included, remember they are not the sole focus. Try to touch the full body (if that's comfortable or agreed upon ahead of time). Modification option: If full body touch is too difficult, you can break up different body parts and slowly introduce new areas.
- No insertion of anything into the vagina or anus.

PHASE 3: Mutual touching with chest and genitals off-limits

- For this phase you'll be facing each other, either sitting up or lying down together. You can prop yourselves up with pillows and use one or two hands to do the touching, depending on what's comfortable and accessible for you.
- Follow the same instructions as phase 1—chest and genitals are off-limits, with one important change: now you'll be mutually touching (at the same time).
- There is no toucher or person being touched—both partners touch simultaneously.
- You won't be able to focus on both your touch and your partner's touch at the same time (that's a lot for the brain to juggle!). As long as you're focusing and refocusing on your TPT sensations, you're on the right track.
- Either partner can say "stop" when feeling ready to conclude and move on to the debriefing portion of the session.

PHASE 4: Mutual touching with chest and genitals on-limits

- Start with phase 3 to warm up and ease into phase 4.
- For this new phase you will follow the same instructions as phase 3, except now you can touch each other's chests and genitals. Though

these typical erogenous zones are now included, remember they are not the sole focus. Try to touch the full body. Modification option: If full body touch is too difficult, you can start with certain body parts and slowly introduce new areas.
- No insertion of anything into the vagina or anus.

PHASE 5: Genital exploration

- For phase 5, we'll return to taking turns touching and being touched. Get into the same position as phase 2, or another position that is comfortable to explore your partner's genitals.
- The toucher explores their partner's genitals nonjudgmentally and with curiosity, reflecting *silently* on what they see and feel (e.g., colors, textures, temperature). Work to avoid value judgments (e.g., good, bad).
- The person being touched is also focusing on temperature, pressure, and texture (TPT). There may be worry or anticipation about what the toucher is seeing and experiencing, and it's important to work on refocusing these thoughts and emotions (aka mental sensations) back to TPT. It's especially common in this phase to repeatedly require refocusing away from self-judgmental thoughts and emotions.
- What's interesting about this phase is that it gives the toucher an opportunity to really look at their partner's genitals without a goal or pressure. Most people have never experienced this before.
- For the person being touched, this phase provides an important opportunity to notice the reactions (mental and physical) that may come up when their genitals are the focus of nonjudgmental attention.
- After practicing this phase a few times, some people report feeling more comfortable with genital touch. If that happens, great. If that doesn't happen, that's also okay. The goal here is noticing and observing the sensations and experience with curiosity and without judgment.

PHASE 6: "Move the hand"

- In past phases, you were instructed to move your partner's hand *away* to a more comfortable area of the body if their touch felt uncomfortable. In this phase, we practice moving the hand *toward* an area of interest.

- What does an "area of interest" mean? This is a place on your body that you're especially interested in allowing your partner to further explore. Just remember that we are not intentionally seeking out or providing pleasure, but rather exploring nonjudgmentally and with curiosity.
- Following the phase 2 instructions and taking turns touching, you'll now incorporate moving the hand *toward*. The person being touched takes their partner's hand, much like moving a computer mouse, and moves it to an area of interest.
- Once you've guided your partner's hand, remove your hand and let your partner explore on their own. Remember, your partner is touching for themselves, not for you. You are merely guiding them to an area of interest.
- Try moving your partner's hand a few times during the exercise before switching roles.

PHASE 7: Genital-to-genital touching

- Get into any comfortable position where you and your partner's genitals can be in contact. For example, one person may lie at the edge of a bed with their partner standing, allowing genitals to touch. Alternatively, you may lie next to each other and have your legs intertwined. Or you might have one partner straddling the other. There will be genital-to-genital contact, but no penetration or insertion of any kind.
- Start with phase 4 (mutual touching) to warm up and ease into phase 7.
- While genitals are touching, use your hands to touch other parts of the body within reach, while focusing on TPT. Modification option: If you wish, you can include some light genital-to-genital movement (remember, this is external only) while continuing to explore TPT with your hands.
- If one or both partners have a penis and an erection occurs, that's fine—just refocus on TPT. Modification option: If early ejaculation is a concern, stop touching genitals and return to phase 4 mutual touching. Once the arousal subsides, you can get back to genital-to-genital touch.

- Alternate your positions a few times between phase 7 genital-to-genital touch and phase 4 mutual touching. In other words, genitals will not be touching the entire time.
- End the session with phase 4 mutual touching.

If penetration is not part of sexual activity for you and your partner—and you don't want it to be—sensate focus exercises will likely end for you at phase 7. If penetration is important to sexual activity for you and/or your partner(s), continue on to phases 8 and 9. If penetration is important to you but you experience pain with it, stop here, at the end of phase 7. We strongly encourage you to consult with a sexual medicine provider about treatment for sexual pain before moving on (see chapter 9 for additional guidance).

PHASE 8: Genital-to-genital touching, with penetration, no movement

- This phase is exactly like phase 7, except that it involves penetration. Penetration may involve use of fingers, a toy, or a penis. Depending on your sexual interests, one or all partners may wish to explore penetration during this phase.
- If penetration requires an erection for you or your partner and it's not happening right this moment, refocus on mutual touching (phase 4) and genital-to-genital touching (phase 7). If an erection develops, you can choose to attempt penetration. If there is a loss of erection, return to mutual touching. Remember that the important piece here is focusing on your experiences of TPT sensations, *not* arousal or erection.
- The partner who is being penetrated will stay still during insertion of the finger, toy, or penis. It remains important for both partners to focus on TPT sensations.
- Don't forget to use plenty of lubricant for penetration (see the guide in chapter 4 for recommendations on lubricants).
- Once there's penetration, it's important that there be no thrusting or movement, so as to allow for specific focus on physical sensations. This is known as *containment*, and the inserted finger, toy, or penis is only to be contained in this phase.

- The person being penetrated can use their pelvic floor muscles to tense or relax, noticing TPT during this process.
- When the person being penetrated is ready, they will say, "Switch." At that point, gently remove the finger, toy, or penis. If the other partner also wishes to explore penetration, you can now switch roles. Otherwise, return to phase 4 mutual touching.
- Practice penetration a few times during this phase, alternating between this and phase 4 mutual touching. Modification option: If there is pain with penetration, remove the finger, toy, or penis and return to phase 4 mutual touching. It's important not to push through pain—rather, this is a sign to consult further with a medical provider, sex therapist, or pelvic floor physical therapist (see chapter 9).
- If an orgasm happens, that's okay—just return to phase 4 mutual touching and end there.
- End the session with phase 4 mutual touching.

PHASE 9: Genital-to-genital touching, with penetration and movement

- This phase is exactly like phase 8, except there is now penetration with gentle movement.
- During penetration (don't forget to use lube!), focus only on TPT, not on getting you or your partner aroused.
- Once there is penetration, you can add slow, gentle movement or thrusting. Remember to focus on TPT.
- The partner who is being penetrated can use pelvic floor muscles to tense or relax, noticing TPT during this process.
- Practice penetration with movement a few times, alternating between this and phase 4 mutual touching. Modification option: If there is pain with penetration, remove the finger, toy, or penis and return to phase 4 mutual touching. It's important not to push through pain—rather, this is a sign to consult further with a medical provider, sex therapist, or pelvic floor physical therapist (see chapter 9).
- When the person being penetrated is ready, they will say, "Switch." At that point, gently remove the finger, toy, or penis. If the other partner also wishes to explore penetration, you can now switch roles. Otherwise, return to phase 4 mutual touching.

- If an orgasm happens, that's okay—just return to phase 4 mutual touching and end there.
- End the session with phase 4 mutual touching.

Some people complete this series of exercises and don't return to them, having gotten what they needed from the practice. Others may return to sensate focus phases to get into a mindful headspace prior to sexual activity. Once you've completed the series, feel free to revisit whatever parts may be useful to you. Sensate focus can look deceptively easy, but it does require sustained effort and motivation to practice what are new skills for most people. Next, we tackle some frequently asked questions about these important exercises.

FREQUENTLY ASKED QUESTIONS ABOUT SENSATE FOCUS

Q: *Do we have to do all of the phases?*
A: You're welcome to practice as many phases as you would like—stopping at any point—though we don't recommend skipping phases, as they're progressive.

Q: *What if touching feels pleasurable?*
A: That's okay! We're working to facilitate a neutral environment, which means that it's fine if you experience pleasure and it's also fine if you don't. If you notice a pleasurable sensation, just redirect your attention back to temperature, pressure, and texture (TPT) sensations.

Q: *What if I get sexually aroused during sensate focus exercises?*
A: This can definitely happen for some people during sensate focus exercises, and it's perfectly fine. Sexual arousal is not against the rules—just treat it as yet another bodily sensation. Arousal may come and go. Here, too, we recommend refocusing on touch sensations.

Q: *What if I feel comfortable and want to be sexual or have an orgasm?*
A: Great question! Historically, sensate focus instructions have several modifications to address orgasm once a session has ended. However, these options are highly dependent upon *why* partners are practicing sensate focus. Sensate focus exercises can be used to address sexual desire discrepancies, as well as difficulties with sexual pain, orgasm, ejaculation, erection, and many other

sexual health issues. Some partners are working on more than one concern at the same time.

Since the answer to this question is dependent on context and this format doesn't allow us to address everyone's specific situation, our blanket recommendation here is to advise against pairing orgasm and sensate focus. The point of these exercises is to focus on the process, not on a destination. When sensate focus leads to sexual activity, there tends to be little to no difference from what you may already be experiencing. We run the risk of reinforcing old patterns. This can lead to feelings of sexual pressure, or it can turn sensate focus into a structured foreplay exercise, which it isn't.

Learning to sit with sexual frustration, allowing arousal to ebb and flow without necessarily leading to orgasm, is a very helpful sexual skill. That said, if you decide to stimulate to orgasm, we advise waiting a minimum of fifteen minutes after the sensate focus session in order to keep the experiences separate. You may also consider physically moving to another location. To keep from adding to a sense of pressure in your partnership, this physical release is best done solo. If the decision to pursue orgasm following sensate focus exercises is becoming a point of contention, pressure, or an ongoing pattern, we strongly suggest working with a sex therapist. See chapter 9 for additional information.

Q: *This feels pretty sexual. . . . How is sensate focus not sex?*

A: It's true that sensate focus exercises have many similar elements to sex: touch, being alone with a partner, being partially or fully naked. They can sometimes also trigger arousal. Table 5 shows the key differences between sensate focus and typical sexual experiences:

TABLE 5. SEX VERSUS SENSATE FOCUS	
(Staircase) Sex	**Sensate Focus**
Goal-oriented	Process-oriented
Focus on partner and self	Focus on self
Tends to be evaluative (e.g., "I'm not aroused enough")	Descriptive (e.g., "What do I notice?")
May be judgmental	Nonjudgmental
Outcome-focused	Sensation-focused
May be distracted	Mindful

You may notice that the descriptions of sensate focus sound a lot like the open-ended, flexible Wheel Model approach to partnered sex, described in chapter 2. That's no coincidence! The descriptions of sex noted here reflect typical Staircase thinking. Our goal is to practice cultivating more open-ended experiences using sensate focus, in a way that will ideally translate—with time and practice—to partnered sex that more closely resembles the Wheel Model.

Q: *What if I have a stress response during sensate focus?*

A: The answer here takes us back to the window of tolerance, first discussed in chapter 5 (it may be helpful to revisit that section). Consider the difference between a gentle nudge and a shove. A gentle nudge feels like an emotional stretch and occurs at the edge of your window of tolerance. The activity may trigger feelings of nervousness or mild anxiety but feels manageable overall. An activity that feels like a shove, however, tends to spark severe anxiety and leads quickly into fight, flight, or shutdown. This is a clear sign that you've moved outside of your window of tolerance. An important aspect of sensate focus exercises is to stay within the gentle nudge.

If you find yourself outside of your window of tolerance during sensate focus, here are a few things you can try:

- If the stress response is an upsetting thought or emotion (what we might refer to as a mental sensation), try refocusing your attention back on the physical sensations of touch to see if that helps to calm your system.
- Take a few moments to focus on breath sensations rather than the physical sensations of touch. Come back to TPT touch sensations as you feel ready.
- Move your hand or your partner's hand to another area of the body, depending on who is touching and being touched.
- Pause and take a break (brief or extended, as you need) from the exercise.

An important note: It's okay to break the nonverbal guideline of sensate focus if you're having a stress response and need to inform your partner. If you're able to get back into your window of tolerance fairly quickly, you may not need to tell your partner about the stress response until the post–sensate focus debrief. If you're not able to get back into your window of tolerance and your stress response feels unmanageable, it's important to be able to communicate this to your partner and stop the exercise. Particularly during a shutdown response, it can be difficult for others to know what you're experiencing.

These options are available to you at any time during sensate focus exercises. Some people who get outside their window of tolerance with sensate focus might stop the exercises altogether and not revisit them. And in some cases, that's the absolute best thing to do. In these circumstances, we recommend meeting with a sex therapist or trauma therapist if possible (see chapter 9 for more detail). In other cases, it may be appropriate to break up the exercises into even smaller steps (to gently stretch your window of tolerance) and try again. There isn't a universal approach to this, as it heavily depends on each person's experience and circumstances.

Q: *What if I can't focus?*

A: This is a common concern and makes sense, since many of us struggle to be present in the moment (and our hustle-and-grind culture doesn't really encourage it!). When you notice that you've become distracted during sensate focus (and you will be!), gently redirect your attention back to TPT touch sensations. You may have to redirect your focus in this way fairly often at first. That's absolutely fine, and it does get easier with time and practice!

For many folks that we work with in sex therapy, establishing a general mindfulness practice apart from sensate focus can be enormously helpful. There are many reasons that we might struggle to focus, including high stress levels, attentional difficulties, anxiety, and so on. Often, practicing our mindfulness skills in other ways (e.g., via online apps or a class) provides a stronger foundation from which to approach sensate focus exercises. We've listed some of our favorite options in the Resources section.

Q: *Why is it so hard to focus on myself?*

A: We commonly get this feedback from our clients. Many of us have been socialized to focus primarily on our partners during physical touch and sexual activity. And there's nothing wrong with that. We don't want to be selfish lovers, after all! The problem occurs when we focus on our partners to the exclusion of our own experiences. This lack of balance leaves us disconnected from our own sexual responses, particularly physical sensations. Sensate focus exercises are a way to practice solely focusing on our own experience. In the long term, this helps us improve and better balance our attention during sexual activity.

Sociocultural influences—including family and faith traditions—are important to consider if you are struggling to focus on your own experiences. Many people, especially those socialized into traditional feminine gender roles or within purity culture, were taught sexual passivity. Sexual passivity can be detrimental to sexual experiences in several ways: deferring to a partner at the expense of your own pleasure or safety, for example, or holding an internalized belief that experiencing pleasure is bad or shameful. Ideally, with sensate focus practice, self-focus gradually becomes easier. If sitting with your own experience of touch sensations remains highly difficult, however, it may be helpful to connect with a sex therapist or somatic therapist for further exploration.

Q: *What if I don't feel comfortable being naked?*

A: We hear you! Being naked can be an incredibly vulnerable experience. Prior to each sensate focus session, have a conversation with your partner about what clothing, if any, will be worn. You and your partner(s) may have different levels of comfort and preference. If you decide to start the exercises fully clothed, try removing one article of clothing the next time, an additional article of clothing after that, and so on and so forth. This may become part of an anxiety hierarchy, like we discussed in chapter 5.

Q: *Is sex off-limits altogether when we're working on sensate focus?*

A: If you experience physical pain with sex, we want you to avoid any activity that triggers that pain (see chapter 4). Outside of this parameter, you and your partner(s) are free to be sexual in any way that you'd like, as long as it's *separate* from a sensate focus session. There are partners who have sexual contact throughout the week when they're practicing sensate focus, and there are partners who don't. It depends on the situation and each person's comfort level. We want to acknowledge how variable our recommendations are with our clients, based on their unique individual and interpersonal needs.

Q: *Can we skip the debriefing portion and just focus on touching?*

A: We strongly encourage you to practice debriefing with your partner after each touch session. This helps to facilitate greater awareness and reflection, as well as communication between partners in a nonjudgmental atmosphere.

Part III

chapter 8

PARTNERS WITH HIGHER LIBIDO

This chapter is for partners who tend to have the higher libido in their relationships. While many books have been written for folks with lower libido, fewer have been written about sexual desire discrepancies, and even fewer for those with higher libido without framing it as a problem. We want to be clear that having higher sexual desire in a relationship is *not* a problem in and of itself. Neither is having lower sexual desire. As we've discussed, the problem occurs when there's a difference in desire that gets mismanaged, creating distress. *We're not trying to lower your libido to match that of your partner(s), nor are we trying to raise your partner's libido to match yours.* The goal is to help you better navigate these differences.

Dr. Stan Tatkin uses the analogy of the tortoise and the hare when discussing partners who have different emotional processing speeds: one person might be an external processor and want to talk things out immediately, whereas another might be an internal processor and want to take time to think things through.[1] He points out that hares can slow down, but tortoises can't speed up. Let's apply this helpful analogy to the subject of desire discrepancies. In this case, the tortoise represents the partner with lower desire, or perhaps more responsive desire, and the hare represents the partner with higher desire, or perhaps greater spontaneous desire. You may have noticed that many of the recommendations and exercises in this book bend more toward the tortoise than the hare. In many cases, when working to manage a desire discrepancy, it's true that the hare can slow down, but the tortoise can't speed up. If the lower-libido partner is experiencing pressure (whether internally from themselves or externally from a partner), they risk leaving their window of tolerance (discussed in chapter 5). They then may either (a) go through the motions of sex in a disconnected or dissociated state or (b) avoid intimacy altogether.

We're not trying to make tortoises into hares or vice versa. We *are* trying to honor all partners, while also integrating important information about psychology, relationship health, and neurobiology. If you're the partner with higher libido, we want you to know that your desire for sex and physical intimacy makes sense and is totally valid. Our goal is to explore and per-haps shift how you communicate that desire to your partner(s)—and also shift how you and your partner(s) are managing your desire differences so that you can break free from negative patterns and feelings of resentment.

A NOTE ABOUT GENDER ROLES

As discussed in chapter 1, our culture tends to overwhelm us with gendered messages and stereotypes about sex. Before we get into more specific recom-mendations for higher-libido partners, we want to acknowledge the common assumption that the higher-libido partner is a cisgender heterosexual man. Turns out, that's not always true! This assumption is based on the cultural messages we receive about gender and sexual orientation. While it is cer-tainly true that in many cisgender heterosexual relationships, the man has the higher libido, there are also many men who are the lower-libido partner in their relationships. In fact, there are many men and nonbinary people who have lower desire, and there are many women and nonbinary people who have higher desire than their partners.

Unfortunately, these folks tend to be missed or even ignored due to cultural assumptions. Additionally, because the dominant cultural narra-tive states that men are supposed to always have high desire and women always have lower desire in comparison, folks who don't fit this script can experience shame and embarrassment. They may even delay seeking help for these concerns. If you or your partner feels shame or embarrassment because you don't fit into these stereotyped roles about libido, we want you to know that you're not alone. Remember: "high" libido and "low" libido are relative to the relational dynamic. You may very easily be the higher-desire partner in one relationship, but the lower-desire partner in another relationship. Again, the difficulty of a sexual desire discrepancy is in the mismanagement of the *discrepancy itself* and the resulting relationship dynamic, not the individual partners.

In your **sexual health journal**, reflect on the following questions: Have you experienced feelings of shame or embarrassment about your level of desire? Have you felt that something was "wrong" with you? What messages or experiences might have provoked these feelings? What has it been like for you to be the higher-desire partner in your relationship?

REVISITING THE SEXUAL PURSUE-WITHDRAW CYCLE

We first introduced the pursue-withdraw relationship dynamic in chapter 3 and expanded on it in chapter 6. Recall that this is a pattern that can arise both in our relationships as a whole as well as in our sexual dynamics specifically. Some people have the same role in the general relationship as they do in the sexual relationship—being the pursuer or withdrawer in both contexts—while others may fall into different roles depending on the situation: for example, a person may be a pursuer in the general relationship and a withdrawer when it comes to sex. Perhaps unsurprisingly, partners who have higher libido or the more spontaneous style of desire are often the sexual pursuers (unless they feel consistently rejected and, over time, stop pursuing). You may have found that the more you pursue sexual contact, the more your partner withdraws. Each partner contributes to this relational dynamic. Rather than continue to use the same (likely ineffective) strategies of pursuit, we want to help partners bridge the libido gap. We know this is a tough situation and can be quite frustrating or upsetting. So the question is, what can you do instead?

There are a few effective ways to help break the pursue-withdraw pattern around sex. As the higher-desire partner, one place to start is to explore your own motivators for sex (if needed, revisit chapter 1 for more about motivators). Are you seeking emotional connection? Physical pleasure? Stress reduction? Validation? An orgasm? Pinpointing your most frequent motivators for sex is helpful for better understanding what it is specifically that you desire when initiating sex. As you gain a better understanding of your sexual motivators, you might be able to diversify the ways in which you can meet these desires. For example, if you're seeking intimate connection with a partner, is sex the only way for you to experience that intimacy? Perhaps there are more options. Let's look at an example.

Akeem and Amara have been struggling with a sexual desire discrepancy in their relationship for three years. Amara is the higher-desire partner in their relationship, and she has been most upset about the infrequency of intercourse. Amara feels most intimate with Akeem when they have penetrative sex. This is what she seeks the most when she initiates sex—that sense of physical closeness. Akeem, however, doesn't experience much physical pleasure from penetrative sex, and his overall sexual interest has lowered a bit since starting an antidepressant medication. When they came in for sex therapy, they were stuck around the issue of infrequent intercourse. Amara often complained about Akeem's low desire and had an assumption that intercourse was the only way to meet her intimacy needs. As they discovered about the Sexual Staircase and started exploring intimacy dates, they discovered something important. During an intimacy date, Amara asked Akeem if he would lie on top of her while they were both naked, so that she could feel the weight of his body and the feeling of his skin against hers. Akeem was open to trying it. As they did, Amara realized that this was one of the sensations of intercourse she most longed for: the pressure of her partner's body against hers, his skin giving her a sense of warmth and comfort. It was a truly intimate moment, and she realized that penetration—while highly enjoyable for her—was not the only way to have physical closeness. After sharing this experience together, they explored other activities on the intimacy date menu. This allowed Amara to better experience what she was looking for in terms of an intimate connection, and it gave Akeem lots of options for exploring pleasure.

Another important strategy for breaking the pursue-withdraw cycle is to change how we communicate our bid for sex—both verbally and nonverbally—with our partner(s). Here are some things we commonly hear that lead the pursued partner to withdraw:

- Making pointed "jokes" about sex that your partner doesn't appreciate
- Touching your partner in a way that they have communicated they dislike
- Focusing on your own desires without taking a partner's preferences, boundaries, or needs into consideration

Notice the main themes in these ineffective strategies: the pursued partner feels pressured, uncomfortable, unheard, and disrespected. Likely these outcomes were not the pursuer's intent. However, if this is the impact of our sexual pursuits, then it's understandable that our partners will very likely withdraw over time.

A quick note here about the difference between *intent* and *impact*: intent is what we set out to communicate, or how we hope the other person will receive our words or actions. Impact, on the other hand, is the other person's actual experience of our words or behavior. When it comes to the pursue-withdraw cycle, the impact of a pursuer's words and actions often does not match their intent, creating frustration for everyone involved. What's important here is for sexual pursuers to acknowledge any negative *impact* of their communication and integrate feedback from their partner(s). This can help to create a more positive cycle.

Disrupting the pursue-withdraw cycle requires more effective communication and awareness of your partner's perspective. Essentially, we want to ensure that the impact of our words and actions better matches our intent. In addition to truly listening to partner feedback, here are some examples of what to try instead:

- "I miss being sexual with you but don't want to pressure you. Sometimes it just helps to tell you how I feel."
- "I've really been wanting more physical intimacy. I'm wondering if there's something we can do together that would feel comfortable for you? Perhaps [name a few options]?"
- "I'd love to do something to pleasure you. Would you be up for that? What can I do that's just for you?"
- "I'd like to have an orgasm. Wondering if you'd be up for joining me in some way? If not, that's okay too."
- "I'm at a 10 for wanting sex right now. Where are you on the willingness scale today?"

Something we often hear from higher-desire partners is that while they would enjoy more sexual contact, what they also often desire is to feel heard, to feel wanted, to feel cared for, and to feel close with their partner(s). If any of those underlying needs resonate with you, we strongly recommend sharing that with your partner(s). Let them know the need behind your sexual pursuit—perhaps it's broader than they (or you) realize. When we express our more vulnerable feelings and needs, rather than reactive emotions like frustration or anger, our partners often respond differently. And even if a partner continues to withdraw, at least we are doing our part to break free from the negative cycle on the pursuer side of the equation.

Here are some questions to reflect on in your **sexual health journal:** When you initiate sex with your partner(s), do you notice that you have a common motivator? Could there be multiple ways to meet your desires or underlying needs? What have you tried in terms of experimenting with different approaches to meeting your desires? If you've stopped initiating due to a history of feeling rejected, in what ways have you tried communicating your feelings to your partner? How did that go?

DIY PLEASURE AND RELATIONSHIP AGREEMENTS

Because the Sexual Staircase script is often deeply ingrained in our approach to partnered sex, we have a tendency to get trapped in an all-or-nothing pattern. If one of your main motivators for sex is physical pleasure or to have an orgasm—as it is for many people!—it's important to consider various options for sexual self-exploration and self-expression. It's critical, particularly when working to break free of the pursue-withdraw cycle, to adopt a sense of flexibility and adaptability around sex. This means identifying ways to engage in sexual pleasure that don't rely on our partners or put pressure on them. Remember one of the foundational sexual health principles: you are responsible for your own pleasure. Keeping this principle in mind helps us to (a) better address our sexual desires and (b) reduce pressure on our partner(s). Let's take a look at some ways to experience sexual pleasure or orgasm by ourselves. You might also consider expanding your nonsexual experiences of pleasure, as discussed in chapter 5. Think about these as DIY—do-it-yourself—pleasure options:

- Fantasizing about sex
- Listening to an erotic story
- Watching a movie or show with sexy scenes
- Using sexually explicit material (SEM)
- Reading an erotic novel

- Masturbating
- Exploring a new sexual toy

As you read through this list of options, notice which ones might be of interest to you. Perhaps some of these are things you're already doing. An important factor to consider when exploring sex by yourself is the agreement in your particular relationship. A *relationship agreement* is the arrangement partners make about their relationship boundaries. It's a mutual understanding of relationship expectations and violations. Because we're often not taught or encouraged to openly talk about these matters, many relationship agreements are assumed and unspoken—leaving the door open to misunderstandings and hurt feelings. Making your agreement explicit and spoken can help to avoid unintentional breaches of trust in relationships. In the context of exploring self-pleasure, this looks like a discussion between partners about whether these DIY options fall inside or outside of your relationship agreement. For example, is watching sexually explicit material considered a relational violation or something that's agreeable—or even encouraged? Do relationship boundaries depend on the type of SEM being used (e.g., visual versus audio)? These are important conversations to have. Here are some examples of what this can sound like:

- "Babe, I don't want you to keep feeling pressure around our sex life. How would you feel if I [insert activity of interest]?"
- "I know we've had tension around sex lately. Can we sit down and talk more about how we can manage this differently? When's a good time for you to talk?"
- "Masturbating is a good way for me to get the release I want without pressuring you, but we've never really talked openly about it. How do you feel about masturbation?"
- "I know we've talked about porn use in the past. I want to understand your concerns because I'm thinking it could be a way for us to better manage our different libidos."

Let's spend a moment specifically on masturbation. For some couples, it can be a hot-button issue, whereas for other partnerships it's an understood and expected part of each person's sexuality. In many relationships, masturbation is enjoyed together (aka mutual masturbation) as a component of partnered sex. Masturbation can be an effective way to meet the desires of higher-libido partners, especially when their primary motivators for sex are physical pleasure or orgasms. Some of the benefits of masturbation and orgasms include:

- Lowering stress levels due to a decrease in stress hormones like cortisol
- Improving sleep
- Releasing feel-good neurotransmitters and hormones like endorphins and oxytocin
- Reducing pain or cramping
- Exercising pelvic floor muscles
- Learning more about what you like and what feels good
- Facilitating genital health by increasing blood flow and oxygen to the genital tissue[2]

We understand that one of the things masturbation cannot do is provide a sense of intimate connection with a partner (though it certainly can help you connect with yourself). This is why, as we've noted, it can be helpful to diversify the ways in which you experience partnered intimacy so that a specific sexual activity, like penetrative sex, is not the *only* option on the table. However, if your higher libido is predominantly about a desire for more regular orgasms (in comparison to your partner), masturbation is a helpful way to manage this motivator. Meeting some of these physical desires on your own will likely reduce pressure on your relationship.

As we've outlined, it's important to explore a variety of ways to bridge a sexual desire difference in relationships. For higher-libido partners, this often requires an exploration and expansion of self-pleasure. It's critical to talk openly about self-pleasure options with partners. Without this communication, we run the risk of engaging in secretive behavior that may violate an assumed relationship agreement and end up aggravating relational conflict in the long term.

PRIVACY VERSUS SECRECY

The section on relationship agreements brings up an important topic: discussing what's considered private versus secret in a relationship. This will be unique to each partnership and works best when it's explicitly discussed together. For example, in many relationships, the fact that partners masturbate in general is known and not a secret. However, there may be certain aspects of masturbation that are considered private information and not openly discussed (e.g., the where, when, and how). There are no specific rules here and every relationship involves its own unique agreements around sexual health, including masturbation. What's important is to have open dialogue so that everyone is on the same page.

THE HIGHER-DESIRE PARTNER'S ROLE IN SENSATE FOCUS

As outlined in chapter 7, sensate focus exercises can be enormously helpful for addressing barriers to partnered sexual intimacy. These exercises may present a number of challenges, however. They may push some lower-desire partners outside or to the edge of their window of tolerance (for a review of this concept, see chapter 5). We see this happen less often with higher-desire partners, who are typically craving more physical touch. Often, the challenge for higher-desire partners is to slow things down with sensate focus exercises and not to push for too much too soon. We know this can be challenging. In sex therapy, we often see higher-desire partners trying to advance sensate focus too quickly or judging the exercises as being too slow. Another challenge may arise if the higher-libido person criticizes their partner's physical responses to the exercises—such as bracing or muscle tension—or tries to use sensate focus exercises as an opportunity to be sexual. While your desire for more touch or sex is absolutely understandable, these behaviors tend to backfire and can actually set things back. Here are examples of unhelpful statements that may actually worsen sexual health concerns:

- "Why can't you just relax?"
- "I barely touched you—why are you so tense?"
- "Can't we just fool around now?"
- "I don't get why we have to do this."
- "This whole thing is taking too long."

These kinds of statements can come across as critical, unsupportive, pressuring, or blaming. It can leave our lower-libido partners feeling alone, rushed, or like they aren't good enough, and it reinforces the idea that they are the "problem." Remember, sexual desire discrepancies are a relational issue. This is where—as the higher-libido partner—we can do our part to improve the management of sexual desire differences, letting our partners know that we're there for them and that we're in this together.

Research shows that how partners respond to sexual concerns can play a significant role in shaping the outcome.[3] Most of the studies in this area have focused on cisgender women with sexual pain and their partners, but the results are also quite informative for those navigating libido discrepancies and practicing sensate focus. In general, researchers have identified three ways that partners tend to respond to sexual difficulties: negative, solicitous, and facilitative.

1. Negative response: As seen in the previous list, in these responses a partner becomes aggressive, hostile, critical, or otherwise hurtful. This can sound like, "Why can't we just have sex?" or "This is taking forever!"
2. Solicitous response: In these responses, a partner becomes too hands-off or afraid of provoking negative reactions (such as anxiety or pain). They might not mention sex or sensate focus exercises, avoiding the subject altogether. This can sound like, "I don't want you to be uncomfortable, don't worry about it"—or, more commonly, there is a complete lack of discussion about sexual concerns.
3. Facilitative response: In these responses, a partner approaches sexual challenges from a more assertive perspective, trying to find creative and flexible solutions without creating a pressured dynamic. This might look like asking how they can be involved in the process and approaching things more collaboratively.

Research has consistently shown that sexual concerns are more effectively managed when partners are perceived to be facilitative in their responses.[4] Here are some things you can say to your partner(s) to be more facilitative regarding sensate focus exercises:

- "We can go at whatever pace feels most comfortable for you."
- "How can I best support you during these exercises?"
- "What can I do to make things more comfortable for you?"

- "It's been a few days since we last did sensate focus—when would be a good time to practice again?"
- "I noticed you tensing up when we were practicing sensate focus. Should we slow things down?"

Negative responses to sexual concerns are just that—negative and unproductive. Solicitous responses often stem from a desire to be supportive but can backfire by creating avoidance. Over time, avoidance typically increases our anxiety and distress and can actually worsen the sexual dynamic. In contrast to solicitous responses, facilitative responses can decrease sexual avoidance while also appropriately responding to a partner's needs. Facilitative responses also tend to reduce distressing emotions, such as anxiety or shame, by approaching sexual concerns from a position of collaboration, respect, and mutual problem-solving. This is particularly true for sensate focus exercises.

Recall the analogy of the tortoise and the hare when it comes to sexual desire differences. It's important to keep in mind that higher-libido partners are better able to slow down than lower-desire partners can speed up. Again, the risk with trying to rush through the process of sensate focus is that even if your partner goes through the motions, they may not be fully present or comfortable. This undermines your overall sexual health goals.

In your **sexual health journal**, explore the following questions: Have you expressed negative or solicitous responses to sexual health concerns? What impact did that have? In what ways can you practice a more facilitative approach? Did you see any sample questions or statements here that you'd like to try out?

SUPPORTING PARTNERS WITH A TRAUMA HISTORY

Some people's libido has been impacted by a history of trauma. Regardless of whether that trauma was sexual or nonsexual, it can affect their sexuality for months or years. For some, trauma decreases libido and leaves them feeling less safe in their bodies, with other people, and in the world. For others, trauma can increase libido and create a hypersexual response as part of an effort to feel more in control. In this section, we'll discuss how you can be supportive if a partner has a trauma history, specifically if their libido has lowered in response to trauma and created a lack of safety with touch or sex.

One of the most common impacts of trauma—especially physical and sexual trauma—is a prolonged stress response and hypervigilance when it comes to being touched. If you've had partners with a trauma history, you may have noticed them pulling away from you or tensing up in the context of physical touch or sex. It's important to try not to take things personally when this stress response happens. This can be challenging because, of course, you're involved and that makes it personal! However, in many ways these reactions are probably not about you and, as we've seen, your response can either improve or worsen the dynamic.

Recall that a stress response can involve activating the sympathetic nervous system (SNS) or parasympathetic nervous system (PNS). Some signs that the SNS or PNS have been activated include an increased or decreased heart rate, muscle tension, quicker breathing or holding of the breath, bracing, sweating, and flushing. If you suspect that your partner may be experiencing a stress response, the first thing you can do is verbally check in with them. Here are some examples of what you might ask:

- "Do you need us to stop touching for a bit?"
- "It seems like you might be triggered right now. Is that happening?"
- "Should we slow things down?"
- "Can I do something to help you feel safe right now?"
- "Would it be helpful for us to take a few minutes to breathe together?"
- "Do you want closeness or some time alone right now?"
- "Would it be better not to touch right now, or is there a type of touch that would feel more comforting—holding hands, rubbing your back?"

As we discussed in the last section, it's important not to rush a partner with sexual activity or physical touch. Trying to move too quickly creates high levels of pressure and can undermine trust and safety. Let your partner know that you're there for them and that you're okay with going slowly. You might also offer them co-regulation, which is when your own nervous system is calm and acts as an anchor for your partner to feel more at ease. This can look like practicing a breathing exercise together, sharing supportive statements, or offering a hug. Here are a few other ideas for how you can be supportive to your partner(s):

- Get informed about trauma and how it may be impacting your partner and your relationship. Consider reading a few books about trauma, listening to podcasts, or watching videos online. Check out the Resources section for some options.
- If your partner is involved in trauma-focused therapy, ask if it would be helpful for you to participate in a therapy session with them.
- Consider participating in your own individual therapy to process your experience and reactions.

Part of creating a safe and respectful relationship is being aware of your partner's vulnerable spots (and your own) and taking care not to ignore them. Though your partner's trauma may have occurred prior to your relationship or be independent of you, please know that you play a critical role in their healing and in reestablishing safety with sex and physical touch.

In your **sexual health journal**, reflect on the following: Have you and your partner ever discussed trauma? If a partner has a trauma history, how have you been involved in their recovery or healing? In what ways might you be willing to learn more about the impacts of trauma?

WHEN HIGH LIBIDO IS A CONCERN

As we've discussed, libido is a spectrum, and there's no one amount of sexual desire that's considered normal or right. There are times when high libido can lead to high levels of sexual activity. Frequent sexual activity may not be a concern at all—this depends on each individual and the dynamics of the relationship(s) they're in. In some cases, however, high levels of sexual activity may reflect trauma or another mental health or medical concern and can become problematic.[5] For example, high levels of sexual activity can be a symptom of bipolar disorder—specifically a state of mania. It can also occur with dementia or as a side effect of some medications. Some people may engage in sex to feel more alive or in control, or to return from feeling dissociated after trauma—again, whether this is problematic depends on the individual. Here are some examples of sexual behavior that *may* be related to trauma or other mental health concerns:

- Risky or dangerous sexual behavior
- Prioritizing sex over daily needs and responsibilities

- Feeling guilt or shame after sex
- Sexual thoughts or urges that cause distress to oneself
- Engaging in sexual behavior that doesn't align with one's values
- Sexual behavior that leads to negative consequences (e.g., repeatedly being late for work, spending significant amounts of money, violating a relationship agreement)
- Sexual behavior that feels difficult to control or manage

Again, it's important to emphasize that high libido and high levels of sexual activity, in and of themselves, are not necessarily a problem. It's when higher libido leads to problematic sexual behavior that concerns may develop. Identifying problematic sexual behavior involves discernment. Sometimes the concern is about how the behavior is impacting you as an individual; other times, it's more about how the behavior impacts your relationship(s). At the individual level, if you have an underlying mental health concern or trauma that you feel may be contributing to your heightened sexual interest or behaviors, it's important to seek professional support. This might be in the form of individual therapy or medication management (e.g., for depression or anxiety). At the interpersonal (relationship) level, navigating concerns about high libido or high levels of sexual behavior is best accomplished via sex or relationship therapy.

Take out your **sexual health journal** and consider these reflection questions: Have you ever been concerned about your sexual behavior? Is there a history of trauma or other mental health concerns that might influence your sexual interest or behaviors? Do any of the examples of problematic sexual behavior resonate for you? If so, write down which ones.

WHEN THE FOUR HORSEMEN MEET HIGH LIBIDO

Sometimes, partners who have lower or more responsive desire accuse a higher-libido partner of having a sex addiction. In our experience, this is often proclaimed with criticism or contempt and reflects a feeling of overwhelm or pressure around a sexual desire discrepancy. While problematic sexual behavior may indeed be present, accusations grounded in the Four Horsemen typically reflect ineffective management of a libido difference and are likely to create more tension and conflict. It's often a sign that your partner is not feeling seen or heard in your relationship. Regardless of whether one's higher libido or sexual behavior is problematic, it's critical to find healthy and respectful ways for all partners to discuss the issue. If contemptuous communication has become the norm in your relationship, professional support is likely going to be the next best step. Consider asking your partner if they would be willing to see a relationship or sex therapist with you. There's more information about how to seek additional support in chapter 9. If you need a refresher on the Four Horsemen, consider revisiting chapter 3.

OPENING UP

As we discussed in chapter 3, a libido difference may lead to discussions about opening up a monogamous relationship and exploring various forms of ethical non-monogamy (ENM). For partners with higher or more spontaneous sexual desire, this may be of particular interest and, as such, it's important to understand how to navigate these conversations.

Relationships inherently take work. This is true regardless of whether we're engaged in monogamy or ENM. The latter, however, can be particularly challenging to navigate given the limited information, education, and ENM role models in our culture. As we covered early on in this book, there is no one-size-fits-all with regard to sex and sexuality, and this includes relationship structures! Monogamy is not for everyone. Neither is ethical non-monogamy. Perhaps most importantly, ENM requires careful consideration and planning. It is not a cure-all for sexual desire discrepancies.

Remember that non-monogamy is a spectrum with a whole host of options and meanings. Considering (and practicing!) ENM requires a ton of communication, particularly around your relationship agreements (i.e., what's okay and what's not okay). Because of this, many folks may need to spend significant time building their communication skills before considering ENM. In short: ENM can be a wonderful option for some partnerships, but it is not something that should be rushed into, nor is it a relationship structure to approach lightly. It can be helpful to work with a therapist who is trained in diverse relationship structures to support you in your experience. If exploring ENM is of interest to you, here are some ways you might start these conversations with a partner:

- "I've been reading about ethical non-monogamy and it sounds interesting. Would you be open to discussing it?"

- "When would be a good time for us to sit down and talk about managing our different libidos? I have an option I want to run by you."
- "Would you be willing to read a book about non-monogamy with me just to explore the concept without pressure?"
- "Would you be willing to see a therapist with me to keep exploring ways to navigate our desire differences?" (If your partner is agreeable, you can then seek out a therapist who has competence working with ENM.)

When you're in a monogamous relationship, bringing up an interest in ethical non-monogamy can feel anxiety provoking. There may be uncertainty about how your partner will respond. Even if you raise the topic and your partner is disinterested, it can still be helpful to communicate this interest to ensure all options have been on the table and discussed. This may serve to increase emotional intimacy and avoid built-up feelings of resentment by helping you to feel more known or understood. In the next chapter, we'll discuss recommendations for seeking out additional support.

chapter 9

WHEN TO KICK IT
UP A NOTCH

This book is designed to offer foundational information, introduce important concepts, and review useful exercises for navigating the often stressful experience of a sexual desire discrepancy. We recognize, however, that this book may be just a starting point for some folks. It's quite common, in fact, to need some additional help navigating sexual health challenges—whether those are about libido or something else. In this final chapter, we offer suggestions for where to turn if you need further support. We've divided the chapter first by profession and then by concern. We find that many people are reluctant to pursue sexual health–related care under the mistaken belief that this somehow reflects a deficit in them or their relationship. As we've seen though, sex is complicated! In fact, it's a sign of wisdom and strength to prioritize and seek the care you need. You deserve no less.

IDENTIFYING YOUR TEAM

Addressing sexual health challenges often requires a multidisciplinary approach. That's because sex, as we've seen, involves a complex interplay of biological, psychological, relational, and sociocultural factors. For many people, addressing sexual health concerns can require a team-based approach that includes providers and professionals with different areas of expertise. This prospect can certainly feel overwhelming, so we want to start with a general overview of who it may be useful to connect with. Here are some professionals to consider adding to your team.

Sexual medicine specialists are, as the name implies, medical providers who have received specialized training in sexual medicine. These can include physicians, physician assistants, and nurse practitioners. Sexual medicine specialists often have backgrounds in fields such as urology and obstetrics/gynecology, though this is not always the case. Certainly, many folks start addressing sexual health by raising their concerns with their primary care provider. It's important to recognize, however, that these professionals may have little experience or expertise in sexual health. Thus, seeking out a sexual medicine specialist is often an important step.

Pelvic physical therapists are physical therapists with advanced specialized training in treating pelvic floor muscle dysfunction, such as weakness or tension. When sexual health concerns are related to the pelvic floor muscles, pelvic physical therapy is a go-to aspect of care. As with general medical providers, most physical therapists are unlikely to have much training or expertise in pelvic floor or sexual health–related concerns. Therefore, specifically seeking out a pelvic physical therapist is crucial.

Sex therapists are licensed mental health professionals who have received advanced specialized training in sexual health. Sex therapy training is typically done after completing graduate school in a related field (such as psychology, marriage and family therapy, social work, or counseling) and obtaining one's licensure as a mental health professional. Advanced sexual health and sex therapy training can then occur in several ways; for example, through a specialized postdoctoral fellowship, a sex therapy certification program, or an informal training agreement with a supervisor/mentor in the field. In North America, the American Association of Sexuality Educators, Counselors and Therapists (AASECT) is the professional organization that certifies sex therapists. AASECT ensures a standardized and minimal level of education, experience, and care. Some sex therapists may not be AASECT certified, in which case you'll want to ask about their training and credentials. For instance, a therapist who has taken a weekend course on sex therapy is not going to have the same level of training as a sex therapist who has studied for years under supervision.

Relationship therapists are licensed mental health professionals who have completed specific training in couple, family, or relationship therapy. Some relationship therapists specialize during graduate school, such as in marriage and family therapy (MFT) programs, while others obtain relationship therapy training as part of an advanced fellowship or postgraduate training. Most folks assume that relationship therapists are well versed in sexual health topics. Unfortunately, this is not always the case. Some relationship therapists have additional training in sex therapy, but many don't. If you're looking for a therapist who can do both sex and relationship therapy, you'll want to ask if they've received training in both areas.

General mental health therapists are professionals who have completed a graduate training program in mental health. This group includes marriage and family therapists, counselors, social workers, and psychologists. In North America, these professionals undergo a licensing process and are regulated by different professional boards. General therapists might use one specific treatment mode, like cognitive behavioral therapy, or a variety of treatment approaches to address various mental health concerns.

Trauma therapists are mental health therapists who have done advanced training in one or more trauma modalities. Some trauma therapists use talk therapy approaches, such as cognitive therapy or behavioral therapy, while others use more somatic (body-based) approaches, such as somatic experiencing or sensorimotor psychotherapy. The most important factor in choosing a trauma therapist, as with other therapists, is to find a good fit by working with a provider you trust and with whom you feel comfortable.

Gender therapists are mental health therapists who have done advanced training in gender health, often specifically focused on helping trans and nonbinary folks navigate a gender transition, dysphoria, the effects of transphobia, or other non-gender-related concerns. Many sex therapists are also gender therapists—though not all, so it's important to ask. Thankfully, more and more therapists are being trained to competently support people across the gender spectrum.

Psychiatrists are medical doctors (physicians) who have specialized in treating mental health concerns. Historically, psychiatrists offered talk and behaviorally focused therapy. This is still true for some, though more often these days, psychiatrists tend to focus on medication management. Psychiatrists are experts in psychotropic medications—for example, helping folks find an antidepressant or antianxiety medication that works best for them. Seeing a psychiatrist can be helpful for folks who have tried different psychotropic medications and haven't found the right medication or dosage to adequately address mental health symptoms. A psychiatrist can also be helpful to consult if you are experiencing sexual side effects from a psychotropic medication. Another option is the increasing number of nurse practitioners—known as psychiatric nurse practitioners—who have specialized training in this area.

Clergy or faith leaders may include pastors, rabbis, Imams, priests, and others. Addressing sexual or relationship health concerns with a trusted faith leader may be helpful for some folks. For example, you might have questions about how your particular faith tradition recommends approaching sexual health or relationship concerns. We have also found it useful, as sex therapists, for clients with strong faith backgrounds to discuss treatment recommendations with their faith leader. As always, treatment should respect and fit within your value system.

MOBILIZING YOUR TEAM: QUESTIONS TO ASK AND COMMON CONCERNS

Unfortunately, there's a general lack of sexual health training in most graduate and medical schools, leaving many mental health and medical providers woefully unprepared to help clients and patients with sexual health concerns.[1] Frustratingly, we've heard from many people whose sexual health concerns were not adequately addressed or were outright dismissed by a professional. Often, we must advocate for ourselves when raising sexual health concerns with mental health or medical providers. As noted, however, it can be tricky to identify which providers have the training and expertise to best help us. Consider asking the following questions to assess whether a professional has been trained in sexual health/medicine:

- What training have you done to specialize in sexual health or medicine?
- Do you regularly attend continuing education programs or conferences on sexual health topics?
- Are you a member of any professional sexual health organizations?
- Do you publish or present on sexual or gender health topics within your profession?
- Have you treated other people with my concerns?

Now that we've discussed the various professionals who may be involved in your sexual health care, let's look at some specific concerns that we've covered throughout the book and who you might consider seeing for additional support.

Relationship Problems

Sex and relationship concerns are, of course, often intertwined, and many therapists provide both sex and relationship therapy. As previously mentioned, however, there are also plenty of relationship therapists with no sex therapy training and many sex therapists with no relationship therapy training. This often surprises folks but is an important distinction to know in order to ensure you get the best care.

It can sometimes be hard to distinguish what is primarily a relationship concern versus a sexual health concern, given how deeply interwoven these aspects of our lives may be. As we've covered in this book, sexual difficulties can certainly harm relationship dynamics, and relationship concerns can negatively impact sex (especially libido). If you're experiencing relationship challenges—particularly high levels of conflict or betrayal, are considering leaving a relationship, or are feeling contempt toward a partner—we recommend seeing a relationship therapist. Partners in such situations tend to experience challenges with sex therapy homework, which often involves intimacy exercises. Again, a provider may be both a sex and relationship therapist, so it's also possible that treatment could begin by focusing on relationship health and, as tensions decrease, slowly move into sex therapy interventions. Two evidence-based treatment approaches that we've integrated throughout the book are *emotionally focused couple therapy* (EFT) and *Gottman Method couple therapy*. These modes of treatment—among others, such as cognitive behavioral couples therapy—are evidence-based following decades of research.

Sexual/Genital Pain

For folks who experience sexual or genital pain, we recommend first locating a sexual medicine specialist near you. As we discussed in chapter 4, it's critically important to determine any physical causes of your pain. Once established, this will typically lead to additional referrals, such as pelvic physical therapy or sex therapy. In the Resources section of this book, you can locate a specialist with the International Society for the Study of Women's Sexual Health (ISSWSH) or the International Society for Sexual Medicine (ISSM). The order in which you see these specialists is important: if you see a pelvic physical therapist prior to meeting with a sexual medicine specialist, the full range of potential medical factors may not get evaluated or treated. Particularly if there is sexual or genital pain that is not specific to muscle dysfunction, pelvic physical therapy or use of dilators may exacerbate the problem if initiated too soon in the treatment process. Additionally, seeing a sex therapist without first evaluating the physical source of pain can unintentionally set people up for the same pain cycle. For example, if medical treatment is required for genitourinary syndrome of menopause (GSM), this should happen prior to or simultaneously with pelvic physical therapy or sex therapy to ensure the genital tissues receive the care they need for optimal health.

Arousal, Orgasm/Ejaculation, and Desire Concerns

For folks who have concerns with arousal, orgasm/ejaculation, or libido, there are two types of specialists you might consider seeing: a sex therapist and a sexual medicine specialist. A sex therapist can help you explore and identify the psychological, social, and relational factors that may be impacting arousal, orgasms/ejaculation, or sexual desire. They can certainly provide support with some of the exercises in this book, as well as additional exercises and treatment options. A sexual medicine specialist can assess the physiological factors that may impact arousal, orgasms/ejaculation, and sexual desire—such as hormones or medication side effects—and do a workup or additional testing to see if there are any medical variables related to your concerns.

Trauma

If you have a history of trauma that has become a significant barrier to mental or sexual health, we recommend seeing a trauma therapist. There are many types of trauma therapies, including cognitive, integrative, somatic (body-centered), behavioral, and emotion focused. We know that this can at times feel overwhelming. As mentioned earlier, an important factor when working through trauma therapy—as with other types of therapy—is to feel like you and the therapist are a good fit, meaning you're comfortable and safe with them and feel like you can open up and trust them. It's also important that whatever type of trauma therapy you pursue takes your window of tolerance into account, moving at a pace that doesn't consistently overwhelm you. Remember, the goal is to slowly widen your window over time.

Mental Health Concerns

If you're experiencing depression, anxiety, mood fluctuations, or other mental health symptoms, we recommend meeting with a general mental health therapist. Some people simultaneously see a primary therapist as well as other specialty therapists (e.g., sex therapist, relationship therapist, trauma therapist). Others may work with a general mental health therapist to stabilize their mental health symptoms before seeing a specialty provider. As we've mentioned, it's important to feel comfortable with your therapist and to feel like you can be open with them. Depending on your symptoms, you might also talk with your primary care provider. They may be able to assist with medication management or refer you to a psychiatrist or other medical provider who specializes in psychotropic medications. Oftentimes, gold-standard treatment for concerns like depression and anxiety involve a combined approach of both therapy and medication management.

Medical Concerns

Many common health concerns—such as diabetes and hypertension—can negatively impact sexual health. For example, challenges with erections may be directly linked to heart health, due to the role our cardiovascular system plays in overall blood flow. When diabetes results in neuropathy (numbness), genital sensitivity and orgasmic functioning may also be impaired. In such instances, working with your primary care provider may be sufficient and a sexual medicine specialist may not be necessary.

Of course, it's important to have regular preventative medical care and checkups for your overall well-being. Most people don't realize that this is also critical for our sexual health! Regular health maintenance may even be able to prevent some sexual health concerns. Making annual checkups with your medical provider a priority is actually a very important piece of maintaining overall sexual health.

Cancer

For folks who have cancer or who have undergone cancer treatment, it perhaps goes without saying that working closely with your oncology team is critically important. We strongly encourage you to keep your oncology providers in the loop about your sexual health concerns (as they may not always ask!). Let them know about any sexual health–related changes or side effects you're experiencing from the cancer treatment, such as changes in sexual desire, lubrication, or erections. Remember that it's incredibly common to experience sexual health changes during or after treatments like chemotherapy, radiation, hormone suppression, or cancer-related surgeries. Additionally, consider meeting with a sexual medicine specialist and a sex therapist to help you and your partner(s) work through any changes to your sexual health. Recall that a sex therapist in particular can provide knowledgeable support throughout these changes and help you explore different ways to experience sexual pleasure.

Gender Health

If you are exploring gender, and certainly if you experience dysphoria, and would like some additional support, you might consider seeing a therapist who specializes in gender health. Some folks prefer working with a therapist who is transgender or nonbinary, while others may work with a cisgender therapist who has gone through specialized training in gender health. It's important to note that not all trans or nonbinary people experience gender dysphoria. If medical interventions such as hormones or surgery feel congruent with your goals, there are also medical providers with specialized training in gender health.

Problematic Sexual Behavior

When sexual behavior becomes problematic or out of control, we highly recommend starting with a sex therapist. Most sex therapy programs include training in this area. If you can't find a sex therapist with this expertise, your next best option may be to see a therapist who specializes in trauma, as their training may be well suited to address some of these concerns.

Sexual Exploration and Enhancement

If you have concerns about sexual functioning (e.g., arousal, orgasms/ejaculation, sexual pain), it often helps to see both a sexual medicine specialist and a sex therapist to address any underlying medical concerns as well as psychological and relational factors that may be at play. If you're interested in learning how to improve sexual intimacy, explore sexual interests, or experience more pleasure, meeting with a sex therapist will likely be most helpful. Sex therapy is an excellent space to gain support in areas like building sexual communication skills; reducing sexual anxiety, guilt, or shame; exploring identity; opening up a monogamous relationship; trying out kink; being more present in your body; and learning new ways to experience sex.

FINAL THOUGHTS ON DESIRE

We're sure that by now, you're well aware that libido is complicated! We've discussed the ecological model and how factors that hit our sexual brakes can be sociocultural, interpersonal, and individual in nature. While we've tried our best to represent the many factors that impact libido, we can't address every factor for every person. Things like sexually transmitted infections (STIs), the aftermath of infidelity, recovery from substance abuse, and many other variables can also significantly impact libido. It's important to identify the factors that are unique and relevant to you and your relationships; many of the exercises and recommendations throughout the book are helpful across multiple situations.

One of our key takeaway messages that we hope to have clearly imparted by now is to get off the Sexual Staircase! Learning to expand your sexual experiences using the flexible, adaptable, open-ended Wheel Model is a critical skill, as our sexualities change across time and circumstance. Libido differences are to be expected in relationships. Remember that the problem isn't the desire difference—it's how those differences get managed or mismanaged.

One of the most important factors—if not *the* most important factor—for sexual desire is sexual satisfaction. What we find pleasurable is often highly individual. Discovering your sexual accelerators can require significant exploration and, for some, adjustment to the very idea of prioritizing their own pleasure. Finding ways to feel good—individually and with partners—can help us maintain positive sexual experiences throughout our relationships. We encourage you to be open to many forms of pleasure—sexual or otherwise.

We recognize that finding good, accurate sexual health information can be difficult and that for many, access to sex therapy is limited. We hope that we've provided helpful information and exercises to improve your relationships and decrease distress around libido differences. For some people, this book alone will provide sufficient support for navigating these differences.

For others, this book will be a springboard to additional resources and support. We hope we've normalized your experiences and provided you with a path forward. Remember, at the end of the day, it's not about matching your libidos. Instead, the key is to honor, understand, and support your differences.

RESOURCES

The following resources may be helpful for additional reading or exploration. Please note that many of the following (especially the books) are cisnormative and heteronormative, are written by nondisabled people, and are mostly authored by white people. That said, we have worked to include a variety of voices and perspectives despite the limitations of the field. The items in each section are arranged alphabetically by title.

BOOKS

Asexuality

Ace: What Asexuality Reveals About Desire, Society, and the Meaning of Sex, by Angela Chen

The Invisible Orientation: An Introduction to Asexuality, by Julie Sondra Decker

A Quick & Easy Guide to Asexuality, by Molly Muldoon and Will Hernandez

Refusing Compulsory Sexuality: A Black Asexual Lens on Our Sex-Obsessed Culture, by Sherronda J. Brown

Body Image

The Body Image Workbook: An Eight-Step Program for Learning to Like Your Looks (2nd edition), by Thomas F. Cash

The Body Is Not an Apology: The Power of Radical Self-Love (2nd edition), by Sonya Renee Taylor

More Than a Body: Your Body Is an Instrument, Not an Ornament, by Lexie Kite and Lindsay Kite

Cancer and Sex

Making Love Again: Hope for Couples Facing Loss of Sexual Intimacy, by Keith Laken and Virginia Laken

Man Cancer Sex, by Anne Katz

Reclaiming Sex & Intimacy After Prostate Cancer, by Jeffrey Albaugh
Sex and Cancer: Intimacy, Romance, and Love After Diagnosis and Treatment, by Saketh R. Guntupalli and Maryann Karinch
Woman Cancer Sex, by Anne Katz

Disability
The Handi Book of Love, Lust & Disability, by Jess Tarpey, Andrew Gurza, and Katy Venables
A Quick & Easy Guide to Sex & Disability, by A. Andrews
Regain That Feeling: Secrets to Sexual Self-Discovery: People Living with Spinal Cord Injuries Share Profound Insights into Sex, Pleasure, Relationships, Orgasm, and the Importance of Connectedness, by Mitchell Tepper
The Ultimate Guide to Sex and Disability: For All of Us Who Live with Disabilities, Chronic Pain & Illness, by Miriam Kaufman, Cory Silverberg, and Fran Odette

Ethical Non-Monogamy
The Ethical Slut: A Practical Guide to Polyamory, Open Relationships, and Other Freedoms in Sex and Love (3rd edition), by Janet W. Hardy and Dossie Easton
The Handbook of Consensual Non-Monogamy: Affirming Mental Health Practice, edited by Michelle D. Vaughan and Theodore R. Burnes (book for clinicians)
Opening Up: A Guide to Creating and Sustaining Open Relationships, by Tristan Taormino
Polysecure: Attachment, Trauma and Consensual Nonmonogamy, by Jessica Fern

Gender
Beyond the Gender Binary, by Alok Vaid-Menon
Gender Trauma: Healing Cultural, Social, and Historical Gendered Trauma, by Alex Iantaffi
How to Understand Your Gender: A Practical Guide for Exploring Who You Are, by Alex Iantaffi and Meg-John Barker
Life Isn't Binary: On Being Both, Beyond, and In-Between, by Alex Iantaffi and Meg-John Barker
Nerve Endings: The New Trans Erotic, edited by Tobi Hill-Meyer

Take Me There: Trans and Genderqueer Erotica, edited by Tristan Taormino
Trans Bodies, Trans Selves: A Resource by and for Transgender Communities (2nd edition), edited by Laura Erickson-Schroth
You and Your Gender Identity: A Guide to Discovery, by Dara Hoffman-Fox

General Sexual Health

Anal Pleasure and Health: A Guide for Men, Women and Couples, by Jack Morin
The Autism Spectrum Guide to Sexuality and Relationships: Understand Yourself and Make Choices that Are Right for You, by Emma Goodall
Bang! Masturbation for People of All Genders & Abilities, by Vic Liu
Curvy Girl Sex: 101 Body-Positive Positions to Empower Your Sex Life, by Elle Chase
Girl Sex 101: A Queer Pleasure Guide for Women and Their Lovers, by Allison Moon and KD Diamond
Hot and Unbothered: How to Think About, Talk About, and Have the Sex You Really Want, by Yana Tallon-Hicks
How to Understand Your Sexuality: A Practical Guide for Exploring Who You Are, by Meg-John Barker and Alex Iantaffi
The Monster Under the Bed: Sex, Depression, and the Conversations We Aren't Having, by JoEllen Notte
The New Male Sexuality: The Truth About Men, Sex, and Pleasure, by Bernie Zilbergeld
Pleasure Activism: The Politics of Feeling Good (Emergent Strategy), by adrienne maree brown
Queer Sex: A Trans and Non-Binary Guide to Intimacy, Pleasure and Relationships, by Juno Roche
Read My Lips: A Complete Guide to the Vulva and Vagina, by Debby Herbenick and Vanessa Schick
Sex After Grief: Navigating Your Sexuality After Losing Your Beloved, by Joan Price
Sex Talks: Five Conversations That Will Transform Your Love Life, by Vanessa Marin with Xander Marin
Shameless: A Case for Not Feeling Bad About Feeling Good (About Sex), by Nadia Bolz-Weber
She Comes First: The Thinking Man's Guide to Pleasuring a Woman, by Ian Kerner

So Tell Me About the Last Time You Had Sex: Laying Bare and Learning to Repair Our Love Lives, by Ian Kerner

This Arab Is Queer: An Anthology by LGBTQ+ Arab Writers, edited by Elias Jahshan

Trans Sex: Clinical Approaches to Trans Sexualities and Erotic Embodiments, by Lucie Fielding (book for clinicians)

The Vagina Bible: The Vulva and the Vagina—Separating the Myth from the Medicine, by Jen Gunter

Kink and BDSM

The Leather Couch: Clinical Practice with Kinky Clients, by Stefani Goerlich (book for clinicians)

The New Bottoming Book, by Dossie Easton and Janet W. Hardy

The New Topping Book, by Dossie Easton and Janet W. Hardy

The Ultimate Guide to Kink: BDSM, Role Play and the Erotic Edge, by Tristan Taormino and Barbara Carrellas

Mental Load and Emotional Labor

All the Rage: Mothers, Fathers, and the Myth of Equal Partnership, by Darcy Lockman

The Emotional Load: And Other Invisible Stuff, by Emma, translated by Una Dimitrijevic

Fair Play: The Game Changing Solution for When You Have Too Much to Do (and More Life to Live), by Eve Rodsky

Fed Up: Emotional Labor, Women, and the Way Forward, by Gemma Hartley

The Mental Load: A Feminist Comic, by Emma

Mindfulness

Better Sex Through Mindfulness: How Women Can Cultivate Desire, by Lori A. Brotto

From Madness to Mindfulness: Reinventing Sex for Women, by Jennifer Gunsallus

Mindfulness for Beginners: Reclaiming the Present Moment—And Your Life, by Jon Kabat-Zinn

Trauma-Sensitive Mindfulness: Practices for Safe and Transformative Healing, by David A. Treleaven (book for clinicians)

Orgasm and Ejaculation

Becoming Cliterate: Why Orgasm Equality Matters—And How to Get It, by Laurie Mintz

Becoming Orgasmic: A Sexual and Personal Growth Program for Women, by Julia Heiman and Joseph LoPiccolo

Coping with Premature Ejaculation: How to Overcome PE, Please Your Partner & Have Great Sex, by Barry W. McCarthy and Michael E. Metz

Learn to Orgasm in 4 Acts, by Betty Dodson

Personal Growth

Burnout: The Secret to Unlocking the Stress Cycle, by Emily Nagoski and Amelia Nagoski

Daring Greatly: How the Courage to Be Vulnerable Transforms the Way We Live, Love, Parent, and Lead, by Brené Brown

All About Love: New Visions, by bell hooks

Self-Compassion: The Proven Power of Being Kind to Yourself, by Kristin Neff

Porn Literacy

Ethical Porn for Dicks: A Man's Guide to Responsible Viewing Pleasure, by David J. Ley

The Feminist Porn Book: The Politics of Producing Pleasure, by Tristan Taormino, Celine Parreñas Shimizu, Constance Penley, and Mireille Miller-Young

His Porn, Her Pain: Confronting America's PornPanic with Honest Talk About Sex, by Marty Klein

Purity Culture and Faith-Based Trauma

Pure: Inside the Evangelical Movement That Shamed a Generation of Young Women and How I Broke Free, by Linda Kay Klein

The Purity Myth: How America's Obsession with Virginity Is Hurting Young Women, by Jessica Valenti

Sex, God & the Conservative Church: Erasing Shame from Sexual Intimacy, by Tina Schermer Sellers

Racial Healing

The Inner Work of Racial Justice: Healing Ourselves and Transforming Our Communities Through Mindfulness, by Rhonda V. Magee

Me Sexy: An Exploration of Native Sex and Sexuality, edited by Drew Hayden Taylor

Mindful of Race: Transforming Racism from the Inside Out, by Ruth King

My Grandmother's Hands: Racialized Trauma and the Pathway to Mending Our Hearts and Bodies, by Resmaa Menakem

The Racial Healing Handbook: Practical Activities to Help You Challenge Privilege, Confront Systemic Racism & Engage in Collective Healing, by Anneliese Singh

Relationship Health

The Art of Receiving and Giving: The Wheel of Consent, by Betty Martin with Robyn Dalzen

Hold Me Tight: Seven Conversations for a Lifetime of Love, by Sue Johnson

Loving Bravely: Twenty Lessons of Self-Discovery to Help You Get the Love You Want, by Alexandra H. Solomon

Marriage Be Hard: 12 Conversations to Keep You Laughing, Loving, and Learning with Your Partner, by Kevin Fredericks and Melissa Fredericks

Mating in Captivity: Unlocking Erotic Intelligence, by Esther Perel

The Power of Attachment: How to Create Deep and Lasting Intimate Relationships, by Diane Poole Heller

The Seven Principles for Making Marriage Work: A Practical Guide from the Country's Foremost Relationship Expert, by John M. Gottman and Nan Silver

Wired for Love: How Understanding Your Partner's Brain and Attachment Style Can Help You Defuse Conflict and Build a Secure Relationship, by Stan Tatkin

Sex and Aging

Better Than I Ever Expected: Straight Talk About Sex After Sixty, by Joan Price

Naked at Our Age: Talking Out Loud About Senior Sex, by Joan Price

The Ultimate Guide to Sex After Fifty: How to Maintain—or Regain—a Spicy, Satisfying Sex Life, by Joan Price

Sexual Arousal and Desire

Come as You Are: The Surprising New Science That Will Transform Your Sex Life (revised and updated), by Emily Nagoski

The Come as You Are Workbook: A Practical Guide to the Science of Sex, by Emily Nagoski

Coping with Erectile Dysfunction: How to Regain Confidence and Enjoy Great Sex, by Michael E. Metz and Barry W. McCarthy

Taking Sexy Back: How to Own Your Sexuality and Create the Relationships You Want, by Alexandra H. Solomon

Sexual Pain

Healing Painful Sex: A Woman's Guide to Confronting, Diagnosing, and Treating Sexual Pain, by Deborah Coady and Nancy Fish

When Sex Hurts: Understanding and Healing Pelvic Pain, by Andrew Goldstein, Caroline Pukall, and Irwin Goldstein

Trauma

The Body Remembers: The Psychophysiology of Trauma and Trauma Treatment, by Babette Rothschild

Reclaiming Pleasure: A Sex Positive Guide for Moving Past Sexual Trauma and Living a Passionate Life, by Holly Richmond

What Happened to You? Conversations on Trauma, Resilience, and Healing, by Oprah Winfrey and Bruce D. Perry

ZINES

Fucking Trans Women, by Mira Bellwether, http://fuckingtranswomen .org/

Trans Sex Zine, Volumes 1 and 2, by Eloise von DeWitt and Bobbi Gass, https://transsexzine.com/

WEBSITES AND ORGANIZATIONS

Academy of Pelvic Health Physical Therapy, aptapelvichealth.org

American Association of Sexuality Educators, Counselors and Therapists (AASECT), aasect.org

The Asexual Visibility and Education Network (AVEN), asexuality.org

Black Lives Matter Meditation for Healing Racial Trauma by Dr. Candice Nicole Hargons, drcandicenicole.com/blm-meditation
EMDR (Eye Movement Desensitization and Reprocessing) Institute, Inc., emdr.com
The Gottman Institute, gottman.com
Herman & Wallace Pelvic Rehabilitation Institute, hermanwallace.com
The International Centre for Excellence in Emotionally Focused Therapy, iceeft.com
International Society for Sexual Medicine (ISSM), issm.info
International Society for the Study of Women's Sexual Health (ISSWSH), isswsh.org
Oh Joy Sex Toy, ohjoysextoy.com
OMG Yes (research-based video site about sexual pleasure for people with vulvas), omgyes.com
Organization for Polyamory and Ethical Non-monogamy, open-love.org
Sensorimotor Psychotherapy Institute, sensorimotorpsychotherapy.org
Sexual Health Solutions (online sexual health courses), sexualhealth solutions.com
Smitten Kitten (online education-based sexual health store), smittenkitten online.com
Somatic Experiencing International, traumahealing.org
Transgender Professional Association for Transgender Health (TPATH), tpathealth.org
The Wheel of Consent, bettymartin.org

COMMUNICATION CARDS/GAMES

Gottman Card Decks (mobile app): gottman.com/couples/apps
Where Should We Begin—A Game of Stories, by Esther Perel: https://game.estherperel.com

SEXUAL AIDS/TOYS

Fin by Dame Products: This can be helpful for folks who struggle with hand grip, arthritis, etc.
Joystick by Bump'n: An accessible sexual aid designed by disabled folks

Ohnut: Wearable and stackable silicone rings to help control the depth of
    penetration
Packer Gear FTM Stroker by California Exotic Novelties: Designed for
    people with clitorises who are trans and/or nonbinary
Starsi by Cute Little Fuckers: An inclusive vibrating toy for people of all
    genders
Liberator: There are a variety of wedge pillows with toy mounts

SEXUAL HEALTH/EROTIC STORIES APPS

Coral: getcoral.app
Dipsea: dipseastories.com
Emjoy: letsemjoy.com
Ferly: weareferly.com
Maeve: withmaeve.com

MINDFULNESS APPS

Calm: calm.com
Headspace: headspace.com
Insight Timer: insighttimer.com

ACKNOWLEDGMENTS

Thank you, first and foremost, to the many people who have trusted us with their sexual healthcare over the years. It's a privilege and an honor to be part of your journeys. Special thanks are due to our agent extraordinaire, Claire Harris, and P.S. Literary Agency for believing in this project early on and supporting us throughout the process. Gratitude to our editor, Catherine Tung. Special thanks to our amazing copyeditor, Raquel Pidal, and our sincere appreciation to Susan Lumenello, Marcy Barnes, and the rest of the team at Beacon Press. We are very appreciative of the talented Jennifer Pearl (Team Computer), who created beautiful graphics to accompany our words. Thank you to early readers and reviewers: Laurie Mintz, Lexx Brown-James, Elaine Fogel, Barry McCarthy, and Monica Johnson. We're so grateful for your thoughtful input and insights. Finally, we want to acknowledge the many pioneers of our field, without whom we would not be where we are today.

Jennifer: Thank you to my incredible partner, Josh. From propping me up on the tough and defeated days to ensuring I never wrote without a delicious latte in hand to running our home when I simply could not—this book would never have been possible without you. Thank you for always giving me the love and freedom to follow my passion.

To both chosen and bio family alike: I would be utterly lost without your love, encouragement, and some solid venting sessions. Thank you in particular to Elliot Tebbe, Erin Steen, and Michelle Gates for your steadfast friendship, unwavering support, and making me laugh until it hurts. Mom and Dad, you instilled in me a love of learning (and perhaps a bit of rebelliousness) from day one. Thank you for these immense gifts—they won't be wasted.

I've been privileged to learn from the most incredible mentors and teachers. To Jay Paul, thank you for bringing a scared and clueless first-generation college student under your wing and pointing her in the right direction. Thank you to my tireless graduate mentors, Sheila Garos and Susan Hendrick, who provided gentle guidance, challenging supervision, and more reference letters than anyone should ever have to write! My deep gratitude to Eli Coleman and Hildy Bowbeer for taking a chance on me and literally changing the direction of my career. To the incredible faculty and supervisors who mentored me at the Institute for Sexual and Gender Health, especially Bean Robinson, Sara J. Mize, Anne McBean, Dianne Berg, Katie Spencer, Rose Munns, and Alex Iantaffi: you are some of the most badass people and sex therapists I've ever met. Thank you, thank you, thank you for sharing your wisdom and passion.

Writing a book is just as difficult as I imagined, yet more rewarding than I dared hope. Lauren, I am eternally grateful that you talked me into this project and allowed me to share your brilliant vision. Some days were delightful, others were daunting, and I could not have asked for a better co-author and friend in this process.

———— • ————

Lauren: Immense gratitude to my family and friends for always supporting me and believing in me. I want to particularly thank my parents who have been my greatest supporters throughout my life, encouraging me to pursue my passions and career goals. Growing up in a sex-positive environment, as I did, is unfortunately less common and I'm determined to help change that.

To the many teachers, mentors, and supervisors who have guided me along my professional path, especially Gregory Shrader, Sheryl Harrison, Lawrence Sideman, Eli Coleman, Alex Iantaffi, and Dave Jackson.

To my husband, John, for loving me, grounding me, and encouraging me throughout this writing process. It's through our relationship that I have learned what it means to be in a partnership, how to communicate more effectively, and how to negotiate differences. I am so grateful to have him by my side.

Finally, to Jenn, without whom this book would not have been written. She helped keep me focused, added her vast expertise, and edited my stream-of-consciousness so that it made sense. She's a champion in this field and a wonderful friend. I'm beyond grateful that she agreed to write this book with me.

REFERENCES

INTRODUCTION: IT'S COMPLICATED

1. Filippo Maria Nimbi and Chiara Simonelli, "The Sex Therapists' Approach to the Evaluation and Management of Low Sex Drive in Men," *Journal of Sexual Medicine* 19, no. 4 (April 2022): 546–52, https://doi.org/10.1016/j.jsxm.2022.02.002.

2. Joseph Henrich, Steven J. Heine, and Ara Norenzayan, "The Weirdest People in the World?" *Behavioral and Brain Sciences* 33, nos. 2–3 (June 2010): 61–83, https://doi.org/10.1017/s0140525x0999152x.

CHAPTER 1: THE LOWDOWN ON LIBIDO

1. Sigmund Freud, *Three Essays on the Theory of Sexuality* (London: Imago Publishing Co., 1949).

2. John D. DeLamater and Janet Shibley Hyde, "Essentialism vs. Social Constructionism in the Study of Human Sexuality," *Journal of Sex Research* 35, no. 1 (1998): 10–18, https://doi.org/10.1080/00224499809551913; Leonore Tiefer, *Sex Is Not a Natural Act and Other Essays* (Boulder, CO: Westview Press, 2004); Deborah L. Tolman and Lisa M. Diamond, "Desegregating Sexuality Research: Cultural and Biological Perspectives on Gender and Desire," *Annual Review of Sex Research* 12 (2001): 33–74; Sari M. van Anders, "Testosterone and Sexual Desire in Healthy Women and Men," *Archives of Sexual Behavior* 41, no. 6 (December 2012): 1471–84, https://doi.org/10.1007/s10508-012-9946-2; Sari M. van Anders, "Beyond Masculinity: Testosterone, Gender/Sex, and Human Social Behavior in a Comparative Context," *Frontiers in Neuroendocrinology* 34, no. 3 (August 2013): 198–210, https://doi.org/10.1016/j.yfrne.2013.07.001.

3. Frederick M. Toates, *Motivational Systems: Problems in Behavioral Sciences* (Cambridge: Cambridge University Press, 1986).

4. Cindy M. Meston and David M. Buss, "Why Humans Have Sex," *Archives of Sexual Behavior* 36, no. 4 (August 2007): 477–507, https://doi.org/10.1007/s10508-007-9175-2.

5. Meredith L. Chivers et al., "Agreement of Self-Reported and Genital Measures of Sexual Arousal in Men and Women: A Meta-Analysis," *Archives of Sexual Behavior* 39, no. 1 (February 2010): 5–56, https://doi.org/10.1007/s10508-009-9556-9.

6. Helen Singer Kaplan, *Disorders of Sexual Desire and Other New Concepts and Techniques in Sex Therapy* (New York: Simon and Schuster, 1979).

7. Rosemary Basson, "The Female Sexual Response: A Different Model," *Journal of Sex & Marital Therapy* 26, no. 1 (2000): 51–65, https://doi.org/10.1080/009262300278641.

8. Jonny Coxon and Leighton Seal, "Medical Management to Support Trans Men in a Gender Identity Clinic," in *Men's Health*, ed. Roger S. Kirby et al. (Boca Raton, FL:

CRC Press, 2021), 260–65; Lisa Grossman and Mary Lake Polan, "Are Hormones the Answer to Low Libido? Individualizing Hormone Therapy for Low Libido in Midlife Women," *Contemporary OB/GYN* 58, no. 2 (February 2013): 22–26; T. Keta Hodgson and Glenn D. Braunstein, "Physiological Effects of Androgens in Women," in *Androgen Excess Disorders in Women: Polycystic Ovary Syndrome and Other Disorders*, 2nd ed., ed. Ricardo Azziz, Didier Dewailly, and John E. Nestler (Totowa, NJ: Humana Press, 2007), 49–61; Alvin M. Matsumoto, "Andropause: Clinical Implications of the Decline in Serum Testosterone Levels with Aging in Men," *Journals of Gerontology Series A: Biological Sciences and Medical Sciences* 57, no. 2 (February 2002): M76–99, https://doi.org/10 .1093/gerona/57.2.m76; James R. Roney and Zachary L. Simmons, "Hormonal Predictors of Sexual Motivation in Natural Menstrual Cycles," *Hormones and Behavior* 63, no. 4 (April 2013): 636–45, https://doi.org/10.1016/j.yhbeh.2013.02.013; Thomas G. Travison et al., "The Relationship Between Libido and Testosterone Levels in Aging Men," *Journal of Clinical Endocrinology & Metabolism* 91, no. 7 (July 2006): 2509–13, https:// doi.org/10.1210/jc.2005-2508.

9. Sharon J. Parish et al., "International Society for the Study of Women's Sexual Health Clinical Practice Guideline for the Use of Systemic Testosterone for Hypoactive Sexual Desire Disorder in Women," *Journal of Women's Health* 30, no. 4 (April 2021): 474–91, https://doi.org/10.1089/jwh.2021.29037; van Anders, "Testosterone and Sexual Desire in Healthy Women and Men."

10. Anita H. Clayton, Sheryl A. Kingsberg, and Irwin Goldstein, "Evaluation and Management of Hypoactive Sexual Desire Disorder," *Sexual Medicine* 6, no. 2 (June 2018): 59–74, https://doi.org/10.1016/j.esxm.2018.01.004; Amber N. Edinoff et al., "Bremelanotide for Treatment of Female Hypoactive Sexual Desire," *Neurology International* 14, no. 1 (March 2022): 75–88, https://doi.org/10.3390/neurolint14010006.

11. Zhahai Spring Stewart and Cascade Spring Cook, "About the Term 'New Relationship Energy,'" Aphrodite's Web, https://www.aphroweb.net/nre_origin.htm; Dorothy Tennov, *Love and Limerence: The Experience of Being in Love* (New York: Stein and Day, 1979).

12. JoAnn Loulan, *Lesbian Sex* (Duluth, MN: Spinsters Ink, 1984), 9.

13. Eric Janssen and James Bancroft, "The Dual-Control Model: The Role of Sexual Inhibition and Excitation in Sexual Arousal and Behavior," in *The Psychophysiology of Sex*, ed. Erick Janssen (Bloomington: Indiana University Press, 2007), 197–222.

14. Cynthia A. Graham et al., "Turning On and Turning Off: A Focus Group Study of the Factors That Affect Women's Sexual Arousal," *Archives of Sexual Behavior* 33, no. 6 (December 2004): 527–38, https://doi.org/10.1023/B:ASEB.0000044737.62561.fd.

15. Kristen P. Mark and Julie A. Lasslo, "Maintaining Sexual Desire in Long-Term Relationships: A Systematic Review and Conceptual Model," *Journal of Sex Research* 55, no. 4–5 (2018): 563–81, https://doi.org/10.1080/00224499.2018.1437592; Laura M. Vowels, Matthew J. Vowels, and Kristen P. Mark, "Uncovering the Most Important Factors for Predicting Sexual Desire Using Explainable Machine Learning," *Journal of Sexual Medicine* 18, no. 7 (2021): 1198–1216, https://doi.org/10.1016/j.jsxm.2021.04.010.

16. Maria Manuela Peixoto, "Problematic Sexual Desire Discrepancy in Heterosexuals, Gay Men and Lesbian Women: Differences in Sexual Satisfaction and Dyadic Adjustment," *Psychology & Sexuality* (November 2021): 1–11, https://doi.org/10.1080 /19419899.2021.1999313; Tiago José Pereira, Paulo P. P. Machado, and Maria Manuela Peixoto, "Sexual and Relationship Satisfaction: The Role of Perceived (Non)Problematic

Sexual Desire Discrepancy in Gay and Heterosexual Men," *Journal of Sex & Marital Therapy* 45, no. 2 (2019): 103–13, https://doi.org/10.1080/0092623x.2018.1488323.

17. David A. Frederick et al., "Debunking Lesbian Bed Death: Using Coarsened Exact Matching to Compare Sexual Practices and Satisfaction of Lesbian and Heterosexual Women," *Archives of Sexual Behavior* 50, no. 8 (November 2021): 3601–19, https://doi.org/10.1007/s10508-021-02096-4.

18. Julie Sondra Decker, *The Invisible Orientation: An Introduction to Asexuality* (New York: Skyhorse Publishing, 2015).

19. Adrienne Rich, "Compulsory Heterosexuality and Lesbian Existence," *Signs: Journal of Women in Culture and Society* 5, no. 4 (Summer 1980): 631–60, https://doi.org/10.1086/493756.

20. Angela Chen, *Ace: What Asexuality Reveals About Desire, Society, and the Meaning of Sex* (Boston: Beacon Press, 2021), 35.

21. Daniel M. Wegner et al., "Paradoxical Effects of Thought Suppression," *Journal of Personality and Social Psychology* 53, no. 1 (January 1987): 5–13, https://doi.org/10.1037/0022-3514.53.1.5.

22. Amelia Nagoski and Emily Nagoski, *Burnout: The Secret to Unlocking the Stress Cycle* (New York: Ballantine Books, 2019), 5.

CHAPTER 2: CULTURAL AND SOCIETAL FACTORS

1. Urie Bronfenbrenner, *The Ecology of Human Development: Experiments by Nature and Design* (Cambridge, MA: Harvard University Press, 1979).

2. George L. Engel, "The Need for a New Medical Model: A Challenge for Biomedicine," *Science* 196, no. 4286 (April 1977): 129–36, https://doi.org/10.1126/science.847460.

3. Kristen P. Mark and Julie A. Lasslo, "Maintaining Sexual Desire in Long-Term Relationships: A Systematic Review and Conceptual Model," *Journal of Sex Research* 55, no. 4–5 (2018): 563–81, https://doi.org/10.1080/00224499.2018.1437592.

4. Jean M. Twenge, Ryne A. Sherman, and Brooke E. Wells, "Sexual Inactivity During Young Adulthood Is More Common Among U.S. Millennials and iGen: Age, Period, and Cohort Effects on Having No Sexual Partners After Age 18," *Archives of Sexual Behavior* 46, no. 2 (February 2017): 433–40, https://doi.org/10.1007/s10508-016-0798-z.

5. Twenge, Sherman, and Wells, "Sexual Inactivity During Young Adulthood Is More Common Among U.S. Millennials and iGen," 433–40.

6. Robert Bozick, "Is There Really a Sex Recession? Period and Cohort Effects on Sexual Inactivity Among American Men, 2006–2019," *American Journal of Men's Health* 15, no. 6 (2021), https://doi.org/10.1177/15579883211057710; Twenge, Sherman, and Wells, "Sexual Inactivity During Young Adulthood Is More Common Among U.S. Millennials and iGen," 433–40.

7. Melissa A. Habel et al., "Heterosexual Anal and Oral Sex in Adolescents and Adults in the United States, 2011–2015," *Sexually Transmitted Diseases* 45, no. 12 (December 2018): 775–82, https://doi.org/10.1097/olq.0000000000000889; Debra Herbenick et al., "Prevalence and Characteristics of Vibrator Use by Women in the United States: Results from a Nationally Representative Study," *Journal of Sexual Medicine* 6, no. 7 (July 2009): 1857–66, https://doi.org/10.1111/j.1743-6109.2009.01318.x; Gui Liu et al., "Trends and Patterns of Sexual Behaviors Among Adolescents and Adults Aged 14 to

59 Years, United States," *Sexually Transmitted Diseases* 42, no. 1 (January 2015): 20–26, https://doi.org/10.1097/olq.0000000000000231; Michael Reece et al., "Prevalence and Characteristics of Vibrator Use by Men in the United States," *Journal of Sexual Medicine* 6, no. 7 (July 2009): 1867–74, https://doi.org/10.1111/j.1743-6109.2009.01290.x; Vanessa Schick et al., "Prevalence and Characteristics of Vibrator Use Among Women Who Have Sex with Women," *Journal of Sexual Medicine* 8, no. 12 (December 2011): 3306–15, https://doi.org/10.1111/j.1743-6109.2011.02503.x.

8. Kennedy Holmes, "Shining Another Light on Spousal Rape Exemptions: Spousal Sexual Violence Laws in the #MeToo Era," *UC Irvine Law Review* 11, no. 4 (April 2021): 1213.

9. Justin J. Lehmiller et al., "Less Sex, but More Sexual Diversity: Changes in Sexual Behavior During the COVID-19 Coronavirus Pandemic," *Leisure Sciences* 43, no. 1–2 (2021): 1–10, https://doi.org/10.1080/01490400.2020.1774016; Amy Muise, Ulrich Schimmack, and Emily A. Impett, "Sexual Frequency Predicts Greater Well-Being, but More Is Not Always Better," *Social Psychological and Personality Science* 7, no. 4 (May 2016): 295–302, https://doi.org/10.1177/1948550615616462.

10. Elina Haavio-Mannila and Osmo Kontula, "Correlates of Increased Sexual Satisfaction," *Archives of Sexual Behavior* 26, no. 4 (August 1997): 399–419, https://doi.org/10.1023/a:1024591318836; Shemeka Thorpe et al., "Black Women's Pleasure Mapping," *Journal of Black Sexuality and Relationships* 7, no. 4 (Spring 2021): 1–23, https://doi.org/10.1353/bsr.2021.0008.

11. Maria Manuela Peixoto, "Problematic Sexual Desire Discrepancy in Heterosexuals, Gay Men and Lesbian Women: Differences in Sexual Satisfaction and Dyadic Adjustment," *Psychology & Sexuality* (November 2021): 1–11, https://doi.org/10.1080/19419899.2021.1999313; Laura M. Vowels, Matthew J. Vowels, and Kristen P. Mark, "Uncovering the Most Important Factors for Predicting Sexual Desire Using Explainable Machine Learning," *Journal of Sexual Medicine* 18, no. 7 (2021): 1198–1216; Laura M. Vowels, Matthew J. Vowels, and Kristen P. Mark, "Identifying the Strongest Self-Report Predictors of Sexual Satisfaction Using Machine Learning," *Journal of Social and Personal Relationships* 39, no. 5 (May 2022): 1191–1212.

12. Gary R. VandenBos, ed., *APA Dictionary of Psychology* (Washington, DC: American Psychological Association, 2007).

13. Donald O. Hebb, *The Organisation of Behaviour: A Neuropsychological Theory* (London: Wiley, 1949).

14. Carla J. Shatz, "The Developing Brain," *Scientific American* 267, no. 3 (September 1992): 60–67, https://doi.org/10.1038/scientificamerican0992-60.

15. Amy M. Burdette, Terrence D. Hill, and Kyl Myers, "Understanding Religious Variations in Sexuality and Sexual Health," in *Handbook of the Sociology of Sexualities*, ed. John Delamater and Rebecca F. Plante (New York: Springer, 2015), 349–70.

16. Linda K. Klein, *Pure: Inside the Evangelical Movement That Shamed a Generation of Young Women and How I Broke Free* (New York: Atria, 2018).

17. Klein, *Pure*, 189.

18. Bretlyn C. Owens, M. Elizabeth Lewis Hall, and Tamara L. Anderson, "The Relationship Between Purity Culture and Rape Myth Acceptance," *Journal of Psychology and Theology* 49, no. 4 (December 2021): 405–18, https://doi.org/10.1177/0091647120974992.

19. Stephenie Davies, Jennifer Katz, and Joan L. Jackson, "Sexual Desire Discrepancies: Effects on Sexual and Relationship Satisfaction in Heterosexual Dating Couples,"

Archives of Sexual Behavior 28, no. 6 (December 1999): 553–67, https://doi.org/10
.1023/A:1018721417683; Kristen P. Mark and Sarah H. Murray, "Gender Differences
in Desire Discrepancy as a Predictor of Sexual and Relationship Satisfaction in a College
Sample of Heterosexual Romantic Relationships," *Journal of Sex & Marital Therapy* 38,
no. 2 (2012): 198–215, https://doi.org/10.1080/0092623x.2011.606877.

20. Rose McKeon Olson and Claudia García-Moreno, "Virginity Testing: A Systematic Review," *Reproductive Health* 14, no. 61 (2017), https://doi.org/10.1186/s12978
-017-0319-0; Jessica Valenti, *The Purity Myth: How America's Obsession with Virginity Is
Hurting Young Women* (Berkeley, CA: Seal Press, 2009).

21. Hanne Blank, *Virgin: The Untouched History* (New York: Bloomsbury, 2008).

22. Virginia R. Brooks, *Minority Stress and Lesbian Women* (Lexington, MA: Lexington Books, 1981); Ilan H. Meyer, "Minority Stress and Mental Health in Gay Men,"
Journal of Health and Social Behavior 36, no. 1 (March 1995): 38–56, https://doi.org
/10.2307/2137286.

23. Meyer, "Minority Stress and Mental Health in Gay Men"; Ilan H. Meyer,
"Prejudice, Social Stress, and Mental Health in Lesbian, Gay, and Bisexual Populations:
Conceptual Issues and Research Evidence," *Psychological Bulletin* 129, no. 5 (2003): 674,
https://doi.org/10.1037/0033-2909.129.5.674.

24. Cristóbal Calvillo, María del Mar Sánchez-Fuentes, and Juan Carlos Sierra, "An
Explanatory Model of Sexual Satisfaction in Adults with a Same-Sex Partner: An Analysis
Based on Gender Differences," *International Journal of Environmental Research and Public
Health* 17, no. 10 (May 2020): 3393, https://doi.org/10.3390/ijerph17103393; Chao
Song et al., "Perceived Discrimination and Relationship Satisfaction Among Same-Sex
Couples: The Role of Dyadic Stress and Sex," *Journal of Sex & Marital Therapy* 48, no. 6
(January 2022): 567–78, https://doi.org/10.1080/0092623x.2021.2022048.

25. Wilson S. Figueroa et al., "Daily Stressors and Diurnal Cortisol Among Sexual
and Gender Minority Young Adults," *Health Psychology* 40, no. 2 (2021): 145–54, https://
doi.org/10.1037/hea0001054; Annesa Flentje et al., "The Relationship Between Minority
Stress and Biological Outcomes: A Systematic Review," *Journal of Behavioral Medicine* 43,
no. 5 (October 2020): 673–94, https://doi.org/10.1007/s10865-019-00120-6; David
M. Huebner et al., "Cardiovascular and Cortisol Responses to Experimentally-Induced
Minority Stress," *Health Psychology* 40, no. 5 (2021): 316–25, https://doi.org/10.1037
/hea0001067.

26. David H. Chae et al., "Discrimination, Racial Bias, and Telomere Length in
African-American Men," *American Journal of Preventive Medicine* 46, no. 2 (February
2014): 103–11, https://doi.org/10.1016/j.amepre.2013.10.020; David H. Chae et al.,
"Racial Discrimination and Telomere Shortening Among African Americans: The Coronary Artery Risk Development in Young Adults (CARDIA) Study," *Health Psychology*
39, no. 3 (2020): 209–19, https://doi.org/10.1037/hea0000832; Marilyn D. Thomas
et al., "Racial Discrimination and Telomere Length in Midlife African American
Women: Interactions of Educational Attainment and Employment Status," *Annals of
Behavioral Medicine* 55, no. 7 (July 2021): 601–11, https://doi.org/10.1093
/abm/kaaa104.

27. Candice N. Hargons et al., "'White People Stress Me Out All the Time': Black
Students Define Racial Trauma," *Cultural Diversity and Ethnic Minority Psychology* 28, no.
1 (2022): 49–57, https://doi.org/10.1037/cdp0000351; Derald Wing Sue et al., "Racial

Microaggressions in Everyday Life: Implications for Clinical Practice," *American Psychologist* 62, no. 4 (2007): 271–86, https://doi.org/10.1037/0003-066x.62.4.271.

28. Lisa Dawn Hamilton and Cindy M. Meston, "Chronic Stress and Sexual Function in Women," *Journal of Sexual Medicine* 10, no. 10 (October 2013): 2443–54, https://doi.org/10.1111/jsm.12249; Katrina Schrode et al., "Minority Stress and Sexual Functioning Among African American Women with At-Risk Partners in South Los Angeles," *Journal of Sexual Medicine* 19, no. 4 (April 2022): 603–12, https://doi.org/10.1016/j.jsxm.2022.02.005.

29. Moniek M. ter Kuile, Daan Vigeveno, and Ellen Laan, "Preliminary Evidence That Acute and Chronic Daily Psychological Stress Affect Sexual Arousal in Sexually Functional Women," *Behaviour Research and Therapy* 45, no. 9 (September 2007): 2078–89, https://doi.org/10.1016/j.brat.2007.03.006.

30. Adrienne Rich, "Compulsory Heterosexuality and Lesbian Existence," *Signs: Journal of Women in Culture and Society* 5, no. 4 (1980): 631–60, https://doi.org/10.1086/493756; Sari M. van Anders et al., "The Heteronormativity Theory of Low Sexual Desire in Women Partnered with Men," *Archives of Sexual Behavior* 51, no. 1 (January 2022): 391–415, https://doi.org/10.1007/s10508-021-02100-x; Michael Warner, "Introduction: Fear of a Queer Planet," *Social Text*, no. 29 (1991): 3–17, http://www.jstor.org/stable/466295.

31. van Anders et al., "The Heteronormativity Theory of Low Sexual Desire in Women Partnered with Men"; Stevi Jackson, "Interchanges: Gender, Sexuality and Heterosexuality: The Complexity (and Limits) of Heteronormativity," *Feminist Theory* 7, no. 1 (April 2006): 105–21, https://doi.org/10.1177/1464700106061462; Kristen Schilt and Laurel Westbrook, "Doing Gender, Doing Heteronormativity: 'Gender Normals,' Transgender People, and the Social Maintenance of Heterosexuality," *Gender & Society* 23, no. 4 (August 2009): 440–64, https://doi.org/10.1177/0891243209340034.

32. van Anders et al., "The Heteronormativity Theory of Low Sexual Desire in Women Partnered with Men."

33. Alex Iantaffi, *Gender Trauma: Healing Cultural, Social, and Historical Gendered Trauma* (London: Jessica Kingsley Publishers, 2021); G. Nic Rider, Jennifer A. Vencill et al., "The Gender Affirmative Lifespan Approach (GALA): A Framework for Competent Clinical Care with Nonbinary Clients," *International Journal of Transgenderism* 20, no. 2–3 (2019): 275–88, https://doi.org/10.1080/15532739.2018.1485069.

34. Michael L. Hendricks and Rylan J. Testa, "A Conceptual Framework for Clinical Work with Transgender and Gender Nonconforming Clients: An Adaptation of the Minority Stress Model," *Professional Psychology: Research and Practice* 43, no. 5 (2012): 460–67, https://doi.org/10.1037/a0029597.

35. Melanie Blackless et al., "How Sexually Dimorphic Are We? Review and Synthesis," *American Journal of Human Biology* 12, no. 2 (March 2000): 151–66, https://doi.org/10.1002/(SICI)1520-6300(200003/04)12:2<151::AID-AJHB1>3.0.CO;2-F; Leonard Sax, "How Common Is Intersex? A Response to Anne Fausto-Sterling," *Journal of Sex Research* 39, no. 3 (2002): 174–78, https://doi.org/10.1080/00224490209552139.

36. Lexie Kite and Lindsay Kite, *More Than a Body: Your Body Is an Instrument, Not an Ornament* (Boston: Houghton Mifflin Harcourt, 2021).

37. Barbara L. Fredrickson and Tomi-Ann Roberts, "Objectification Theory: Toward Understanding Women's Lived Experiences and Mental Health Risks," *Psychology of*

Women Quarterly 21, no. 2 (June 1997): 173–206, https://doi.org/10.1111/j.1471
-6402.1997.tb00108.x.

38. William H. Masters and Virginia E. Johnson, *Human Sexual Inadequacy* (Boston: Little, Brown, 1970).

39. Susan L. Bryant, "The Beauty Ideal: The Effects of European Standards of Beauty on Black Women," *Columbia Social Work Review* 11, no. 1 (2019): 80–91, https://doi .org/10.7916/cswr.v11i1.1933; Emma Dabiri, *Twisted: The Tangled History of Black Hair Culture* (New York: Harper Perennial, 2020); Molly Silvestrini, "'It's Not Something I Can Shake': The Effect of Racial Stereotypes, Beauty Standards, and Sexual Racism on Interracial Attraction," *Sexuality & Culture* 24, no. 1 (February 2020): 305–25, https:// doi.org/10.1007/s12119-019-09644-0.

40. Whitney Howzell, "The Influence of Colorism on Sexual Desirability Among Black Americans," PhD diss., Widener University, 2019, https://www.proquest.com /openview/a4cb1753af9c1a6cc8ff6f3938b554b5/1.pdf?pq-origsite=gscholar&cbl =18750&diss=y.

CHAPTER 3: INTERPERSONAL FACTORS

1. John M. Gottman and Nan Silver, *The Seven Principles for Making Marriage Work: A Practical Guide from the Country's Foremost Relationship Expert* (New York: Harmony Books, 2015).

2. Gottman and Silver, *The Seven Principles for Making Marriage Work.*

3. Gottman and Silver, *The Seven Principles for Making Marriage Work.*

4. Zhahai Spring Stewart and Cascade Spring Cook, "About the Term 'New Relationship Energy'," https://www.aphroweb.net/nre_origin.htm.

5. Terri D. Conley et al., "The Fewer the Merrier? Assessing Stigma Surrounding Consensually Non-monogamous Romantic Relationships," *Analyses of Social Issues and Public Policy* 13, no. 1 (December 2013): 1–30, https://doi.org/10.1111/j.1530-2415 .2012.01286.x.

6. Nichole Fairbrother, Trevor A. Hart, and Malcolm Fairbrother, "Open Relationship Prevalence, Characteristics, and Correlates in a Nationally Representative Sample of Canadian Adults," *Journal of Sex Research* 56, no. 6 (2019): 695–704, https://doi.org/10 .1080/00224499.2019.1580667; Mara L. Haupert et al., "Prevalence of Experiences with Consensual Non-Monogamous Relationships: Findings from Two National Samples of Single Americans," *Journal of Sex & Marital Therapy* 43, no. 5 (2017): 424–40, https:// doi.org/10.1080/0092623X.2016.1178675; Ethan Czuy Levine et al., "Open Relationships, Nonconsensual Nonmonogamy, and Monogamy Among U.S. Adults: Findings from the 2012 National Survey of Sexual Health and Behavior," *Archives of Sexual Behavior* 47, no. 5 (2018): 1439–50, https://doi.org/10.1007/s10508-018-1178-7.

7. Monique Haicault, "La Gestion Ordinaire de La Vie En Deux," *Sociologie Du Travail* 26, no. 3 (1984): 268–77, https://doi.org/10.3406/sotra.1984.2072.

8. Liz Dean, Brendan Churchill, and Leah Ruppanner, "The Mental Load: Building a Deeper Theoretical Understanding of How Cognitive and Emotional Labor Over*load* Women and Mothers," *Community, Work & Family* 25, no. 1 (2022): 13–29, https://doi .org/10.1080/13668803.2021.2002813.

9. Sari M. van Anders et al, "The Heteronormativity Theory of Low Sexual Desire in Women Partnered with Men," *Archives of Sexual Behavior* 51 (August 2021): 391–415, https://doi.org/10.1007/s10508-021-02100-x.

10. Abbie E. Goldberg, Nanette K. Gartrell, and Gary Gates, *Research Report on LGB-Parent Families* (Los Angeles: Williams Institute, UCLA School of Law, 2014), https://williamsinstitute.law.ucla.edu/wp-content/uploads/LGB-Parent-Families-Jul -2014.pdf.

11. Nathan D. Leonhardt et al., "Relationship Satisfaction and Commitment in the Transition to Parenthood: A Couple-Centered Approach," *Journal of Marriage and Family* 84, no. 1 (2022): 80–100, https://doi.org/10.1111/jomf.12785; Natalie O. Rosen et al., "Trajectories of Sexual Well-Being Among Couples in the Transition to Parenthood," *Journal of Family Psychology* 35, no. 4 (2021): 523–33, https://doi.org/10.1037 /fam0000689.

CHAPTER 4: INDIVIDUAL FACTORS

1. Katrina Karkazis and Rebecca Jordan-Young, "Debating a Testosterone 'Sex Gap,'" *Science* 348, no. 6237 (May 2015): 858–60, https://doi.org/10.1126/science.aab1057; Elisa Maseroli and Linda Vignozzi, "Are Endogenous Androgens Linked to Female Sexual Function? A Systemic Review and Meta-Analysis," *Journal of Sexual Medicine* 19, no. 4 (April 2022): 553–68, https://doi.org/10.1016/j.jsxm.2022.01.515; Sari M. van Anders, "Beyond Masculinity: Testosterone, Gender/Sex, and Human Social Behavior in a Comparative Context," *Frontiers in Neuroendocrinology* 34, no. 3 (August 2013): 198–210, https://doi.org/10.1016/j.yfrne.2013.07.001.

2. Sara B. Chadwick et al., "Multifaceted Sexual Desire and Hormonal Associations: Accounting for Social Location, Relationship Status, and Desire Target," *Archives of Sexual Behavior* 46, no. 8 (April 2017): 2445–63, https://doi.org/10.1007/s10508-017-0959-8; Jukka Hintikka et al., "Original Research—Endocrinology: Hypogonadism, Decreased Sexual Desire, and Long-Term Depression in Middle-Aged Men," *Journal of Sexual Medicine* 6, no. 7 (July 2009): 2049–57, https://doi.org/10.1111/j.1743-6109.2009.01299.x; F. Jockenhövel et al., "Comparison of Long-Acting Testosterone Undecanoate Formulation Versus Testosterone Enanthate on Sexual Function and Mood in Hypogonadal Men," *European Journal of Endocrinology* 160, no. 5 (2009): 815–19, https://doi.org/10 .1530/EJE-08-0830; Jessica C. Raisanen et al., "Average Associations Between Sexual Desire, Testosterone, and Stress in Women and Men Over Time," *Archives of Sexual Behavior* 47, no. 6 (2018): 1613–31, https://doi.org/10.1007/s10508-018-1231-6; Sari M. van Anders, "Testosterone and Sexual Desire in Healthy Women and Men," *Archives of Sexual Behavior* 41, no. 6 (2012): 1471–84, https://doi.org/10.1007/s10508-012-9946-2; Sari M. van Anders, Katherine L. Goldey, and Patty X. Kuo, "The Steroid/Peptide Theory of Social Bonds: Integrating Testosterone and Peptide Responses for Classifying Social Behavioral Contexts," *Psychoneuroendocrinology* 36, no. 9 (October 2011): 1265–75, https:// doi.org/10.1016/j.psyneuen.2011.06.001.

3. Rosemary Basson et al., "Role of Androgens in Women's Sexual Dysfunction," *Menopause* 17, no. 5 (September 2010): 962–71, http://doi.org/10.1097/gme.0b013 e3181d59765; Susan R. Davis et al., "Circulating Androgen Levels and Self-Reported Sexual Function in Women," *JAMA* 294, no. 1 (2005): 91–96, https://doi.org/10.1001 /jama.294.1.91; Raisanen et al., "Average Associations Between Sexual Desire, Testosterone, and Stress in Women and Men Over Time"; Patricia Schreiner-Engel et al., "Low Sexual Desire in Women: The Role of Reproductive Hormones," *Hormones and Behavior* 23, no. 2 (June 1989): 221–34, https://doi.org/10.1016/0018-506X(89)90063-9; van Anders, "Testosterone and Sexual Desire in Healthy Women and Men"; Sari M.

van Anders et al., "Associations Between Testosterone Secretion and Sexual Activity in Women," *Hormones and Behavior* 51, no. 4 (April 2007): 477–82, https://doi.org/10.1016/j.yhbeh.2007.01.003; Sari M. van Anders and Emily J. Dunn, "Are Gonadal Steroids Linked with Orgasm Perceptions and Sexual Assertiveness in Women and Men?" *Hormones and Behavior* 56, no. 2 (August 2009): 206–13, https://doi.org/10.1016/j.yhbeh.2009.04.007; Sari M. van Anders, Katherine L. Goldey, and Sarah N. Bell, "Measurement of Testosterone in Human Sexuality Research: Methodological Considerations," *Archives of Sexual Behavior* 43, no. 2 (2014): 231–50, https://doi.org/10.1007/s10508-013-0123-z.

4. Katie K. Crean-Tate, Jennifer A. Vencill et al., "Management of Genitourinary Syndrome of Menopause in Female Cancer Patients: A Focus on Vaginal Hormonal Therapy," *American Journal of Obstetrics & Gynecology* 222, no. 2 (February 2020): 103–13, https://doi.org/10.1016/j.ajog.2019.08.043; Risa Kagan, Susan Kellogg-Spadt, and Sharon J. Parish, "Practical Treatment Considerations in the Management of Genitourinary Syndrome of Menopause," *Drugs & Aging* 36, no. 10 (2019): 897–908, https://doi.org/10.1007/s40266-019-00700-w.

5. Koen Demyttenaere and Liesbeth Jaspers, "Review: Bupropion and SSRI-Induced Side Effects," *Journal of Psychopharmacology* 22, no. 7 (2008): 792–804, https://doi.org/10.1177/0269881107083798.

6. Monika Staruch et al., "Sexual Activity During Pregnancy," *Neuroendocrinology Letters* 37, no. 1 (2016): 53–58, https://www.researchgate.net/publication/299072479_Sexual_activity_during_Pregnancy.

7. Rosie Charter et al., "The Transgender Parent: Experiences and Constructions of Pregnancy and Parenthood for Transgender Men in Australia," *International Journal of Transgenderism* 19, no. 1 (2018): 64–77, https://doi.org/10.1080/15532739.2017.1399496; Lee K. Roosevelt, Sarah Pietzmeier, and Robinson Reed, "Clinically and Culturally Competent Care for Transgender and Nonbinary People: A Challenge to Providers of Perinatal Care," *Journal of Perinatal & Neonatal Nursing* 35, no. 2 (April/June 2021): 142–49, https://doi.org/10.1097/JPN.0000000000000560.

8. Charlotte Cassis et al., "What Happens to Female Sexual Function During Pregnancy?" *European Journal of Obstetrics & Gynecology and Reproductive Biology* 258 (March 2021): 265–68, https://doi.org/10.1016/j.ejogrb.2021.01.003; Sunullah Soysal et al., "Differences in Sexual Function Between Trimesters During Pregnancy: An Observational Study," *Gynecology Obstetrics & Reproductive Medicine* 27, no. 2 (2021): 109–15, https://doi.org/10.21613/GORM.2020.1073.

9. Stephanie Buehler, *Counseling Couples Before, During, and After Pregnancy: Sexuality and Intimacy Issues* (New York: Springer Publishing Co., 2018).

10. Charter et al., "The Transgender Parent."

11. Mattea Romano et al., "Postpartum Period: Three Distinct but Continuous Phases," *Journal of Prenatal Medicine* 4, no. 2 (April–June 2010): 22–25.

12. Catherine Forster et al., "Psychological and Sexual Changes After the Cessation of Breast-Feeding," *Obstetrics and Gynecology* 84, no. 5 (November 1994): 872–76.

13. Christine M. Curley and Blair T. Johnson, "Sexuality and Aging: Is It Time for a New Sexual Revolution?" *Social Science & Medicine* 301 (May 2022): 114865, https://doi.org/10.1016/j.socscimed.2022.114865; Terrie Beth Ginsberg, Sherry C. Pomerantz, and Veronika Kramer-Feeley, "Sexuality in Older Adults: Behaviours and Preferences," *Age and Ageing* 34, no. 5 (September 2005): 475–80, https://doi.org/10.1093/ageing

/afi143; Shilpa Srinivasan et al., "Sexuality and the Older Adult," *Current Psychiatry Reports* 21, no. 97 (2019), https://doi.org/10.1007/s11920-019-1090-4.

14. Adapted from Joan Price, *The Ultimate Guide to Sex After 50: How to Maintain—or Regain—a Spicy, Satisfying Sex Life* (New York: Cleis Press, 2014).

15. Thierry Almont et al., "Sexual Health Problems and Discussion in Colorectal Cancer Patients Two Years After Diagnosis: A National Cross-Sectional Study," *Journal of Sexual Medicine* 16, no. 1 (January 2019): 96–110, https://doi.org/10.1016/j.jsxm.2018.11.008; Leslie R. Schover, "Sexual Quality of Life in Men and Women After Cancer," *Climacteric* 22, no. 6 (2019): 553–57, https://doi.org/10.1080/13697137.2018.1526893.

16. Roanne Millman et al., "Patient Interest in the Lowdown on Down There: Attendance at a Vulvovaginal and Sexual Health Workshop Post-Cancer Treatment," *Supportive Care in Cancer* 28, no. 8 (2020): 3889–96, https://doi.org/10.1007/s00520-019-05162-9.

17. Crean-Tate, Vencill et al., "Management of Genitourinary Syndrome of Menopause in Female Cancer Patients"; Craig D. Zippe et al., "Female Sexual Dysfunction After Radical Cystectomy: A New Outcome Measure," *Urology* 63, no. 6 (June 2004): 1153–57, https://doi.org/10.1016/j.urology.2003.12.034.

18. Elizabeth Cathcart-Rake et al., "Querying Patients with Cancer About Sexual Health and Sexual and Gender Minority Status: A Qualitative Study of Health-Care Providers," *American Journal of Hospice and Palliative Medicine* 37, no. 6 (2019): 418–23, https://doi.org/10.1177/1049909119879129; E. M. Krouwel et al., "Discussing Sexual Health in the Medical Oncologist's Practice: Exploring Current Practice and Challenges," *Journal of Cancer Education* 35, no. 6 (2019): 1072–88, https://doi.org/10.1007/s13187-019-01559-6; Jennifer Barsky Reese et al., "Patient-Provider Communication About Sexual Concerns in Cancer: A Systematic Review," *Journal of Cancer Survivorship* 11, no. 2 (2016): 175–88, https://doi.org/10.1007/s11764-016-0577-9; Marjan J. Traa et al., "The Sexual Health Care Needs After Colorectal Cancer: The View of Patients, Partners, and Health Care Professionals," *Supportive Care in Cancer* 22, no. 3 (2014): 763–72, https://doi.org/10.1007/s00520-013-2032-z.

19. Lucie Fielding, *Trans Sex: Clinical Approaches to Trans Sexualities and Erotic Embodiments* (New York: Routledge, 2021).

CHAPTER 5: CONNECTION WITH SELF

1. Charlie Glickman, "The Language of Sex Positivity," *Electronic Journal of Human Sexuality* 3 (July 2000): 1–5, http://www.ejhs.org/volume3/sexpositive.htm.

2. Lori A. Brotto et al., "A Randomized Trial Comparing Group Mindfulness-Based Cognitive Therapy with Group Supportive Sex Education and Therapy for the Treatment of Female Sexual Interest/Arousal Disorder," *Journal of Consulting and Clinical Psychology* 89, no. 7 (2021): 626–39, https://doi.org/10.1037/ccp0000661; Izabela Jaderek and Michal Lew-Starowicz, "A Systematic Review on Mindfulness Meditation–Based Interventions for Sexual Dysfunctions," *Journal of Sexual Medicine* 16, no. 10 (October 2019): 1581–96, https://doi.org/10.1016/j.jsxm.2019.07.019; Chelom E. Leavitt, Eva S. Lefkowitz, and Emily A. Waterman, "The Role of Sexual Mindfulness in Sexual Wellbeing, Relational Wellbeing, and Self-Esteem," *Journal of Sex & Marital Therapy* 45, no. 6 (2019): 497–509, https://doi.org/10.1080/0092623X.2019.1572680.

3. Nicola Finley, "Lifestyle Choices Can Augment Female Sexual Well-Being," *American Journal of Lifestyle Medicine* 12, no. 1 (2018): 38–41, https://doi.org/10.1177

/1559827617740823; Jaderek, and Lew-Starowicz, "A Systematic Review on Mindfulness Meditation–Based Interventions for Sexual Dysfunctions."

4. Stephenie R. Chaudoir, Katie Wang, and John E. Pachankis, "What Reduces Sexual Minority Stress? A Review of the Intervention 'Toolkit,'" *Journal of Social Issues* 73, no. 3 (September 2017): 586–617, https://doi.org/10.1111/josi.12233; Mathijs F. G. Lucassen et al., "Rainbow SPARX: A Novel Approach to Addressing Depression in Sexual Minority Youth," *Cognitive and Behavioral Practice* 22, no. 2 (May 2015): 203–16, https://doi.org/10.1016/j.cbpra.2013.12.008; Della V. Mosley et al., "Critical Consciousness of Anti-Black Racism: A Practical Model to Prevent and Resist Racial Trauma," *Journal of Counseling Psychology* 68, no. 1 (March 2020): 1–16, https://doi.org/10.1037 /cou0000430.

5. World Association for Sexual Health, "Declaration on Sexual Pleasure," https:// worldsexualhealth.net/declaration-on-sexual-pleasure.

6. Louisa Allen, "Pleasure's Perils? Critically Reflecting on Pleasure's Inclusion in Sexuality Education," *Sexualities* 15, no. 3–4 (2012): 455–71, https://doi.org/10.1177 /1363460712439654.

7. Adapted from Julia R. Heiman, and Joseph LoPiccolo, *Becoming Orgasmic: A Sexual and Personal Growth Program for Women*, revised and expanded ed. (New York: Fireside Books, 1988), 58.

8. Daniel J. Siegel, *Mindsight: The New Science of Personal Transformation* (New York: Bantam Books, 2010).

9. Deb Dana, *Anchored: How to Befriend Your Nervous System Using Polyvagal Theory* (Boulder, CO: Sounds True, 2021), 130.

10. Stephanie S. Faubion, Richa Sood, and Ekta Kapoor, "Genitourinary Syndrome of Menopause: Management Strategies for the Clinician," *Mayo Clinic Proceedings* 92, no. 12 (December 2017): 1842–49, https://doi.org/10.1016/j.mayocp.2017.08.019; Ellen Laan, Alessandra H. Rellini, and Tricia Barnes, "Standard Operating Procedures for Female Orgasmic Disorder: Consensus of the International Society for Sexual Medicine," *Journal of Sexual Medicine* 10, no. 1 (January 2013): 74–82, https://doi.org/10.1111/j .1743-6109.2012.02880.x; Elizabeth S. Rubin et al., "A Clinical Reference Guide on Sexual Devices for Obstetrician–Gynecologists," *Obstetrics & Gynecology* 133, no. 6 (June 2019): 1259–68, DOI:10.1097/AOG.0000000000003262; Emily Stabile, "Getting the Government in Bed: How to Regulate the Sex Toy Industry," *Berkeley Journal of Gender, Law & Justice* 28, no. 161 (2013), http://dx.doi.org/10.2139/ssrn.2222079.

11. Debra Herbenick et al., "Women's Vibrator Use in Sexual Partnerships: Results from a Nationally Representative Survey in the United States," *Journal of Sex & Marital Therapy* 36, no. 1 (2010): 49–65, https://doi.org/10.1080/00926230903375677; Laan, Rellini, and Barnes, "Standard Operating Procedures for Female Orgasmic Disorder"; Jordan E. Rullo et al., "Genital Vibration for Sexual Function and Enhancement: Best Practice Recommendations for Choosing and Safely Using a Vibrator," *Sexual and Relationship Therapy* 33, no. 3 (2018): 275–85, https://doi.org/10.1080/14681994.201 7.1419558; Jordan E. Rullo et al., "Genital Vibration for Sexual Function and Enhancement: A Review of Evidence," *Sexual and Relationship Therapy* 33, no. 3 (2018): 263–74, https://doi.org/10.1080/14681994.2017.1419557; Robert L. Segal, Kambiz Tajkarimi, and Arthur L. Burnett, "Viberect Penile Vibratory Stimulation System: Evaluation of Its Erectogenic Efficacy," *Canadian Journal of Urology* 20, no. 4 (August 2013): 6844–47.

12. Debra Herbenick et al., "Prevalence and Characteristics of Vibrator Use by Women in the United States: Results from a Nationally Representative Study," *Journal of Sexual Medicine* 6, no. 7 (2009): 1857–66, https://doi.org/10.1111/j.1743-6109.2009 .01318.x; Michael Reece et al., "Prevalence and Characteristics of Vibrator Use by Men in the United States," *Journal of Sexual Medicine* 6, no. 7 (July 2009): 1867–74, https://doi .org/10.1111/j.1743-6109.2009.01290.x.

13. Vanessa Schick et al., "Prevalence and Characteristics of Vibrator Use Among Women Who Have Sex with Women," *Journal of Sexual Medicine*, no. 8 (December 2011): 3306–15, https://doi.org/10.1111/j.1743-6109.2011.02503.x.

14. Alan McKee, "Positive and Negative Effects of Pornography as Attributed by Consumers," *Australian Journal of Communications* 34, no. 1 (January 2007): 87–104; Chris Rissel et al., "A Profile of Pornography Users in Australia: Findings from the Second Australian Study of Health and Relationships," *Journal of Sex Research* 54, no. 2 (2016): 227–40, https://doi.org/10.1080/00224499.2016.1191597.

15. Marty Klein, *His Porn, Her Pain: Confronting America's PornPanic with Honest Talk About Sex* (Santa Barbara, CA: Praeger, 2016).

16. S. E. M. Gauvin and K. E. Merwin, "Sexual Communication Among Sexual and Gender/Sex Diverse Folks: An Overview of What We Know and Suggestions for Where to Go," *Current Sexual Health Reports* 14 (March 2022): 47–62, https://doi.org/10.1007 /s11930-022-00328-9.

17. Emily Rothman, Nicole Daley, and Jess Adler, "A Pornography Literacy Program for Adolescents," *American Journal of Public Health* 110, no. 2 (February 2020): 154–56, https://doi.org/10.2105/AJPH.2019.305468.

CHAPTER 6: CONNECTION WITH PARTNER(S)

1. John M. Gottman and Nan Silver, *The Seven Principles for Making Marriage Work: A Practical Guide from the Country's Foremost Relationship Expert* (New York: Harmony Books, 2015).

2. Murray Bowen, "Theory in the Practice of Psychotherapy," in *Family Therapy: Theory and Practice*, ed. Philip J. Guerin (Cincinnati: Gardner Press, 1976), 42–90.

3. Elahe Ghanbarian et al., "Differentiation of Self and Mate Retention Behaviors: The Mediating Role of Communication Patterns," *Evolutionary Psychology* 18, no. 4 (2020), https://doi.org/10.1177/1474704920972051; Arzun Telli, and Çiğdem Yavuz Güler, "Differentiation of Self, Forgiveness, Jealousy, and Conflict Resolution Responses Among Married Individuals: The Mediating Role of Relationship Satisfaction, Relationship Adjustment, and Emotional Dependency," *Contemporary Family Therapy*, (August 2021), https://doi.org/10.1007/s10591-021-09603-8.

4. Betty Martin with Robyn Dalzen, *The Art of Receiving and Giving: The Wheel of Consent* (Eugene, OR: Luminare Press, 2021).

5. William H. Masters and Virginia E. Johnson, *Human Sexual Response* (Boston: Little, Brown, 1966); William H. Masters and Virginia E. Johnson, *Human Sexual Inadequacy* (Boston: Little, Brown, 1970); Linda Weiner and Constance Avery-Clark, *Sensate Focus in Sex Therapy: The Illustrated Manual* (New York: Routledge, 2017).

6. Gottman and Silver, *The Seven Principles for Making Marriage Work*.

7. John M. Gottman and Joan DeClaire, *The Relationship Cure: A 5 Step Guide to Strengthening Your Marriage, Family, and Friendships* (New York: Harmony Books, 2002).

8. John Gottman and Nan Silver, *What Makes Love Last? How to Build Trust and Avoid Betrayal* (New York: Simon & Schuster, 2013).

9. Gottman and Silver, *The Seven Principles for Making Marriage Work.*

CHAPTER 8: PARTNERS WITH HIGHER LIBIDO

1. Stan Tatkin, "Tortoises and Hares," PACT Institute, June 16, 2012, https://www.thepactinstitute.com/blog/Tortoises%20and%20Hares.

2. Michele Lastella et al., "Sex and Sleep: Perceptions of Sex as a Sleep Promoting Behavior in the General Adult Population," *Frontiers in Public Health* 7 no. 33 (March 2019), https://doi.org/10.3389/fpubh.2019.00033; Sari M. van Anders et al., "Associations Among Physiological and Subjective Sexual Response, Sexual Desire, and Salivary Steroid Hormones in Healthy Premenopausal Women," *Journal of Sexual Medicine* 6, no. 3 (March 2009): 739–51, https://doi.org/10.1111/j.1743-6109.2008.01123.x; Beverly Whipple and Barry R. Komisaruk, "Elevation of Pain Threshold by Vaginal Stimulation in Women," *Pain* 21, no. 4 (April 1985): 357–67, https://doi.org/10.1016/0304-3959 (85)90164-2.

3. Natalie O. Rosen et al., "Harmful or Helpful: Perceived Solicitous and Facilitative Partner Responses Are Differentially Associated with Pain and Sexual Satisfaction in Women with Provoked Vestibulodynia," *Journal of Sexual Medicine* 9, no. 9 (September 2012): 2351–60, https://doi.org/10.1111/j.1743-6109.2012.02851.x; Natalie O. Rosen et al., "Beyond a 'Woman's Problem': The Role of Relationship Processes in Female Genital Pain," *Current Sexual Health Reports* 6, no. 1 (2014): 1–10, https://doi.org/10.1007/s11930-013-0006-2.

4. Rosen et al., "Harmful or Helpful."

5. Andrew H. Evans et al., "Impulsive and Compulsive Behaviors in Parkinson's Disease," *Movement Disorders* 24, no. 11 (August 2009): 1561–70, https://doi.org/10.1002/mds.22505; Lilybeth Fontanesi et al., "Hypersexuality and Trauma: A Mediation and Moderation Model from Psychopathology to Problematic Sexual Behavior," *Journal of Affective Disorders* 281 (February 2021): 631–37, https://doi.org/10.1016/j.jad.2020.11.100.

CHAPTER 9: WHEN TO KICK IT UP A NOTCH

1. Dena M. Abbott et al., "Providing Sexuality Training for Psychologists: The Role of Predoctoral Internship Sites," *American Journal of Sexuality Education* 16, no. 2 (2021): 161–80, https://doi.org/10.1080/15546128.2021.1892555; Eli Coleman et al., "Summit on Medical School Education in Sexual Health: Report of an Expert Consultation," *Journal of Sexual Medicine* 10, no. 4 (April 2013): 924–38, https://doi.org/10.1111/jsm.12142; Debra Mollen et al., "Sexuality Training in Counseling Psychology," *Counselling Psychology Quarterly* 33, no. 3 (2020): 375–92, https://doi.org/10.1080/09515070.2018.1553146; Christina Warner et al., "Sexual Health Knowledge of US Medical Students: A National Survey," *Journal of Sexual Medicine* 15, no. 8 (August 2018): 1093–1102, https://doi.org/10.1016/j.jsxm.2018.05.019.

INDEX

ABOUT THE AUTHORS

Lauren Fogel Mersy, PsyD (she/her) is a licensed clinical psychologist and an AASECT-certified sex therapist practicing in a suburb of Minneapolis, Minnesota. She owns a virtual private practice specializing in sex and relationship therapy. Dr. Fogel Mersy received her doctorate in clinical psychology from the Arizona School of Professional Psychology and completed her postdoctoral training at the University of Minnesota Medical School's Institute for Sexual and Gender Health. She has received advanced training in relationship therapy, including emotionally focused couple therapy and Gottman Method couple therapy.

––––––––––– • –––––––––––

Jennifer A. Vencill, PhD, ABPP (she/her) is an assistant professor, board-certified clinical health psychologist, and AASECT-certified sex therapist at the Mayo Clinic in Rochester, Minnesota. Her clinical and research interests include sexual health and function, health disparities and minority stress in marginalized sexual and gender communities, mixed orientation relationships, and LGBTQ+ mental and sexual health. Dr. Vencill sits on the editorial board of the *International Journal of Sexual Health*, *Psychology of Sexual Orientation and Gender Diversity*, and the *Journal of Positive Sexuality*. She received her doctorate in Counseling Psychology from Texas Tech University and completed her postdoctoral training as the first Michael E. Metz fellow in sexual health at the University of Minnesota Medical School's Institute for Sexual and Gender Health.